Motivating Students by Design

Practical Strategies for Professors

Brett D. Jones

2018

Second Edition

Copyright © 2018, 2015 by Brett D. Jones.

All rights reserved. No part of this book may be reproduced, distributed, or transmitted in any form or by any means, including photocopying, recording, or other electronic or mechanical methods, now known or hereafter invented, without the prior written permission of the author, except in the case of brief quotations embodied in critical reviews and certain other noncommercial uses permitted by copyright law. For permission requests, write to Brett D. Jones at brettdjones@gmail.com.

Printed by CreateSpace
Available from Amazon.com and other book stores

The cover image was designed by Brett D. Jones.

Motivating Students by Design: Practical Strategies for Professors / Brett D. Jones. 2nd edition.

ISBN-13: 978-1981497010
ISBN-10: 1981497013

Contents

Chapter 1: Introduction 1

Chapter 2: Understanding Motivation and the MUSIC® Model of Motivation 5

Chapter 3: Designing Instruction Using the MUSIC® Model of Motivation 17

Chapter 4: Strategies to eMpower Students 43

Chapter 5: Strategies to leverage Usefulness 75

Chapter 6: Strategies to Support Success 93

Chapter 7: Strategies to Trigger Interest 141

Chapter 8: Strategies to Foster Caring 167

Chapter 9: The MUSIC® Model of Motivation Theory and Research 193

Afterword 205

References 207

Appendices 227

About the Author 238

Acknowledgments

We learn about motivation from those around us from the time we're born. So from that perspective, I'm thankful for all of the individuals with whom I've spent a lot of time over the years, including my two brothers, my parents, my grandparents, my wife, and my children. And, I've learned from my college roommates and other friends over the years. I would also like to thank many former students for allowing me to try some good and not-so-good motivation strategies on them. Similarly, my doctoral students and faculty colleagues have helped me refine my thinking about motivation and have collaborated with me on many different research projects. Many of these students and colleagues are listed with me as co-authors of the publications in the *References* section of this book.

The text of this book was strengthened by the comments of my reviewers, including Sehmuz Akalin (Educational Psychology doctoral student, Virginia Tech), Noel Byrd (Project Director in the Office of the Executive Vice President and Provost, Virginia Tech), David Grant (Associate Professor, Virginia-Maryland College of Veterinary Medicine, Virginia Tech), and Stephan Munz (Educational Psychology doctoral student, Virginia Tech). Thank you for your edits and advice!

I have written and edited the second edition of this book entirely on my own; therefore, you may find some mistakes throughout the book. Please excuse my minor mistakes. I've checked it in detail several times, but I'm not perfect. By doing everything myself, I'm able to reduce the production costs of the book, which results in a less expensive book for you. I figured a missing period or two here and there wouldn't bother you if you saved a few dollars! And really, I don't make much money off the sale of the book. My primary motivation for writing the book is to help professors improve their instruction, so that ultimately, students are more engaged in their courses and learn more.

Dedication

This book is dedicated to all the bad teachers and professors I've had over the years. Without them, I would never have had the inspiration to want to improve instructors' teaching, especially at the college level where I attended some pretty bad lectures.

I would also like to dedicate this book to all the good teachers I've had over the years. Without them, I wouldn't have the knowledge and skills necessary to write this book. Fortunately, I had more good teachers than bad ones. I would especially like to thank my parents for being the best teachers of all. Only now as a parent can I begin to understand all of the sacrifices my parents made for my education and well-being.

New to the Second Edition

This second edition of the book is about 75% longer than the first edition because I added a couple chapters, included new strategies and examples, and updated several sections, as summarized here.

- Chapters 2 and 3 are mostly new to this edition, as are a few paragraphs in Chapter 1. In Chapters 2 and 3, I explain the MUSIC® Model of Motivation more completely and how it can be used to design instruction.

- In Chapters 4 to 8, I included 47 new examples of instructional strategies and provided more explanations in some of the examples from the first edition.

- Near the beginning of Chapters 4 to 8, I included a "Relevant Theories" section in which I provide a very brief explanation of some of the primary theories that are most directly relevant to the strategies discussed in that chapter. I acknowledge that my brief descriptions are entirely insufficient to completely explain the theories; however, the descriptions should provide you with a general sense of the theories and include references if you're interested in learning more about the theories.

- In Chapter 9, I updated the research citations and provided a little more explanation throughout.

CHAPTER 1

Introduction

Do your students need to be motivated to engage in your courses? Probably so. As Evelyn Van de Veen (2015) noted: "even at one of the most prestigious universities of the world [Harvard], you cannot take student motivation or student effort for granted" (para. 3). And even if your students are motivated to do well in your course and have the best intentions, they may have other goals and obligations that compete for their attention and time. So what can you do to help them engage more fully in your courses? The motivation strategies and model presented in this book are intended to answer this question. The fundamental concepts behind these strategies are based on decades of research and they're intended to provide you with guidance as you design and implement instruction.

Is teaching an art or science?

You may have had some excellent teachers who seemed to have a one-of-a-kind teaching ability. Or maybe you've read about outstanding teachers in books or seen them in movies, on television, or online. Some people believe that excellent teachers are born with a natural teaching ability or that they possess some unknowable qualities. I contend, however, that although teaching is an art that can take many different forms, it is based firmly in a science that is knowable, at least to some extent.

Some teachers may learn the science of teaching on their own based on their prior experiences as a student or as a teacher through trial and error. Others may learn this science through coursework, books, articles, or websites. These types of experiences can provide teachers with the tools necessary to become a successful "artist." Similar to how excellent artists use their tools to craft beautiful art works, so too must you use the strategies in this book to craft your teaching.

The aim of this book is to give you some of the scientific knowledge needed for your craft. It's up to you to use this knowledge creatively in ways that are appropriate for your course context and that fits your unique background and personality.

Who is the audience for this book?

This book is intended to be read by any type of instructor that teaches students of any age. However, the examples provided throughout the book are most directly related to college professors. I use the term "professors" in this book as a broad term to include professors, teachers, lecturers, instructors, and anyone who designs and implements instruction for learners in higher education. The strategies in this book have been found to be useful to both novice and more experienced professors.

What are the purposes of this book?

I titled this book *Motivating Students by Design* because the premise of the book is that professors can motivate students by designing their courses intentionally. Over the years, research has provided evidence for this premise (Wentzel & Wigfield, 2009). In this book, I explain how professors can use the *MUSIC® Model of Motivation* (Jones, 2009), which is a model that I developed to help professors in all disciplines intentionally design instruction to motivate students.

The purposes of this book are to:

- describe five important research-based principles related to motivating students;
- explain these five principles succinctly, but in enough detail to allow you to understand the mechanisms by which they work;
- provide general guiding strategies that will allow you to implement these principles in your teaching; and
- provide several examples of these strategies with the hope that you will be able to use some of them, or modify them for use, in your teaching.

To achieve these purposes, I used a format that I thought would be most readable to busy students and professors. Consequently, I focused on the purposes above and was guided by the goals listed in Table 1.1.

Table 1.1. *Goals of this Book*

This book is intended to…	This book is **NOT** intended to…
• explain how to implement teaching strategies consistent with current motivation research and theories,	• explain everything known to man and woman about every motivation theory,
• build on your current teaching successes,	• drastically change your teaching approaches (unless your teaching is very poor, in which case you might want to try some drastic changes!!),
• teach you what you need to know to effectively motivate your students,	• teach you everything you need to know to become a successful professor,
• give you control to read the chapters and strategies that are most relevant to your teaching,	• be read linearly from cover to cover (although it can be),
• be succinct and rather informal, and	• be a formal weighty tome, and
• summarize the implications of current motivation-related research and theories.	• include many studies that show similar results and provide hundreds of academic references.

In the first edition of this book I intentionally avoided explaining too many motivation theories. However, because some readers have an interest in using this book as a resource for motivation theories, I included short explanations of motivation theories throughout this edition. I have identified the theory sections as "Relevant Theories" to allow you to find these sections easily if you're interested and to allow you to skip them if you're uninterested.

How should you read this book?

You should definitely read Chapters 2 and 3 because they provide a key foundation that you'll need to understand how to effectively implement the strategies presented in the other chapters. You can simply select strategies in this book without reading Chapters 2 and 3, but they may not work if you don't understand the mindset needed to implement them effectively.

Chapters 4 through 8 focus on motivation strategies related to specific aspects of the motivation model presented in Chapters 2 and 3. You can read Chapters 4 through 8 in any order because they don't build on one another cumulatively. You will know which ones you need and want to read after reading Chapters 2 and 3. In the final chapter, Chapter 9, I provide a little more background and research related to the motivation model presented in this book. You only need to read this chapter if you're interested in the background research.

Why are quotations from famous individuals included throughout the book?

The quotations included throughout the book serve several purposes. All of the quotations are intended to relate to the topic of the section in which they appear. Some of the quotations are meant to reinforce the ideas in the section. Other quotations are meant to get you thinking more about the ideas in the section. And other quotations are intended to be humorous.

CHAPTER 2

Understanding Motivation and the MUSIC® Model of Motivation

To effectively implement the strategies in this book, you need to understand the basic principles of motivation in education and the MUSIC® Model of Motivation. In this chapter, I briefly define motivation and explain the MUSIC® Model of Motivation.

What is motivation?

Motivation is the extent to which one intends to engage in an activity. Once individuals are engaged in an activity, their motivation can increase, decrease, or stay the same, depending on the extent to which they intend to *continue* to engage in it. When individuals continue to engage in an activity over time, we may say that they are persistent, determined, or have grit. Engagement is important because it most directly affects outcomes such as learning and performance (see Figure 2.1). Increased learning and performance is important because they are almost always the primary goals of college courses.

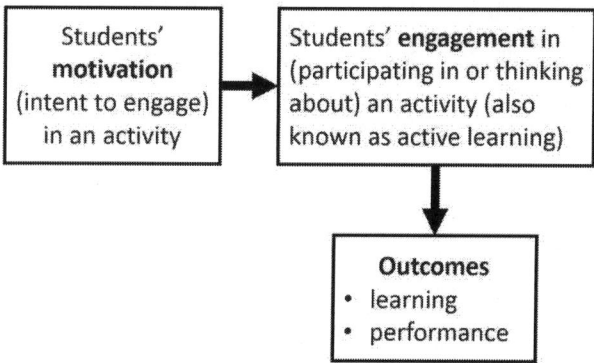

Figure 2.1. *The relationship between motivation, engagement, and outcomes*

Let's look at these four underlined parts of the definition of motivation more closely: Motivation is the extent to which one intends to engage in an activity.

- Extent: The *extent* part of the motivation definition refers to the magnitude of the intent, which has been referred to as the "energizing of behavior" (Hebb, 1955, p. 244). The extent of an individual's motivation for an activity can vary along a continuum from no motivation to high motivation. When the magnitude of the intent is high, people say things like, "He's really motivated to do that."

- Intent: Motivation is considered an *intent* because it describes what individuals intend to do, not what they have already done (Christenson, Reschly, & Wylie, 2012). Once individuals *engage* in an activity, motivation refers to their intent to *continue* to engage in the activity. Many motivation scientists consider motivation to be a goal-directed process because individuals' intentions often (or maybe always) emanate from their goals.

- Engagement: Individuals engage in an activity by *participating in* some aspect of the activity, which is why it is sometimes referred to as "active learning" (Chi & Wylie, 2014). Participation can be labeled *behavioral* engagement because it can be observed, such as when students take notes in class (Fredricks, Blumenfeld, & Paris, 2004). Individuals also engage by *thinking about* some aspect of the activity, which is why this type of engagement is labeled *cognitive* engagement. Cognitive engagement is often unseen by observers. Consider the case of a student who is looking out of a window during a lecture but is thinking deeply about the ideas presented in the lecture. This student may appear to be behaviorally unengaged, but in fact, s/he is very cognitively engaged in thinking about the content.

- An activity: Individuals intend to engage in particular activities, not all activities. Therefore, the activity in which individuals intend to participate indicates the direction of their motivation. In other words, individuals direct their motivation towards particular activities to reach their goals. Students who are motivated by the goal of "getting an A" might engage in activities such as coming to class and taking notes during class.

I like to use this definition of motivation when talking to professors because it succinctly captures the essence of what I believe that many instructors mean when they refer to motivation. And, this definition is consistent with current theoretical and empirical research about the relationship between motivation and engagement (e.g., Anderman & Patrick, 2012; Froiland & Davison, 2016; Froiland & Worrell, 2016; Reeve, Jang, Carrell, Jeon, & Barch, 2004; Schunk & Mullen, 2012). Although this is a good, practical definition of motivation for instructors, it does have some limitations. For example, this definition of motivation doesn't address how individuals' *unconscious* intentions interact with and affect their conscious intentions. However, it is beyond the scope of this book to address this level of breadth and depth within the field of motivation.

So far, my explanations have focused on individuals' motivation to engage in activities with only one goal in mind; however, individuals are motivated to engage in many different activities towards many different goals. Consider the motivation of your students. They're probably motivated to engage in a lot of different activities, such as participating in other college courses, playing sports, playing video games, working, eating, sleeping, and hanging out with friends and family. Because it's only feasible to engage in one or a couple activities at a time (e.g., eating and hanging out with friends), students are constantly making decisions about which activities to engage in by weighing the costs and benefits of each. Figure 2.2 shows how students' cost and benefit analysis and decisions can be represented in the MUSIC model.

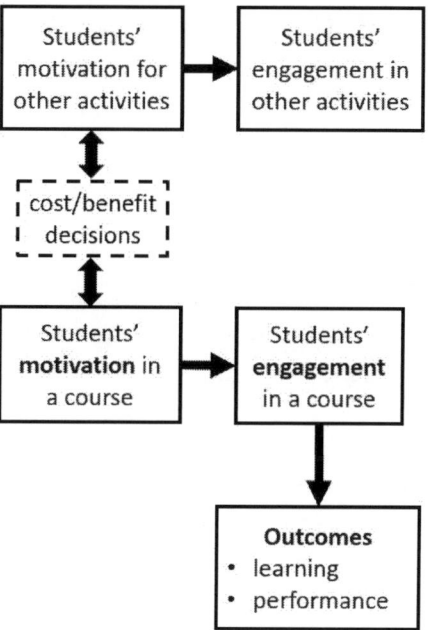

Figure 2.2. *Individuals weigh the costs and benefits of different activities when deciding in which activities to engage.*

Let's assume that the bottom part of Figure 2.2 (which is similar to Figure 2.1) demonstrates students' motivation for and engagement in *your* course. When students are motivated in your course, the bottom arrow pointing to the right shows that they're more likely to engage in your course activities. Yet, students have other options, as indicated by the double-headed vertical arrow above the rectangle labeled "Students' motivation in a course." Even if they are motivated to engage in your course, there may be fewer costs and/or more benefits to engaging in the other activities represented at the top of Figure 2.2; and thus, they may not engage in your course at that time because they decide to engage in other activities. The dotted rectangle labeled "cost/benefit decisions" between these different motivations represents the idea that students must decide which motivations are least costly and/or most beneficial. Based on their cost/benefit analysis (e.g., considering the time, effort, and emotional costs involved), students decide whether they're more motivated to engage in your course or in other activities at that time.

What students choose to engage in at any particular time of day is based on many variables, and may be affected by both conscious and unconscious factors. My research suggests that *time* is one of these variables: students will compare the amount of time they have available with the amount of time it takes to complete the activities, and then, choose activities in an order that allows them to most effectively reach their goals (at least that's the intent, surely it doesn't always work out that way!). When students decide to participate in many activities, the amount of time and effort they can devote to any one particular course is limited, as is evident in the undergraduate student's comment that follows.

"I put forth the minimal amount of effort in order to get an A because I am taking 18 credits, working 10 hours a week, I have an internship 9 hours a week, two clubs I'm an officer in, extracurriculars and I'm a transfer student trying to make friends."

Students will also consider the relative *importance* of completing various tasks towards their long-term goals (Osborne & Jones, 2011). For example, if they're enrolled in two courses that require the same amount of time, but they don't have time to engage fully in both, they'll likely spend more time on the course they value more (e.g., the course is more relevant to their future career). This comment from an undergraduate student provides an example: "Of all my classes, I definitely do not put the most effort into this one. I am more focused on my in-major classes."

Given this fairly complex model of students' motivation, how can instructors use this information to design and implement instruction? I answer this question in the next section.

What key motivation principles do you need to consider when designing and implementing instruction?

Students are motivated when their learning environment is *designed* to engage them. How? I examined decades of motivation research and theories and identified five groups of teaching strategies that can effectively motivate students to engage in learning: empowerment, usefulness, success, interest, and caring. I call these five groups of strategies the "components" of a motivation model. A quick glance at Figure 2.3 reveals why I used MUSIC as an acronym to help instructors remember these components (hint: the initial sounds of each word forms the acronym MUSIC). Consequently, I titled this model the "MUSIC® Model of Motivation" (Jones, 2009).

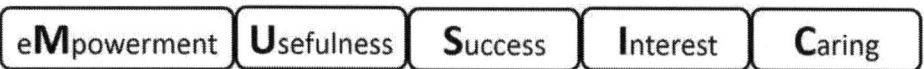

Figure 2.3. *The components of the MUSIC® Model of Motivation*

The need for this type of integrated motivation model has been noted by experts in the field of motivation (Wentzel & Wigfield, 2009, p. 6). The MUSIC model is not based on gimmicks or my personal ideas; rather, I built the model on the work of researchers, primarily in the disciplines of psychology, education, and motivation science (see Chapter 9 for more explanation). I labeled the components with words that would convey to educators the essence of the strategies. For short, I refer to this model throughout the book as the "MUSIC model." (Note that although MUSIC® is a trademark of Brett D. Jones, I do not include the trademark symbol throughout the remainder of the book.)

The MUSIC model is comprised of the five key principles listed here. The instructor needs to ensure that students:

1. feel empowered by having the ability to make decisions about some aspects of their learning,
2. understand why what they are learning is useful for their short- or long-term goals,
3. believe that they can succeed if they put forth the effort required,
4. are interested in the content and instructional activities, and
5. believe that others in the learning environment, such as the instructor and other students, care about their learning and about them as a person.

All five principles are focused on students' *perceptions* of their learning environment. I refer to students' "MUSIC perceptions" as the extent to which students perceive that: they have control of their learning environment in the course (*empowerment*), the coursework is *useful* to their goals, they can *succeed* at the coursework, the instructional methods and coursework are *interesting*, and others in the course (such as the instructor and other students) *care* about whether they succeed in the coursework and care about their well-being. Students' MUSIC perceptions are subjective, internal representations of their experiences; and as a result, MUSIC perceptions can vary across classes and can vary between students in the same class. Thus, the MUSIC model is consistent with the situative perspective, which "interprets individuals' beliefs and behaviors as arising through participation in social, cultural, and historical contexts or systems" (Turner & Nolen, 2015, p. 168).

Students' MUSIC perceptions are important because researchers have documented that these perceptions are related to students' motivation, engagement, and subsequently, outcomes. Thus, in Figure 2.4, I've add MUSIC perceptions to the left side of Figure 2.2.

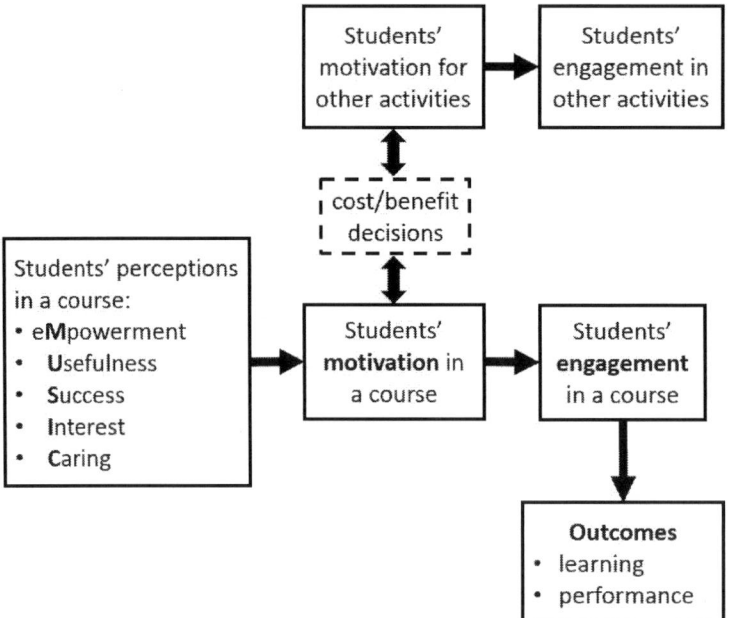

Figure 2.4. *The relationship between students' MUSIC perceptions and their motivation, engagement, and outcomes.*

Although I present the five MUSIC perceptions as distinct from one another, I acknowledge that these perceptions interact, likely in complex ways that are not completely understood by researchers. In fact, researchers have documented that these five MUSIC perceptions are correlated, but they've also conducted quantitative statistical analyses to demonstrate that they're distinct (Chittum & Jones, 2017; Jones,

Li, & Cruz, 2017; Jones, Sahbaz, Schram, & Chittum, 2017; Jones & Sigmon, 2016; Jones & Skaggs, 2016; Jones, Tendhar, & Paretti, 2016; Jones & Wilkins, 2013; Parkes, Jones, & Wilkins, 2015; Schram & Jones, 2016). That is, students can perceive empowerment, usefulness, success, interest, and caring differently within a course. From a practical standpoint (until researchers can figure out how these complex interactions work), I contend that it's useful for instructors to consider students' MUSIC perceptions separately because it's possible to assess each perception and select teaching strategies that influence each.

How does the MUSIC model work?

To examine how the MUSIC model works, let's continue to "back-up" in the figures that I've presented so far. Figure 2.5 adds an "External Variables" rectangle to the left side of Figure 2.4 to indicate that students' MUSIC perceptions are affected by (a) instructors' teaching strategies and (b) other environmental conditions. Here you can see the power of the MUSIC model because instructors can intentionally motivate students by design through implementing teaching strategies intended to directly affect the students' MUSIC perceptions. For example, teaching students effective learning strategies can increase their perceptions that they can *succeed* in the course.

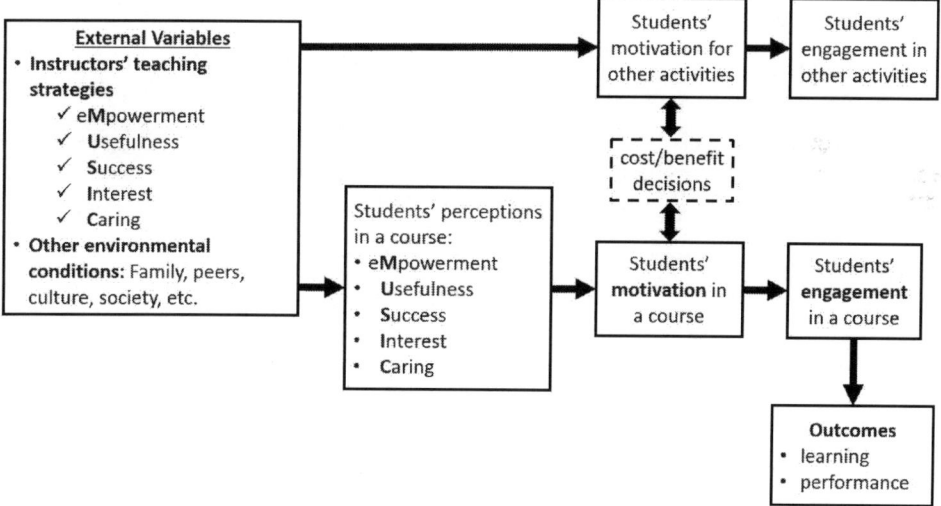

Figure 2.5. *The process through which external variables, such as instructors' teaching strategies, can affect students' MUSIC perceptions, motivation, engagement, and outcomes.*

To summarize, when instructors design and implement a course consistent with MUSIC model strategies, students' increased MUSIC perceptions can lead to increases in students' motivation and engagement, which then leads to positive outcomes, such increased learning and improved performance. The aim of this book is to provide you with many teaching strategies that can help you to teach in ways consistent with the MUSIC model.

Also shown in Figure 2.5 is that "other environmental conditions," such as students' family and peers, and the culture and society in which they learn and live, also affect students' MUSIC perceptions (Bernard, 2012; Kovas, Malykh, & Petrill, 2014). Generally, instructors have little to no control over these conditions that exist outside of the immediate course environment; and therefore, these environmental conditions not a central focus of this book. Although I completely acknowledge that these other environmental conditions can be as important or even more important to students' motivation in a course, my intent in this book is to provide strategies over which you have the most control. For this reason, this book is focused on the MUSIC model strategies.

I want to describe another critical piece of motivating students: considering psychological variables. Psychologists have identified many variables that affect students' motivations. The left side of Figure 2.6 lists some of these "internal psychological variables," including *cognition* (such as their thoughts, beliefs, goals, and values), *affect* (such as their emotions, moods, and feelings), needs and desires (including psychological and physiological needs, for example, the need for nourishment), identity beliefs (beliefs about who one is), and personality characteristics (such as openness, conscientiousness, extroversion, agreeableness, and neuroticism). The interaction among cognition, affect, needs/desires, identity beliefs, and personality characteristics is complex, and certainly beyond the scope of this book, but psychologists use these internal variables to explain human motivation, behavior, and performance (for more information, see Cerasoli, Nicklin, & Nassrelgrgawi, 2016; Ryan, 2012; Shah & Gardner, 2008; Wentzel & Wigfield, 2009).

To complete my explanation of Figure 2.6, I need to explain the meaning of the arrows in the figure. The double-headed arrow between "External Variables" and "Internal Variables" indicates that while the external variables influence the internal variables, the internal variables also affect the external variables. For example, the culture in which one lives (an external variable) can affect students' values (an internal variable). For this reason, a student living in the culture of rural Virginia may have different values than a student living in an urban area of California. Conversely, students' internal variables can affect the external variables. For example, knowing the goals and values of their students (internal variables), instructors teaching at a college serving many students from urban areas of California should

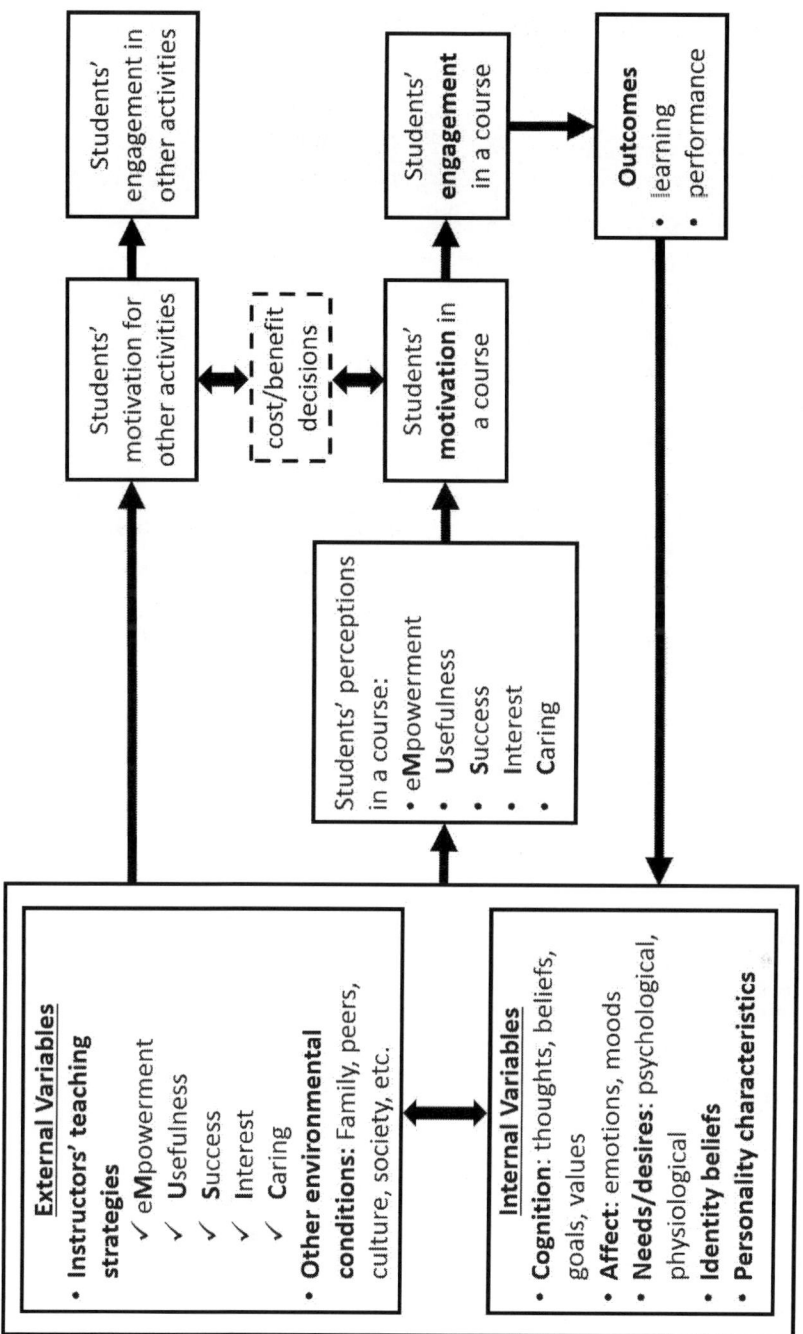

Figure 2.6. *The MUSIC® Model of Motivation as it relates to students in a course*[1]

---

[1] From *Motivating Students by Design: Practical Strategies for Professors* by Brett D. Jones, available at www.theMUSICmodel.com. Copyright © 2018 by Brett D. Jones. Photocopying allowed for personal use.

consider MUSIC model strategies (external variables) that are most appropriate for these students (of course, many instructors have students with a wide variety of internal variables). In sum, the external and internal variables shown in Figure 2.6 are constantly interacting in complex ways.

The two arrows in Figure 2.6 leading from the rectangle around the external and internal variables (pointing to the right) indicate that the complex interactions between students' external and internal variables affect their MUSIC perceptions in a course, as well as their motivation for other activities. This is a vitally important part of the MUSIC model because instructors are only able to influence students' motivation to the extent that they select strategies that affect students' MUSIC perceptions. Therefore, instructors must be cognizant as to how other environmental conditions and internal variables interact with their strategies to affect students' MUSIC perceptions. Although this may sound complicated, the strategies in this book can help you to navigate this process.

"I never teach my pupils. I only attempt to provide the conditions in which they can learn." – Albert Einstein (cited in iz Quotes, 2015a)

The final arrow I want to explain is the one pointing left from "Outcomes" to the external and internal variables rectangle. This arrow indicates that the process of the MUSIC® Model of Motivation is cyclical. When students achieve an outcome, it affects the external and internal variables. Let me give you a few examples. Lucy receives a C grade on her biology course assignment (this is an "Outcome" of her level of engagement in the course). This outcome affects several of her "internal variables," including her beliefs about her ability in biology. Before this assignment, she believed that she was good at biology, but her C grade has lowered her ability belief. If other students in the class also received low grades on this assignment, it could affect the instructor's teaching strategies (an external variable). For instance, the instructor might change some strategies to try to help students or s/he might decrease the difficulty level of the next assignment. These changes to the teaching strategies could then affect Lucy's MUSIC perceptions, motivation, and engagement in ways that would affect her grade (the outcome) on the next assignment. As you can see, this cycle can continue throughout a course or learning experience (Dietrich, Viljaranta, Moeller, & Kracke, 2017). In fact, the cycle occurs constantly throughout individuals' lives as they engage in different activities (related and unrelated to courses), receive different outcomes, and changes occur in the external and internal variables. The goal of the MUSIC model is for the instructor to make changes to teaching strategies that will create a positive cycle in which students become more motivated, engaged, and achieve more desirable outcomes.

An important take away message from the MUSIC model is that motivating strategies are within your control, at least to some extent. Although instructors don't have complete control over students' motivations because of students' internal variables and other external variables, research indicates that instructors can have a significant impact on students' motivation in a course (Christenson et al., 2012; Wentzel & Wigfield, 2009). Another important message from the MUSIC model is that you need to be cognizant of these internal and other external variables when designing your course; otherwise, they may undermine your motivational strategies.

Finally, Figure 2.6 is not intended to illustrate *all* of the variables and interconnections that affect students' motivations. However, it includes many of the key variables that have been identified by researchers, and I find that it's a very practical and useful way for instructors to conceptualize the factors that affect students' motivation, engagement, and learning.

Why does the MUSIC model work?

The MUSIC model is a multidimensional approach to motivation that is effective because students' motivations in a course can vary and students can have very different perceptions of instruction (as any professors who have read their end-of-course evaluations will attest). Using the multidimensional MUSIC model gives you a good chance of motivating more of your students more of the time because it's not limited to any one theory or research agenda. It's likely that there are multiple pathways to motivating students and the MUSIC model provides five different (but often related) pathways to motivating students (i.e., through perceptions of empowerment, usefulness, success, interest, and caring). For example, some students may be motivated primarily by their success perceptions in a course, whereas other students may be more motivated by the usefulness of the content. And sometimes the MUSIC model components are interrelated in complex ways. For instance, one study found that telling students about the usefulness of a task increased their interest and performance in the task, but only when they had higher perceptions of success related to the task (Durik, Shechter, Noh, Rozek, & Harackiewicz, 2015). I may mention some of these types of complex relationships in this book, but until I believe there is enough research evidence to make broader claims, I won't highlight them in this book.

Given these sometimes complex interactions among MUSIC model components, it may be helpful for you to think of the model as a system comprised of several parts, including the students, the instructor, the instructional materials, and the learning environment. All of these parts must interact effectively to produce the desired outcome, which is usually students' learning. Changes to one part of the system can have a range of effects on the other parts of the system.

The MUSIC model is a balanced approach that doesn't favor any motivation theories over others. Instead, the approach is designed to engage students as they oscillate between periods of high and low motivation and engagement. Because the MUSIC model is a conceptual model, it can be applied to any type of teaching approach. And because it was developed based on research from a variety of disciplines with students of all ages, there's no reason to believe that it doesn't apply to all types of learning environments (see Chapter 9 for more information about the development of the MUSIC model). Certainly, however, some aspects of the MUSIC model will be more salient in some courses than others.

Developing the MUSIC model mindset

You can implement a few strategies from this book in one of your courses and see some improvement in students' motivation and engagement. But the real aim of this book is to encourage you to develop a MUSIC mindset, because it can have a more enduring and profound effect on your teaching. What is a MUSIC mindset? Well, instructors who have a MUSIC mindset:

- believe that they can affect students' motivation to some extent,
- understand the five MUSIC model principles,
- understand how to design instruction using the MUSIC model,
- assess students' MUSIC perceptions,
- and use data to intentionally select and implement strategies consistent with the MUSIC model.

Instructors who have the MUSIC mindset think of motivating students not as an add-on or afterthought, but as something that permeates their instructional design. I provide practical strategies for using the MUSIC model to design instruction in the next chapter.

CHAPTER 3

Designing Instruction Using the MUSIC® Model of Motivation

Everything instructors do in a course can potentially affect students' MUSIC perceptions and motivation. Therefore, all aspects of a course need to be designed with a consideration of the MUSIC model. Of course, it's impractical to focus on every aspect of a course, especially when you first design it. But as you become more familiar and comfortable with the concepts in the MUSIC model, it will become easier for you to do. The purpose of this chapter is to provide an overview of how you can use the MUSIC model to design instruction.

How can you use the MUSIC model to design instruction?

The goal of using the MUSIC model is to increase students' motivation (and thus, their engagement and learning); therefore, the focus of the model is on motivation. Other aspects of instructional design are also important, but the aim of the MUSIC model is to delve into the motivational aspects of design that are typically not included in instructional design models to any significant extent. Consequently, you can use the MUSIC model by itself or to complement other instructional design models (e.g., Dick, Carey, & Carey, 2015; Shambaugh & Magliaro, 2006). Furthermore, you can use the MUSIC model very "casually" by looking through this book and trying some of the strategies. Or, you can use the model more systematically by following the design cycle explained in this chapter.

A systematic design approach

Figure 3.1 shows five steps in the basic MUSIC model design cycle that you can use if you prefer a more systematic approach to instructional design. This design cycle contains elements found in any good instructional design model, including: (1) selecting course objectives, (2) selecting strategies, (3) implementing strategies, (4) assessing the effectiveness of the strategies, and (5) evaluating the assessment results. A unique feature of the MUSIC model design cycle is that the instructor intentionally selects MUSIC strategies and assesses students' MUSIC perceptions (which is why the title of this book is *Motivating Students by Design*).

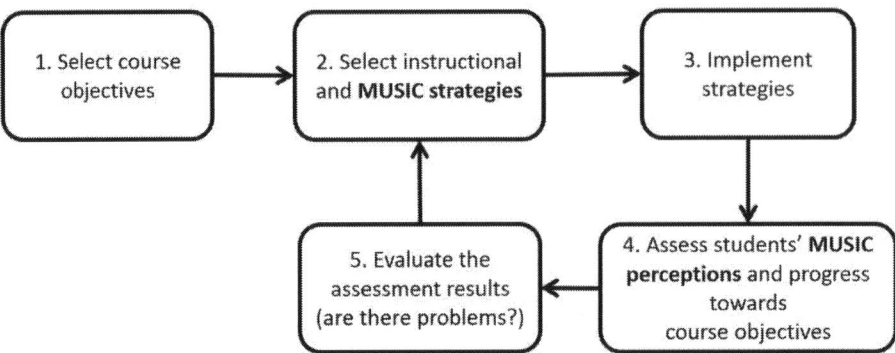

Figure 3.1. *The MUSIC model design cycle*

The MUSIC model design process is cyclical, in that it keeps repeating until there are no problems; that is, until all students are motivated and meet all the course objectives. I'm still in the cycle after 18 years of teaching, so either I'm a slow learner or it's darn near impossible to perfect instruction when you have students with diverse backgrounds and personalities.

The first time you design a course, you will begin at Step 1 in the upper-left side of the design cycle in Figure 3.1 by selecting course objectives. In Step 2, you will select instructional and MUSIC strategies. Entire books and articles are devoted to explaining how to select instructional strategies and I recommend that you consult those resources because the purpose of this book is not to focus on that aspect of the instructional design. Instead, the purpose is to focus on the MUSIC strategies, which are provided throughout this book. If you're teaching a course that you've taught previously, you can use the information from Step 5 in the cycle (Evaluate the assessment results [are there problems?]). If this is your first time teaching the course, you can use whatever information is available, including your prior experiences in other courses. The next steps in the cycle are to implement the strategies by teaching the course (Step 3), to assess students' MUSIC perceptions and progress towards course objectives (Step 4), and to evaluate the assessment results (are there problems?) (Step 5). I explain how to assess students' MUSIC perceptions and evaluate the results in the next section. Please consult other resources for how to assess students' progress towards course objectives. And again, this cycle includes only the basics needed for instructional design, but I find Figure 3.1 useful because it shows how the MUSIC model can be integrated into a broader instructional design process.

Evaluating results

Effective instructors understand one critical point: they will feel uncomfortable in some parts of this design cycle, especially during the evaluation phase (Step 5). It's okay to feel uncomfortable, and in fact, it's a necessary part of the process if you want to improve. You may receive some feedback that's unfair and unwarranted because the issue raised by the student is due to the *student's* lack of preparation or not following directions instead of a deficit on your part. And most of us don't like being criticized by students ("What does this 20 year old know anyway!"). But we can only improve if we know our weaknesses, and everyone has weaknesses in some aspect of his/her instructional design. So the sooner you learn to accept feedback as potentially helpful, and don't take it too personally (easier said than done), the sooner you will improve as an instructor. Unwarranted criticism from students (e.g., students who didn't follow or read directions) can still be useful if you use it to consider whether there is more you could have done to help these students.

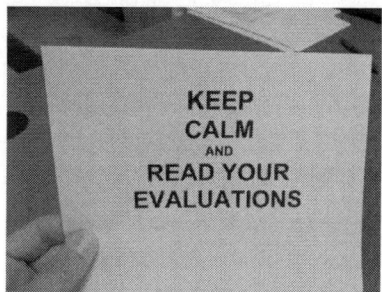

However, I would caution you not to take any one student's strong opinions too seriously if s/he is an outlier. You want to consider all students' feedback, but don't redesign your course to make one student happy, because your changes might cause other problems. It's nearly impossible to satisfy all students because they all have different backgrounds and expectations. Some of my best words of wisdom are: (a) design the best course you can with the time you have available (because there is always limited time), and (b) in making decisions before and during the course, focus on students' motivation and learning. If you do these things, you should sleep well at night knowing that you did what you could for that particular course.

Implementing a MUSIC model intervention

Instructors have asked me what they can do to implement *the* MUSIC model strategies or *the* MUSIC model intervention. Let me be very clear that there is no one type of MUSIC model instruction or intervention. Instructors can do many things to design instruction that is consistent with the MUSIC model. What makes instruction consistent with the MUSIC model is that it meets the five key principles listed in Chapter 2. Instructors can do many different things to meet these principles.

Therefore, although I have identified particular strategies that are consistent with the MUSIC model, that doesn't mean that they are the *only* way to be consistent with the MUSIC model. The strategies provided throughout this book are intended to give you some examples that may be consistent with the MUSIC model if they are implemented appropriately for your students. Clearly, you must use your professional judgment to decide which strategies can help you to meet the five key MUSIC model principles with your students.

How can you assess students' MUSIC perceptions?

All of the MUSIC model principles should be considered when designing instruction. However, you probably already use many strategies consistent with the MUSIC model. Your instruction probably also has a few weaknesses that you could improve upon to motivate students more effectively. But how can you assess the strengths and weaknesses of your instruction? At least four methods can be used to diagnose your instructional strengths and weaknesses related to students' MUSIC perceptions.

1. <u>Reflecting on your experiences.</u> Reflect on your experiences in teaching this course previously. At what times in the course were students less motivated? Use your prior experience when considering which MUSIC components to consider first. Jot down some notes each week about students' engagement that week so that you can remember everything at the end of the course when you're working on redesigning the course. Reviewing your end-of-course teaching evaluations is also a good idea. For a more quantitative reflection on your experiences, you can complete the *MUSIC® Model of Academic Motivation Inventory (College Professor version)* that is provided in the next section.

2. <u>Surveying students.</u> You can survey students *during* your course or near the *end* of it. Some professors have surveyed students as early as an hour after the beginning of a course (McGinley & Jones, 2014); but obviously, students' perceptions continue to evolve throughout the course. Near the beginning of the course, students have less information on which to base their perceptions. Nonetheless, these perceptions influence their motivation at that time. To survey students, ask them questions related to each of the five MUSIC model components. Example quantitative and qualitative (open-ended) questions are provided in the next section. You can place the inventory in an online form (e.g., Google Forms) for efficient data collection and analysis.

3. <u>Talking to students.</u> You can talk to students before or after class, or chat over email. Find out which aspects of the course they find less motivating. It can help to let students know that you value their opinions about the course

and that you'll listen to their ideas about how to make it more engaging. In addition to this type of informal feedback, you could interview students more formally at the end of a course when you've already submitted their grades and they're more likely to discuss their beliefs honestly.

4. <u>Soliciting peer feedback.</u> Ask some of your colleagues or administrators to review your syllabus and attend your class. You may have a center for teaching and learning at your school that will provide this service. Ask them to look specifically for evidence that you teach in a manner consistent with each of the MUSIC model components. For example, they could complete the Professor version of the MUSIC® Model of Academic Motivation Inventory.

What tools can I use to assess students' MUSIC perceptions?

In this section I provide several tools you can use to assess students' MUSIC perceptions. These tools are available for free online at www.theMUSICmodel.com in the *User Guide for Assessing the Components of the MUSIC® Model of Motivation*. If you plan to use these tools, please read and closely follow the instructions for each tool in the *User Guide*. Also, many versions of the MUSIC Inventory have been translated to different languages and all of the translations are available for free in the *User Guide*. Validity information for the quantitative measures are also provided in the *User Guide*.

The following three tools are presented in this section.

- <u>MUSIC® Model of Academic Motivation Inventory (Professor version, short-form)</u>. Use this quantitative inventory to assess *your* beliefs about students' perceptions of your course. It's often helpful to compare your perceptions with your students' perceptions to identify differences.

- <u>MUSIC® Model of Academic Motivation Inventory (College Student version, short form)</u>. Use this quantitative inventory to assess *students'* perceptions of your course. Using this inventory is the quickest way to assess students' MUSIC perceptions in a course.

- <u>Open-ended MUSIC questions for students</u>. Use these questions to obtain students' suggestions for improving a course.

MUSIC® Model of Academic Motivation Inventory (Professor version, short-form[2])

In what course do you want to assess students' motivation? _____

Respond to the items below <u>in relation to this one course</u> using this scale:

1	2	3	4	5	6
Strongly disagree	Disagree	Somewhat disagree	Somewhat agree	Agree	Strongly agree

Note that the word "<u>coursework</u>" refers to anything that students do in the course, including assignments, activities, readings, etc.

Students believe that:

_____ 1. in general, the coursework is useful to them.
_____ 2. the instructional methods used in this course hold their attention.
_____ 3. they are confident that they can succeed in the coursework.
_____ 4. they have the freedom to complete the coursework their own way.
_____ 5. I am willing to assist them if they need help in the course.
_____ 6. they enjoy the instructional methods used in this course.
_____ 7. they can be successful in meeting the academic challenges in this course.
_____ 8. the coursework is beneficial to them.
_____ 9. they have options in how to achieve the goals of the course.
_____ 10. they enjoy completing the coursework.
_____ 11. they are capable of getting a high grade in this course.
_____ 12. I care about how well they do in this course.
_____ 13. they have control over how they learn the course content.
_____ 14. throughout the course, they could be successful on the coursework.
_____ 15. the coursework is relevant to their future.
_____ 16. I am respectful of them.
_____ 17. the coursework is interesting.
_____ 18. the knowledge they gain in this course is important for their future.
_____ 19. I am friendly.
_____ 20. they have flexibility in what they are allowed to do in this course.

---

[2] From *Motivating Students by Design: Practical Strategies for Professors* by Brett D. Jones, available at www.theMUSICmodel.com. Copyright © 2018 by Brett D. Jones. Photocopying allowed for personal use.

Instructions for Scoring the MUSIC® Model of Academic Motivation Inventory (Professor version, short form)

To obtain a score for each of the five scales, place the item numbers from the prior page into the appropriate cell in Table 3.1 below. Then, average the 4 numbers in each row by adding the 4 numbers and dividing by 4 (because there are 4 items per scale). The final scale score represents an average of the items in the scale.

Table 3.1. *Table to Score the MUSIC Inventory Scales (Professor version)*

					Sum of the row values	Scale score (=sum/4)
eMpowerment	item 4+	item 9+	item 13+	item 20+	= ___ /4	= ___
Usefulness	item 1+	item 8+	item 15+	item 18+	= ___ /4	= ___
Success	item 3+	item 7+	item 11+	item 14+	= ___ /4	= ___
Interest	item 2+	item 6+	item 10+	item 17+	= ___ /4	= ___
Caring	item 5+	item 12+	item 16+	item 19+	= ___ /4	= ___

NOTE: Do not sum or average all 20 items because this produces a meaningless value. It's inconsistent with the principles of the MUSIC model to assume that motivation is the sum of the five MUSIC scales. Although this may be true in some cases, it is possible that students are highly motivated and engaged when only one or two of their MUSIC perceptions are high and the others are low.

Look at your scale score for each MUSIC component. Higher numbers indicate that your instruction is more consistent those components of the MUSIC model. Lower numbers indicate that you may be able to implement more strategies consistent with those MUSIC components. These results cannot be interpreted precisely. Instead, they're intended to help you diagnose areas of possible strengths and weaknesses. To corroborate your beliefs, assess *students'* perceptions by asking students to complete the College Student version of the MUSIC Inventory provided on the next page.

MUSIC® Model of Academic Motivation Inventory (College Student version, short-form[3])

The items for the MUSIC® Model of Academic Motivation Inventory (College Student version, short form) are provided in Table 3.2; however, they must be reformatted according to the instructions provided in the *User Guide* (available at www.theMUSICmodel.com) before you use them. For example, students should not see the scale titles (e.g., Success) and the items must be ordered randomly. The scoring instructions are also provided in the *User Guide*.

Table 3.2. *The items for the MUSIC® Model of Academic Motivation Inventory (College Student version, short-form)*

MUSIC Scales	Items
eMpowerment	• I have the freedom complete the coursework my own way. • I have options in how to achieve the goals of the course. • I have control over how I learn the course content. • I have flexibility in what I am allowed to do in this course.
Usefulness	• In general, the coursework is useful to me. • The coursework is beneficial to me. • I find the coursework to be relevant to my future. • The knowledge I gain in this course is important for my future.
Success	• I am confident that I can succeed in the coursework. • I feel that I can be successful in meeting the academic challenges in this course. • I am capable of getting a high grade in this course. • Throughout the course, I have felt that I could be successful on the coursework.
Interest	• The instructional methods used in this course hold my attention. • I enjoy the instructional methods used in this course. • I enjoy completing the coursework. • The coursework is interesting to me.
Caring	• The instructor is willing to assist me if I need help in the course. • The instructor cares about how well I do in this course. • The instructor is respectful of me. • The instructor is friendly.

---

[3] From *Motivating Students by Design: Practical Strategies for Professors* by Brett D. Jones, available at www.theMUSICmodel.com. Copyright © 2018 by Brett D. Jones. Photocopying allowed for personal use.

Open-Ended Questions Related to the MUSIC Model

You can use any questions you want to use to assess students' perceptions of the MUSIC model components. However, I typically include one open-ended question per MUSIC model component, similar to the ones provided here. Don't provide students with the title of the MUSIC component as I have shown here; these titles are for your information only.

1. eMpowerment: What could be changed in this course to make you feel you had more choices in the course?

2. Usefulness: What could be changed in this course to make it more useful to you?

3. Success: What could be changed in this course to help you feel you could be more successful in it?

4. Interest: What could be changed in this course to make it more interesting and enjoyable?

5. Caring: What could be changed in this course to make you feel that the instructor or other students care about whether you learn the course content and care about you as a person?

Final Comments About Using the Assessment Tools

Now you have some tools to use in assessing students' perceptions of your courses. However, you aren't limited to these tools. Be creative and ask questions that will provide data you can use to redesign your course in relation to the MUSIC model components.

Because students' MUSIC perceptions are affected by a variety of factors, students' perceptions can vary from class to class and week to week. You may want to ask students to complete the MUSIC Inventory several times during the semester to assess how your instructional strategies are affecting their motivation over time. It's also possible that if you teach one section of a course in the morning and another in the afternoon that students' perceptions in one section will differ from students' perceptions in the other section. If so, it's worth investigating why the differences exist.

You can use these same assessments when you're designing a specific class (such as a 50 minute or 3 hour class) or activity (such as a 20 minute activity) by changing the wording from "course" or "coursework" to "class" or "activity." In addition, in the instructions to students, tell them what they are responding to. For example, "These items ask you about the activity you just completed," "These items ask you about the two classes this week related to momentum," or "These items ask you about Chapter 4: The Civil War."

How can I use this book to design my instruction?

This book is primarily intended to help you select MUSIC strategies, which is Step 2 in the MUSIC model design cycle shown again in Figure 3.2. One way to use this book is to skim through Chapters 4 through 8 and quickly identify some strategies that might be useful to you. Although this approach might be sufficient, I would encourage you to spend a few more minutes to read the following sections and complete the worksheet that follows, because doing so will force you to think through the process more systematically and will serve you and your students better.

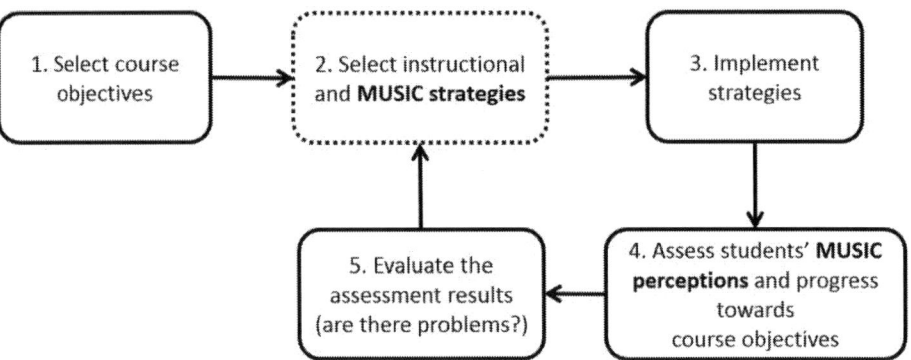

Figure 3.2. *The MUSIC model design cycle*

Steps in the design process for a <u>new</u> course

For a new course, you will complete the design cycle in the order shown in Figure 3.2, starting with Step 1 (Select course objectives). If you've already taught the course, please skip to the next section below, titled "Steps in the design process for an <u>existing</u> course." As I mentioned previously, you will need to use the design cycle in Figure 3.2 to complement other instructional design models (e.g., Dick, Carey, & Carey, 2015; Shambaugh & Magliaro, 2006) because the MUSIC model is not a comprehensive course design model. Instead, it's intended to help you design a more motivating and engaging course than is possible by using a typical course design model (because those models usually don't delve deeply into motivation theory and practice; rather, they acknowledge the importance of motivation, but don't tell you how to design for it in any detail). Because all good design models include steps similar to those in Figure 3.2 (in some form or other), you can simply consider the MUSIC model when you come to steps that are similar to Steps 2, 4, and 5 as you use another design model.

When you're working on selecting instructional and MUSIC strategies (Step 2), try to imagine how students will perceive empowerment, usefulness, success, interest, and caring. Then, work towards selecting strategies that will increase students' perceptions of these MUSIC model components (this book is full of ideas). Also, realize that you can think about incorporating MUSIC model strategies at different levels of your course (as shown in Figure 3.3). At the top level, you can consider changes that affect the entire course, such as attendance and grading policies. You can also consider changes at the unit or chapter level in which you focus specifically on one or more units or chapters. The units/chapters in a course are usually comprised of classes and activities within classes that you can also consider. Don't try to do everything at once because it will be overwhelming; instead, select an activity, class, unit/chapter, or course policy and focus on one of them at a time.

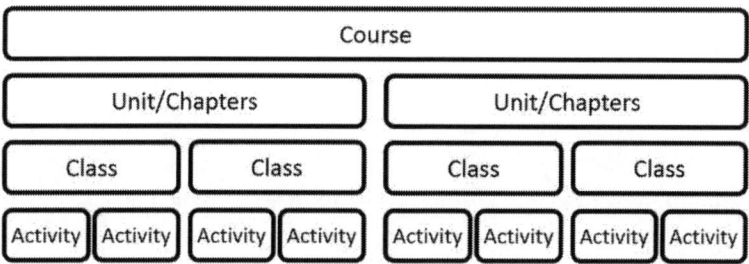

Figure 3.3. *Levels of a course*

After you've completed your design, consider the statements in Table 3.3. If your design is consistent with the MUSIC model, you will answer "true" to these statements. Of course, you cannot be sure of the veracity of your answers until you assess students' perceptions, but you need to make your best estimate during your initial design. And if you believe that any of the statements are not likely to be true, you either need to address them now or in the future.

Table 3.3. *A Brief Checklist to use at the End of Designing a Course or Activity*

MUSIC component	Statements to consider
eMpowerment	• The design gives students choices, control, or freedom to make decisions within the course.
Usefulness	• The design will lead students to believe that the course content, assignments, or activities are useful for their future.
Success	• The design will allow students to believe that they can achieve at a high level on the coursework if they put forth effort.
Interest	• The design will lead students to believe that the instructional methods or coursework are interesting and enjoyable.
Caring	• The design will help students believe that the instructor or others in the course care about whether they succeed in the course or care about their well-being.

After you select the instructional and MUSIC strategies, you implement the strategies by teaching the course (Step 3 in Figure 3.2). After you do that, you can follow the steps in the next section because now you have an existing course.

Steps in the design process for an <u>existing</u> course

For an existing course, you begin your course redesign by assessing students' MUSIC perceptions and progress towards course objectives (Step 4 in Figure 3.2). Previously in the chapter I explained the means by which you can assess students' MUSIC perceptions, including reflecting on your experiences, surveying students, talking to students, and soliciting peer feedback. After you collect some data, you can move to Step 5: evaluating the assessment results to determine whether or not problems exist that you want to address. This step is the most critical part of the redesign process because your evaluation will affect the strategies you select.

Remember, teaching is an art and science. This combination of art and science is evident as you evaluate the assessment results and select appropriate strategies. Here, you must use the science behind the MUSIC model with the flair of an artist to create an instructional design that allows your students to meet the instructional objectives.

When I work with faculty to redesign a course, I find it useful to use both quantitative and qualitative data because both provide useful information about students' MUSIC perceptions. I also find it useful to examine data from both the students' and the instructor's perceptions. I encourage you to use a variety of data to identify areas of weakness and strengths in your instruction. Once you have collected and reviewed the results from the data, completing the questions on the following page can help you to focus your course redesign.

Questions to Help You Focus Your Redesign[4]

1. Are students not meeting some course objectives because of a lack of motivation or engagement? If so, activities related to those course objectives should be considered for redesign. (Possible data sources: grades, scores on tests and rubrics, other assessments and evaluations of student work)

2. Which components of the MUSIC model do *you* believe that *students* perceive to be lower? (Possible data sources: Professor version of the MUSIC Inventory)

3. Which components of the MUSIC model do students rate lowest on quantitative scales? (Possible data sources: College Student version of the MUSIC Inventory)

4. What issues do students raise in response to open-ended questions about each component of the MUSIC model? (Possible data sources: open-ended questions related to each MUSIC component)

5. Do all of the data you collected align and point to a few weaknesses that you can address related to the MUSIC components? If so, what are they? If not, can you reconcile the differences in a manner that will help you to identify weaknesses?

Given your responses to the above 5 questions, which of these statements captures the primary weaknesses or problems you've noted? (*select all that apply*)

o Students don't believe that they have choices, control, or freedom to make decisions within the course. If so, select empowerment strategies (Chapter 4: eMpowerment Strategies).

o Students don't believe that the course content, assignments, or activities are useful for their future. If so, select usefulness strategies (Chapter 5: Usefulness Strategies).

o Students don't believe that they can achieve at a high level in some aspects of the coursework. If so, select success strategies (Chapter 6: Success Strategies).

o Students don't believe that the instructional methods or coursework are interesting or enjoyable. If so, select interest strategies (Chapter 7: Interest Strategies).

o Students don't believe that the instructor or others in the course care about whether they succeed in the course or care about their well-being. If so, select caring strategies (Chapter 8: Caring Strategies).

Based on your answers to all of these questions, identify the MUSIC components that you want to address and order them in terms of importance. Start addressing the most important MUSIC component by reading the corresponding chapter.

---

[4] From *Motivating Students by Design: Practical Strategies for Professors* (2nd Ed.) by Brett D. Jones, available at www.theMUSICmodel.com. Copyright © 2018 by Brett D. Jones. Photocopying allowed for personal use.

And remember that because the MUSIC components are related to each other it's possible that by increasing students' perceptions of one component, you may also change students' perceptions of other components. Therefore, as you make changes to one component, consider how those changes will affect the other components to ensure that your changes will have a positive effect on all MUSIC components.

After you've completed your re-design, consider the statements in Table 3.3 (provided on a prior page). If your design is consistent with the MUSIC model, you will answer "true" to these statements.

Sharing the results with students

When you assess students' perceptions during a course (as opposed to at the end of the course), I encourage you to share the results with your students. Typically, instructors report the means from the MUSIC Inventory (or create a bar graph with the means) and show it on a screen in front of the class. Then, the instructor discusses his/her perceptions of it and any changes that s/he is considering. Listening to students and acknowledging their perspectives can enhance students' sense of empowerment and caring in the course. Therefore, simply showing students the results and discussing them in a respectful manner could lead to increases in students' perceptions of the MUSIC model components and increase in their course engagement. Of course these perceptions will be further reinforced if you actually make changes during the semester to address one or more of their suggestions.

Redesigning an Existing Course: A Specific Example

In this section, I provide an example of the design process I described in the prior section. This example is taken from a course I taught and represents a typical process that I use with other faculty to redesign their existing courses (for example, in a neuroscience lab; Tu & Jones, 2017).

Course Background

The course I will use for this example was titled *Psychological Foundations of Education* and it was offered in a typical 15-week spring semester. I had "inherited" this course from another faculty member who had designed the course. I taught it a few times and had made some minimal changes to the original course design, but as with all of my courses, I wanted to try to engage students even more. This course served upper-level undergraduate students and master's students. All of the students were expected to enroll in (or plan to enroll in) a graduate education program in preparation to become a teacher in a K-12 school. This course was required for all students enrolled in a degree that that led to becoming licensed as a K-12 teacher. Students completed this online, asynchronous course at their own pace, although they had weekly deadlines for the quizzes and assignments. In a typical week, students read a chapter in the textbook and completed an online quiz related to the chapter content. In addition, students were provided with practice quiz questions, a chapter overview video, and some online learning activities to help them understand the course concepts. Students were graded on the quizzes, a case study assignment, and a final exam. Students also received points towards their grade for completing an introductory statement (in which they introduced themselves to me) and a course survey near the end of the course.

Spring Semester: Assessing Students' MUSIC Perceptions and Progress

I began the course redesign in a spring semester by assessing students' MUSIC perceptions and progress towards course objectives (Step 4 in Figure 3.2). Because it was an online course, I never met the students in person, but I exchanged emails with them, which gave me some sense their content questions and concerns. By the end of the course, I had collected the following types of assessment data.

Grades. The final grades for the class were distributed as 53% in the A-range, 43% in the B-range, and 4% in the C-range for an average percentage of about 89%. Overall, I interpreted these grades to indicate that students were generally meeting the course objectives. I didn't detect that any chapters or quizzes were more difficult than the others besides possibly one chapter in which students seemed to struggle a little more to learn the concepts.

MUSIC Perceptions (quantitative data). I assessed students' MUSIC perceptions by administering the MUSIC Inventory (College Student, short version) through an online survey near the end of the course. Students received a few points towards their grade for completing the survey. As described in the *User Guide* for the MUSIC Inventory, I computed the scale score by averaging the four items in each scale. (Note: If you want to be less scientific, you can select one or two questions from each scale as a representative scale item; however, using all four items for each scale makes the scores obtained more reliable.) The results from the 47 students who completed the survey are presented in Figure 3.4 (all students who completed the course also completed the survey for a 100% response rate).

32 • CHAPTER 3: DESIGNING INSTRUCTION

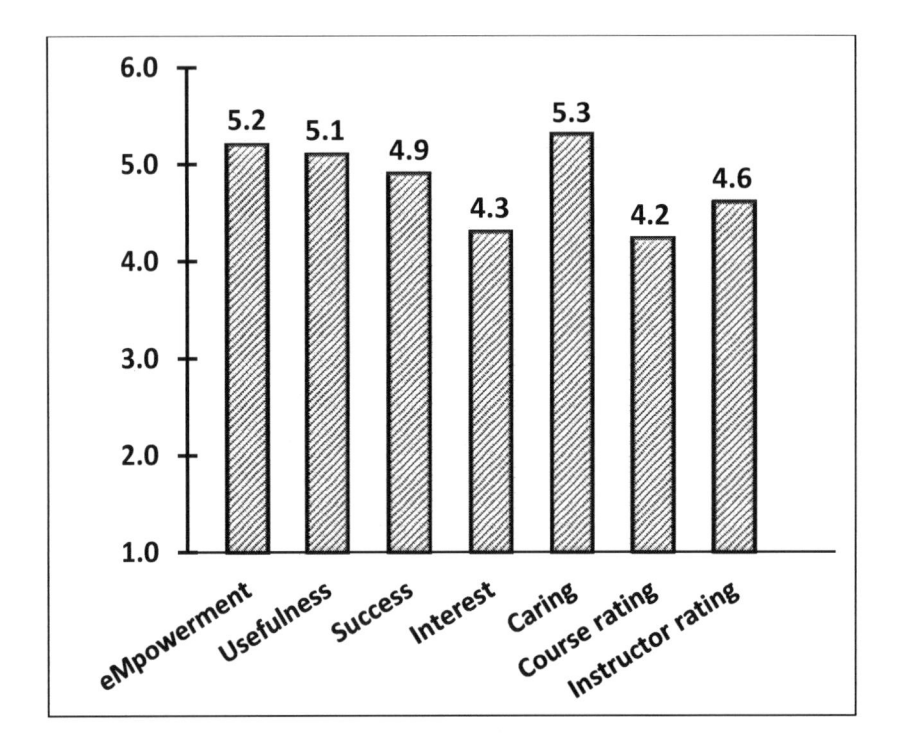

Figure 3.4. *Survey results near the end of the spring semester*

Overall Course and Instructor Ratings. The survey also included one item that asked students to rate the course ("My overall rating of the course." 1 = *terrible*, 6 = *excellent*) and another item that asked them to rate the instructor ("My overall rating of the instructor for this course." 1 = *terrible*, 6 = *excellent*). The results are displayed in Figure 3.4. The course and instructor ratings can be useful to consider in addition to the MUSIC scale scores because they provide an indication of students' overall perceptions. And importantly, whether we like it or not, they are often used for faculty salary, promotion, and tenure decisions.

MUSIC Perceptions (qualitative data). It would have been nice if the survey had also included one open-ended item per MUSIC component as discussed in the previous section, but instead, I asked many different open-ended items related to specific aspects of the course and one general open-ended item that stated: "Please type any comments or suggestions that you have for improving the course."

Evaluating the Assessment Results for Course Redesign

After conducting this assessment of students' MUSIC perceptions (Step 4 in Figure 3.2), it was time to evaluate the assessment results and identify any problems or areas of weaknesses (Step 5 in Figure 3.2). To follow the recommendations in the prior section, I asked myself the questions in the "Questions to Help You Focus Your

Redesign" section and I've copied them here and provided my responses as bulleted items below each question.

1. Are students not meeting some course objectives because of a lack of motivation or engagement? If so, activities related to those course objectives should be considered for redesign.
    - I primarily relied on the quiz grades, case study assignment grade, final exam grades, and course grade to determine that students were generally meeting the course objectives. I couldn't identify any pattern to suggest that some objectives were not met more than others. The grades on the case study assignment were very high, indicating that almost all students met the objectives related to that assignment.

2. Which components of the MUSIC model do you believe that students perceive to be lower?
    - I was concerned about students' level of <u>interest</u>. Although the textbook was very readable and interesting, the course lacked variety, which can lead students to become bored as they complete similar activities each week.
    - I thought students might rate <u>empowerment</u> lower because they were mostly told what to do, although they had choices as to when to do things before the deadlines.

3. Which components of the MUSIC model do students rate lowest on quantitative scales?
    - Overall, the scores on the MUSIC Inventory scales were fairly high, but the <u>Interest</u> component was clearly rated the lowest (see Figure 3.4).
    - The course rating was lower than the instructor rating, and neither rating was too high (see Figure 3.4).

4. What issues do students raise in response to open-ended questions about each component of the MUSIC model?
    - I asked students many questions related to various aspects of the course, but here I will focus on this more general question: "Please type any comments or suggestions that you have for improving the course." I noted two themes in the responses.
        a. Some students suggested including more variety because a lot of emphasis was placed on quizzes. Students wrote: "I think there should be a wider variety of activities for this course" and "It would

be beneficial to vary the assignments, possibly adding more things like the [current case study] assignment."
   b. Some students suggested including more projects to provide more variety, but also to make the course more useful to them. Students wrote: "I felt that I got more out of the [case study] project than the readings because I was actually doing something that's helping me in the long run as a teacher" and "Additional instruction on the methods for promoting different aspects of education."

5. Do all of the data you collected align and point to a few weaknesses that you can address related to the MUSIC components? If so, what are they? If not, can you reconcile the differences in a manner that will help you to identify weaknesses?
   - Generally, the data aligns and indicates that the course could be more <u>interesting</u> and <u>useful</u>.

Given my responses to the 5 questions above, I identified two of the following statements (these are from the previous section) that capture the primary weaknesses I noted. My comments are provided below each statement.

- Students don't believe that they have choices, control, or freedom to make decisions within the course. If so, select empowerment strategies (Chapter 4: eMpowerment Strategies).
  - I didn't see many student concerns related to empowerment, so I didn't focus on empowerment as a top priority, but I wanted to keep it in mind for future revisions.
- Students don't believe that the course content, assignments, or activities are useful for their future. If so, select usefulness strategies (Chapter 5: Usefulness Strategies).
  - I did find some evidence for this and I wanted to improve the perceived usefulness of the course.
- Students don't believe that they can achieve at a high level in some aspects of the coursework. If so, select success strategies (Chapter 6: Success Strategies).
  - I didn't see success perceptions as one of the major weaknesses of the course.

- o Students don't believe that the instructional methods or coursework are interesting or enjoyable. If so, select interest strategies (Chapter 7: Interest Strategies).
  - This was the biggest problem that I noted. The course lacked variety, which can lower students' interest.
- o Students don't believe that the instructor or others in the course care about whether they succeed in the course or care about their well-being. If so, select caring strategies (Chapter 8: Caring Strategies).
  - This was not a theme I noted in the data.

Given these findings, I prioritized the <u>interest</u> and <u>usefulness</u> components of the MUSIC model as the two most important to address in my course redesign. At this point, I was finished with Step 5 in Figure 3.2 and I was ready to move on to Step 2 again: Select instructional and MUSIC strategies. Therefore, Chapters 5 and 7 in this book included the strategies that were most likely to be relevant.

Selecting Strategies to Increase Perceived Interest and Usefulness

As I explained previously in the design of a new course, you can think about incorporating MUSIC model strategies at different levels of your course (as shown previously in Figure 3.3). Because I wanted to increase students' interest and usefulness, I did not see a need to make policy changes at the course level. I wanted to keep all of the chapter units in place, so I didn't see a need to change anything at that level. And because it was an online course, I didn't have classes. Therefore, I decided to focus at the activity level by designing activities that could be used to increase students' perceptions of interest and usefulness (see Figure 3.5).

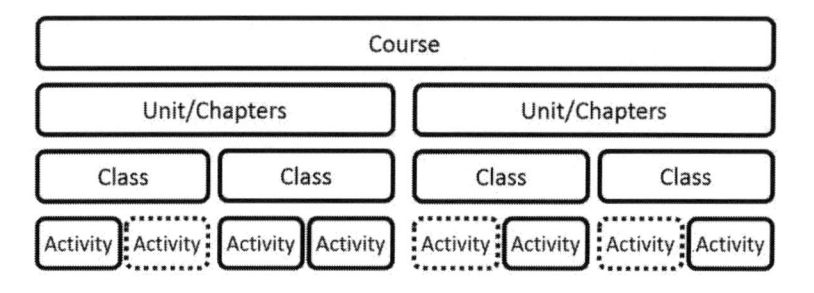

Figure 3.5. *Redesigning at the activity level*

<u>Interest</u>. The data indicated that the course could be more interesting, primarily because it lacked variety. The course focused too heavily on textbook reading and quizzes which led students to become bored of the same assignments throughout the

course. To increase students' perceptions of interest I focused primarily on the strategies in this book related to Interest Strategy 3 ("I.3") in Chapter 7: Stimulate emotional arousal in students to avoid boredom. One of these strategies involves varying instructional activities across the course. To do so I did the following.

- I added three new assignments to add variety to the types of assignments that were provided. Variety should increase students' interest.

- I revised the overview videos and created additional new videos that they could watch after completing the readings. The new videos were intended to trigger interest by including activities that required students to actively participate.

Usefulness. The data indicated that the course could be more useful to students' goals, which including becoming K-12 teachers. Although the content was perceived as useful, the assessments were focused more on obtaining knowledge and less on applying it to teaching (although many examples and quiz questions focused on classroom applications of course concepts). To increase students' perceptions of usefulness I focused primarily on the strategies in this book related to Usefulness Strategy 2 ("U.2") in Chapter 5: Ask students or someone else to share the reasons they find the course content useful.

I chose strategy U.2 primarily because I wanted students to explain to themselves and others how the course concepts could be useful to them as future teachers in their teaching context. To do so, of the three new assignments that I created to increase students' interest, I designed two of them to specifically require students to look in the textbook and "identify 5 ideas that you are most likely to implement as a teacher." I hypothesized that these assignments would be perceived as useful to their future because all of the students were intending to become teachers in the future.

At this point I was ready to move on to Step 3 in Figure 3.2 and implement these strategies.

Fall Semester: Assessing Students' MUSIC Perceptions and Progress

I implemented the revisions (i.e., three new assignments and new and revised videos) in the fall semester immediately following the spring semester in which I collected the data. At the end of the fall semester, I moved on to Step 4 in Figure 3.2 and collected more data using the same quantitative items from the spring semester to assess the effects of the revisions. Figure 3.6 shows a comparison of students' scores at the end of the spring semester (the darker shaded bars) with 20 students' scores at the end of the fall semester (the lighter shaded bars).

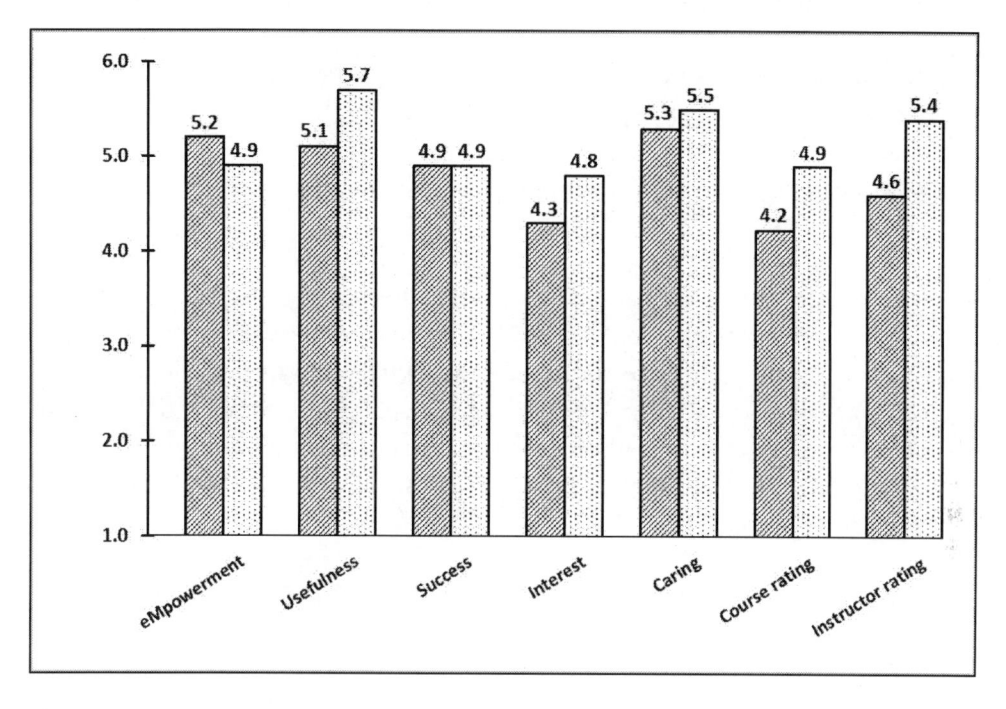

Figure 3.6. *Survey results near the end of the spring semester (darker shaded bars, n = 47) and the end of the fall semester after redesign (lighter shaded bars, n = 20)*

Let's begin by looking at the changes in interest and usefulness scores because the revisions were targeted at increasing students' interest and usefulness perceptions. I considered the revisions to be successful because they increased students' ratings on both interest and usefulness about one-half point. There was little to no difference between semesters in students' ratings of empowerment, success, and caring. However, students rated empowerment a little lower and caring a little higher after the revisions. In addition, the course and instructor ratings were significantly higher after the revisions.

Students were also asked this open-ended question at the end of the fall semester after answering several other open-ended questions: Is there anything else you wanted to tell me about the course? The students' comments included the following.

- "I hope the rest of my graduate courses are as interesting."

- "I really enjoyed this course. It is probably the most useful and relevant course I have taken so far here at Virginia Tech."
- "It is a course that focuses on practicability. I think this course is useful if I become a teacher."

At this point, I was finished assessing students' MUSIC perceptions (Step 4 in Figure 3.2) and now I was ready to evaluate the assessment results (Step 5 in Figure 3.2).

Evaluating the Assessment Results from Fall Semester

Taken together, the quantitative results indicated that the course revisions were successful in having a positive effect on students' perceptions, especially their interest and usefulness perceptions. And these quantitative results were supported by students' responses to the open-ended items. Hurray, it was time to celebrate! Although more could still be done to improve students' ratings, my only concern about my revisions was that students' empowerment scores dropped slightly. I wanted to keep an eye on that, but because it was still relatively high, I wasn't too concerned about it.

Obviously, it's possible that the changes in students' perceptions from the spring to fall semesters were due to factors other than the course revisions. For example, the students in the fall semester were different from the students in the spring semester. A more scientific study was needed to eliminate other possible causes of the changes in perceptions. But that is somewhat irrelevant here because the purpose of this example was to model a process that you can use to revise your courses in ways that are consistent with the MUSIC model. I hope this example was helpful in doing that.

At this point, I'm going to stop cycling through the design cycle in Figure 3.2, but you can imagine that the next step is to determine which areas of the course are now weakest after these most recent revisions and select new strategies to continue the cycle and improve the course even further.

Judging the Motivational Impacts of a New Strategy

In some instances, you will hear about or think of a new teaching strategy and wonder whether it will work well in your course. Let me give you an example to explain how you can use the MUSIC model to help you think about the possible effectiveness of a new teaching strategy.

In my graduate courses (that ranged from about 12 to 27 students each semester), I often posed questions or cases and asked students to discuss them with two or three other students. Over the years, I noticed that some groups would finish their discussion early and begin talking about topics unrelated to the course. As I paid closer attention, I found that many times these students were friends or knew each other because they were in their other courses together. It's not surprising that students sit next to people they know; however, I found that their short discussions and side conversations had a negative effect on the quality of their discussions. Therefore, I started assigning them to seats randomly. Yes, I assigned seats to my graduate students. I anticipated that this might affect their motivation, so I considered the pros and cons related to each component of the MUSIC model, as summarized in Table 3.4.

Table 3.4. *Pros and Cons of Assigning Seats*

MUSIC component	Pros of assigning seats	Cons of assigning seats
eMpowerment	• None	• Students will feel manipulated and controlled
Usefulness	• Students might have better discussions with others they don't know as well or who differ from them in some ways; and thus, learn more	• Students might have similar purposes as their friends for enrolling in the course, which could lead to discussions that are more relevant to their goals
Success	• Students are less likely to engage in off-topic discussions, and thus, remain focused and learn more • Students can learn from others who differ from them or who know more about particular topics	• Students can't choose to sit with others who may be able to help them more or who are more focused and interested in learning; that is, they may get stuck with someone who is unengaged or uninterested in learning
Interest	• Students might like sitting next to strangers because they get tired of sitting with others they know (but feel obliged to sit with them)	• They may not like their assigned partners as much as their friends
Caring	• Students might find commonalities with other students • Students might make new friends	• Students can't build on existing relationships with their friends

I hypothesized that the greatest strength of assigning seats (related to the course objectives) would be associated with the success component: students would have more productive conversations with others and learn more because they would be forced to talk to others that may be more different from themselves than their friends, or at least, others whom they didn't know as well. I hypothesized that the greatest weakness would be that I was perceived as controlling, which would disempower them from the moment they walked in the door each class.

To minimize the weakness listed in Table 3.4 (i.e., to reduce the negative effects of disempowerment), I explained my rationale for the assigned seat policy at the beginning of the course. I also randomly assign students to a different seat each week (to reduce the cons related to the success, interest, and caring components in Table 3.4). Of course by changing the seating each week, students were able to sit with some of their friends some of the weeks. I used a website (www.random.org) to assign seats randomly and showed the seating chart on the screen in the front of the room as they entered the class (see Figure 3.7). To provide a little empowerment, I started assigning students to groups of four and allowing the groups to choose where they wanted to sit in the room. This choice allowed students who want to sit in a certain location the opportunity to come a few minutes earlier and claim that location in the room (e.g., students who want to sit in the front of the room).

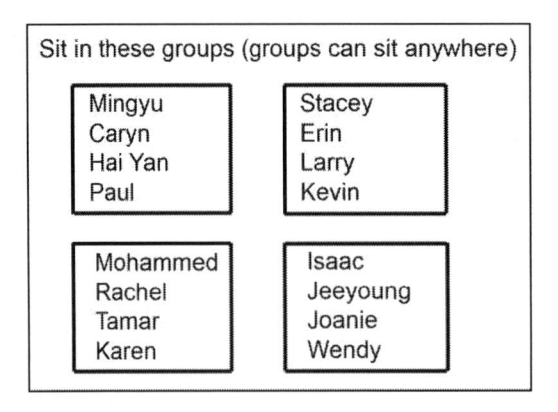

```
Sit in these groups (groups can sit anywhere)

  Mingyu        Stacey
  Caryn         Erin
  Hai Yan       Larry
  Paul          Kevin

  Mohammed      Isaac
  Rachel        Jeeyoung
  Tamar         Joanie
  Karen         Wendy
```

Figure 3.7. *Example seating chart shown at the beginning of class*

After trying this strategy for several years, I found that my hypotheses about what would happen were pretty accurate. The conversations and products they produced from the discussions were of higher quality than when I didn't assign seats; and, the amount of off-topic discussions was much less. Therefore, I continue to assign seats. Some students still comment on the end-of-course evaluations that they wish they had been allowed to choose their seat. But I can live with those comments knowing that our in-class discussions are better and that they seem to be learning more.

I hope this example helped you to see how the MUSIC model can be used to identify motivational strengths and weaknesses related to a teaching strategy or approach. And importantly, how to minimize the motivational weaknesses associated with them.

Where did the teaching strategies in this book come from?

I included teaching strategies in this book that are consistent with the MUSIC model when implemented appropriately. Some of the strategies in this book have been tested with well-designed studies. Other strategies haven't been tested empirically, but they're consistent with theories and research. Unfortunately, in education and psychology, researchers haven't had time to study every teaching strategy in every possible context. Therefore, they develop principles and theories based on empirical research to describe phenomena. I have included teaching strategies that are consistent with motivation principles, theories, and research, even if they haven't been tested empirically. Some of the teaching strategies are based on my personal experience as a professor at the college level for almost two decades or based on the experience of my colleagues whom I've either observed teaching or talked to about their teaching. I consider these individual successes and failures to be case studies that can provide useful information.

Strategies specific to certain aspects of instruction

Everything you do in a course will affect students' perceptions related to all five MUSIC components. However, I thought it might be helpful to point out some specific strategies that may be more important to consider when designing certain aspects of instruction, such as writing your syllabus, creating your attendance policy and class rules, designing your assignments, creating exams, and designing your lectures (if you lecture).

In Table 3.5, I note where some of these strategies are located in this book. As you can see, empowerment strategies are prevalent when creating class rules, assignments, and active learning; usefulness and interest strategies are key when designing effective lectures; and success strategies are prevalent when creating assignments and exams. Again, all of the MUSIC components should be considered during all aspects of the course design, but some MUSIC components are likely more salient than others in certain aspects of instruction.

Table 3.5. *Strategies Related to Specific Aspects of Instruction*

Aspect	Relevant Strategies
Syllabus	M.4.2, S.2.8, S.1.5, S.5.1, S.5.2, C.1.2, C.1.4, C.2.1
Attendance policy	M.4.2, S.5.4, C.4.2
Class rules	M.1.8, M.3.2, Empowerment Strategy 4, C.2.1
Assignments	Empowerment Strategy 1, M.4.2, Usefulness Strategy 3, S.2.7 to S.2.12, S.2.16, S.2.18, S.2.21, Success Strategy 3, S.4.3, S.4.4, S.4.7, C.1.5
Exams	M.4.2, U.3.7, S.2.12, S.2.13, S.2.17, S.4.1, S.4.2, S.5.2
Lecturing	Usefulness Strategy 1; U.2.4; S.2.19, Interest Strategies 1, 2, and 3
Active learning	Many strategies throughout the book; too many to list here, although Empowerment Strategies 2 and 5 focus on this

Note: This is not intended to be a comprehensive list of relevant strategies.

CHAPTER 4

Strategies to eMpower Students

Problem

Students don't believe that they have choices, control, or freedom to make decisions within the course.

Solution

You need to ensure that students feel <u>empowered</u> by having the ability to make decisions about some aspects of their learning.

Overview of eMpowerment

Are you more motivated to do something when *you* decide to do it or when *others* tell you to do it? Do you like to have a choice of options or do you prefer to have only one option? Most people like to make their own decisions and have some options (although sometimes not too many options).

<u>Key Point:</u> Students are more motivated and engaged when they feel empowered; that is, when they have the freedom to control some aspect of their environment and they can make decisions about things that affect them. Empowerment in the MUSIC model refers to giving students some *power* over some aspects of their learning. It places the students in control by giving them the freedom to make decisions. When you empower students, they have a sense of freedom and autonomy.

It's critical to note that you can only empower students to do things that are within their abilities or slightly beyond their abilities. If you give them too much freedom beyond their abilities, they will feel helpless and will likely have difficulty knowing how to even begin the activity. Therefore, you want to increase students' perceptions of empowerment, but also keep their perceptions of *success* at a reasonable level so that they believe they can succeed if they put forth the required effort. This demonstrates another point: it's important to consider the other four components in the MUSIC model when you make changes to one of the components.

Empowerment can be a very powerful motivator, but it can also be very scary to learners. As the principal of my daughter's middle school told parents at an orientation: students coming from elementary school to middle school are most motivated and excited about the freedom they have to change classes, to have their own lockers, etc., but these same freedoms are the things that they're also most anxious about.

If you like your class to be scripted and well organized, and you like to know exactly what students will say and do, you may struggle with giving students empowerment. Even though empowering students may be easier for some instructors than others, all instructors can learn how to do it. You can be well organized and still empower students; in fact, you need to be well organized when you empower students if you want to be an effective instructor. You need to have clear goals (e.g., have clear instructions for assignments), the students need to know the purpose of what they're doing, and you need to help them achieve the goals. The strategies in this chapter will provide you with examples of how you can do these things.

Finally, empowerment does *not* mean that the learner feels *more capable* or *values* the activity or topic. Rather, the learner simply feels the freedom of control over some aspect of their learning. Perceptions about capability and values are important, but they're included in other components of the MUSIC model (perceptions of capability are related to the *success* component and values are related to the *usefulness* component).

In this chapter, I present the following five empowerment strategies and provide several examples of each.

- M.1 Provide students with choices during class and within assignments.
- M.2 Incorporate learner-directed approaches.
- M.3 Explain to students the amount of control they have in the course.
- M.4 Don't give rewards that may be perceived as controlling.
- M.5 Avoid controlling language and allow students to talk more.

Relevant Theories

In this section, I provide very brief explanations of some of the theories that are most directly relevant to the empowerment strategies in the MUSIC model. These are not comprehensive explanations, so please look-up the citations if you are interested in more information.

- Need for autonomy (Deci & Ryan, 1985, 2000; Murray, 1938). Need for autonomy was identified by Murray (1938) as a psychological need. More recently, Deci and Ryan (1985) have described it as a construct within cognitive evaluation theory, which is a subtheory of self-determination theory. Individuals have a need for autonomy, which is a psychological need that is innate in all humans. "The need for autonomy (or self-determination) encompasses people's strivings to be agentic, to feel like the 'origin' (deCharms, 1968) of their actions, and to have a voice or input in determining their own behavior. It concerns the desire to experience an internal perceived locus of causality with regard to action—that is, to experience one's actions as emanating from the self" (Deci & Ryan, 1991, p. 243). Students are more likely to be motivated and perform at higher levels when they experience autonomy (Cerasoli et al., 2016).

- Control theories. Although many control theories relate more closely to the success component of the MUSIC model than the empowerment component (see Chapter 6 for an explanation), some control theories are also related to students' perceptions of empowerment. It's beyond the scope of this book to explain these nuances, but if you're interested, Skinner (1996) wrote an article that delves into this topic.

- Interest Theories (Hidi & Renninger, 2006; Krapp, 2005; Schraw & Lehman, 2001). Interest arises from a combination of situational interest and individual interest. "*Situational interest* is a temporary state aroused by specific features of a situation, task, or object" (Schiefele, 2009, pp. 197-198). In contrast, "*individual interest* is conceptualized as a relatively stable affective-evaluative orientation toward certain subject areas or objects" (Schiefele, 2009, pp. 198). Students are more likely to be motivated when they are interested in the object, activity, or topic of study. When students are empowered, they can pursue activities most closely aligned with their interests (Linnenbrink-Garcia, Patall, & Messersmith, 2013).

Empowerment Strategy 1

Provide students with choices during class and within assignments.

One of the simplest ways to empower students is to give them some choices. Choices can be empowering because they force students to take control and make decisions. In this section, I begin with examples that give students very minimal choices and then progress through examples that give students more choices.

It's important to note that you don't want to give students too many choices. If students are overwhelmed with their choices, it can lead to a lack of motivation and engagement (Schwartz, 2005). Instead, you want to provide "empowerment in bounds," for which you set the boundaries and allow students to make choices within those boundaries. This is similar to a soccer or football game in which the teams are allowed to do what they want to do within the rules and boundaries of the field.

The choices need to be appropriate for students' abilities. Students who have more knowledge and skills can generally be given more choices that allow them to use their abilities, whereas students with less knowledge and skills will be more motivated in a more structured environment with fewer choices until they obtain the confidence needed to handle harder challenges. The main point here is that empowerment through choice is okay as long as it doesn't negatively affect other components of the MUSIC model, such as success perceptions.

Empowerment can also increase other components of the MUSIC model. For example, increasing empowerment through choice can increase students' levels of interest because they can choose things in which they're most interested (Linnenbrink-Garcia et al., 2013).

Example M.1.1 – Allowing Choice of Assignment Order

Allow students to choose the order in which they complete assignments. This may be the simplest way to give students a little bit of autonomy. For example, if students are working in groups on three different assignments, you could allow them to complete the assignments in any order they desire (when none of the assignments are prerequisites for the others).

Example M.1.2 – Allowing Choices Within Assignments

Allow students to make choices within an assignment. In this case, all students complete the same assignment, but they have choices within the assignment. Let me give you a few examples.

- A sociology professor asks students to summarize in writing three of the five theories from their readings given a rubric with specific grading criteria. This assignment allows students to choose three theories from among the five theories.

- A psychology professor asks students to create a case study that demonstrates one of the concepts from the textbook reading. Students are given a grading rubric with specific criteria. This assignment allows students to choose the concept and the details of the case.

- A professor requires students to post discussion topics in an online discussion forum and requires the other students to respond to three of the discussion topics. Students are given a choice as to which discussions they want to respond to.

- A history professor requires students to select an individual from history and describe everything that is in the person's wallet or a bag s/he is carrying (e.g., pictures, pay stubs, things that are important to them). A literature professor uses a similar strategy by asking students to select a character from a book. Another idea is to have students create an Instagram account for the historical figure. These ideas require students to not only choose the person, but also the artifacts that they would be carrying with them.

Example M.1.3 – Allowing Choice of Assignments to Complete

Allow students to choose which assignments they want to complete. You can do this by giving each assignment a point value and providing more assignments than students need to complete to receive an A in the course. For example, you may make available 20 assignments worth 10 points each (for a total of 200 points possible). Yet, to receive an A, students need to accumulate only 150 points of the 200 points, which would allow them to complete fewer than 20 assignments and still receive an A. Students can decide the grade they want to receive and work to achieve their grade goal.

You will likely want to make important assignments worth more points than assignments that require less time and effort. Also, you can consider making some of the assignments mandatory; for instance, assignments that you want all students to complete because the content is critical to the course objectives.

You have to think through different scenarios that can happen, such as what will happen if students do poorly on many assignments? Will they still be able to achieve an A? Is that appropriate? You may implement a policy that students receive zero points on an assignment unless they receive at least a 70% on the assignment (or some other percentage of the assignment).

An advantage of this strategy is that there is no need for extra credit assignments, students can simply complete more of the assignments to improve their grade.

Example M.1.4 – Allowing Choice of Assignment Topic

Allow students to choose the topic of their assignments, as long as their final product relates to the course content and course objectives. A common way to implement this strategy is to allow students to choose the topic of an assigned paper. It seems that professors have been doing this with paper assignments since the beginning of time. A more updated version of this assignment is to ask students to present their topic in a video format instead of as a paper. Students can upload their videos to YouTube and send you the URL for their video.

Chris Walsh, a faculty member at Boston University, provides a slight twist on this idea with a strategy that he has used in his American and African literature, contemporary American novel, and composition courses (Walsh, n.d.). He calls this strategy "the blank syllabus" because he leaves some of the assigned readings blank for some of the classes. For students' first writing assignment, they review the readings that he has listed in a course anthology, select a reading that they believe the entire class should read, and write a paper to advocate for including their reading choice in the course syllabus. If the class size is small, Dr. Walsh includes all of the student-selected readings in the syllabus. If the class is large, he asks students to vote for the readings they want to include in the syllabus. He claims that this strategy "energizes and engages students by encouraging them to 'own' the material and the course itself. They discover things independently and report back to their peers and me with enthusiasm" (Walsh, n.d., p. 1).

Example M.1.5 – Allowing Choice of Assignment Format

Allow students to choose the *format* of an assignment. They might consider formats such as a traditional paper, a video, a video blog (vlog), a project product, a model, a photograph, a skit, etc. (search online and ask students for newer electronic possibilities such as PowToon: https://www.powtoon.com). For some assignments, you might allow students to choose to work in collaboration with other students. If you allow students to choose a project product, you'll probably want students to write at least a one-paragraph proposal to explain their format and what will be included in their project. The proposal will help you to ensure that the quality of the project will meet the course objectives and that the scope of the project is consistent across students, regardless of format. You should give students a rubric (or ask them to give you one that you will first approve) so that they know how they'll be assessed.

An assignment format you may suggest to students as an alternative format is a concept map or mind map, which are graphic organizers that students can create by placing concepts or ideas in ovals, organizing the ovals in a way that shows the relationships among them, and then connecting the ovals together with lines that may or may not be labeled (Novak & Gowin, 1984). Mind maps are slightly different in that the main topic is placed at the center of the map and the ovals and lines extend from the main topic (Buzan & Buzan, 1993). Also, mind maps may include images or colors. Maps can be created with paper and pencil or electronically (search online for tools such as https://bubbl.us). Some students have reported that they enjoy the "complete control over the design" of their mind map (Jones, Ruff, Snyder, Petrich, & Koonce, 2012, p. 11), as well as the fact that creating the map was interesting and that the map was useful for organizing their thoughts and for studying later on. In the Appendix of their online article, Jones et al. (2012) provide example directions to students about how to create a mind map (that you could copy and give to your students), as well as a grading rubric (that you could copy and use to grade students' mind maps).

Example M.1.6 – Allowing Students to Find or Create Resources

Allow students to find or create course resources. You may feel pressure to keep your course updated by finding new information resources in books, articles, or websites. Of course you should be knowledgeable about the latest information in your field. Sometimes, however, it's possible to empower *students* to find or create these resources and then share them with you and the others in the class. In doing so, students may not only be more motivated, but they may also learn more because they have to search through some part of the discipline content, which can expose them to many more resources. By leaving a blank space on your syllabus for some of the resources they find, you can require all students to read some of these newly found resources by either choosing from what students have found or having the students vote on the resources they want included.

Example M.1.7 – Soliciting Ideas for Grading Criteria

Solicit students' ideas for grading criteria. Many assignments require you to develop grading criteria, which could be in the form of a rubric or other less formal guidelines. Typically, professors develop these criteria and then show them to students, preferably before students complete the assignment so that they know how they'll be graded. To give students some empowerment, you can ask students to review your criteria and make suggestions for changes. They may suggest new criteria that are important to them and that they believe would more accurately reflect their effort and abilities. Another alternative is to ask students to develop the criteria by themselves from scratch. You can still review and approve their final criteria, making modifications or suggestions if needed. But often the hard-working students want credit for their hard work and will make the criteria reasonable and fair.

Example M.1.8 – Allowing Students to Create Rules

Allow students to help create classroom rules and policies. I provide some specific examples of classroom rules in Caring Strategy 2 in Chapter 8 (Example C.2.1), but I wanted to make the point here that you can empower students by allowing them to edit the classroom rules and policies you've developed. Or, you can allow *them* to develop the classroom rules and policies. The idea is that students are more likely to feel empowered and to "buy-in" to the rules and policies when they have some input into developing them.

Simon Bates and Alison Lister, faculty at the University of British Columbia, have used this strategy in their introductory physics courses (Bates & Lister, 2013). At the beginning of the course, they asked students to decide on the acceptable use guidelines for their use of technology in the classroom. To get students started, they used Google Docs to post some basic ground rules for students to consider. Then, over the next week, students edited the Google Doc and the class abided by the rules they had created.

Example M.1.9 – Allowing Students to Express Thoughts

Allow students to express their thoughts and ideas. When students express their thoughts and ideas, they have control over what they share. Students must decide not only what they believe about something, but they must also decide which aspects of their beliefs to share with others. Allowing students to participate in small group discussions is one way to allow students to express their thoughts and ideas, but there are other ways as well.

You can require students to create a personal online journal (called a blog, which is short for "Web log"). Because blogs can be viewed publicly on the

Internet, students are immediately writing for a worldwide audience (although bloggers can restrict who is able to see their blog if you want to restrict it to only you or the students in your course). Students can set-up free blogs at a variety of sites (for example, www.blogger.com is a free blogging site backed by Google) and start writing. You can ask students to blog broadly about any course content by sharing their reflections on the content, maybe thinking about questions they still have or misconceptions that they have corrected. Or, you can ask students to focus more narrowly on one or more course topics listed by you. By creating your own blog, you can use it to refer back to students' blog content in your blog (using the "trackback" feature). Doing so can show students that you're paying attention to and are interested in what they're writing. You can encourage students to read and refer to each other's blogs and to comment on other students' specific blog posts. Used in this way, blogging is more like a cooler version of more formal, clunky discussion boards, with other features that discussion boards don't have.

You can ask students to create vlogs (short for "video log" or "video blog") to accomplish some of the same things as a blog, but vlogs also have some other features. With vlogs, students video record themselves speaking and they can add images, movies, and text. Blogs and vlogs can be used by students to reflect on their learning over time. Over time, students may see changes in their beliefs, attitudes, and abilities, which can help them feel empowered because they're in control of their learning.

Professors Kelly Parkes and Sara Kajder required students to blog every other week and vlog on the alternate weeks (Parkes & Kajder, 2010). They used WordPress (https://wordpress.com) because it allowed students to customize the design of their blog, upload video clips, and link to websites and photos. If you're wondering how you can grade blogs and vlogs, see the online journal article by Parkes and Kadjer (2010) because they include some nice rubrics that you can modify for your own use.

Example M.1.10 – Giving Students Opportunities to Lead Instruction

Give students opportunities to lead or co-lead instruction. When students lead or co-lead instruction in the class, they're able to make decisions about what they want to do and how they want to do it. Making these types of decisions can make them feel empowered. But be careful in using this strategy because while this strategy empowers the students leading the instruction, it may do nothing to engage the other students in the class. The novelty of having a peer instructor can be engaging to the other students, and sometimes students have good, unique ideas that the regular professor would never have thought about including in instruction. However, students are usually novice and nervous instructors with little content knowledge about the subject they're teaching (why would they be enrolled in the course if they were as knowledgeable as the regular professor?). As a result, they will need support in preparing to teach; otherwise, the outcome can be a poor presentation with information that's not completely accurate or off the mark in some way. At worst, I've seen it create misconceptions in students' knowledge, which violates the principle of *do no harm*.

Most of the time simply allowing students to teach is not enough to result in an engaging or meaningful class. Personally, as a graduate student, I hated it when the professor assigned a topic each week to a graduate student in my class to teach because I wanted instruction from the professor, not my peers. Not everyone shared my sentiment, but be aware that some students will, especially if the instruction by the students is poor. (That said, in graduate courses it's possible that some students are more knowledgeable than the professor in some particular course topics, and you may want graduate students to teach the class when that's the case.)

If you allow students to lead instruction, you should give them resources with information that includes tips for different types of teaching or presentation strategies. For example, what are the important elements needed to create an effective PowerPoint presentation? What other types of presentations are possible for the assignment (such as group activities, class discussion, etc.)?

It's probably best to have students submit their instructional plans (lessons) to you as they develop their ideas and then again when they're finished creating them (but before they teach the class). By reviewing their plans early, you can give them tips to make sure that they're headed in the right direction. To ensure that they submit their plans to you, require them to do so on the syllabus and give them a grade for it. It's fine to give them full credit for that part of their grade if they simply hand-in something. In other words, you're not grading the quality of their presentation at that point, you're just giving them credit for submitting their plans to you on time to make sure they do it. Remember, you're still the professor and you're responsible for the quality of the instruction, even if someone else is delivering it on any one particular day.

Example M.1.11 – Setting Reasonable Due Dates

Set deadlines for assignments and tests, but don't set the due dates too close together. In an online course where students study and then complete online tests, have regular due dates for assignments to keep students on track at a reasonable pace. But instead of setting two due dates in one week, consider setting one due date on which both assignments are due. This provides students with more freedom in deciding when to complete the coursework during that time. Find the balance between providing too many due dates (which can limit their empowerment) and not enough (which can hinder their success if they aren't good at regulating their study time and they procrastinate until right before the assignment is due).

						November
26	27	28	29	30	31	1
2	3	4	5	6	ASSIGNMENT DUE! 7	8

Example M.1.12 – Using Games That Require Decisions

Use games that put students in charge of making decisions. Games can be engaging because they empower students and allow them to feel successful. Obviously, players aren't always successful, which can negatively affect their motivation if they continually fail to succeed. You can use games in many different ways, but the focus for this strategy is on games that provide students with choices and place them in an active role in their learning.

Games can empower students by allowing them to play different roles, such as members of Congress (*Government in Action*; http://www.mhpractice.com/products/GinA) and historical figures (*Reacting to the Past*; http://reacting.barnard.edu/). Here is a description of a game called *Reacting to the Past*.

> "Students learn by taking on roles, informed by classic texts, in elaborate games set in the past; they learn skills—speaking, writing, critical thinking, problem solving, leadership, and teamwork—in order to prevail in difficult and complicated situations. That is because Reacting roles, unlike those in a play, do not have a fixed script and outcome. While students will be obliged to adhere to the philosophical and intellectual beliefs of the historical figures they have been assigned to play, they must devise their own means of expressing those ideas persuasively, in papers, speeches or other public presentations; and students must also pursue a course of action they think will help them win the game." (http://reacting.barnard.edu/curriculum, para. 1)

Obviously, *Reacting to the Past* is quite sophisticated and the content is not applicable to all college courses. However, I include this example because it shows what's possible when instructors think creatively about how to place students in situations that allow them to make decisions.

Believe it or not, you can even make your entire course a game. Shannon Duvall, a professor of computer science at Elon University, did this in her undergraduate *Computer Graphics and Game Programming* course (Duvall, n.d.). The syllabus read like a game manual and Dr. Duvall renamed things so that the students were players, the assignments were quests, she was the Game Master, the tests were challenges, and the classes were player summits. By completing quests (assignments) and challenges (tests), students earned coins (plastic pirate gold pieces) that they could use for various things during the course. She used a project-based approach in which students were required to create a game engine and a 2D video game. I encourage you to read her article (Duvall, n.d.) if you're interested in this type of course.

Example M.1.13 – Giving Total Freedom on Assignments

Allow students to do whatever they want to do for an assignment. Okay, I'll admit that I don't recommend this strategy for all courses because it's an extreme example. But it worked well for a geography professor at Virginia Tech, Dr. Timothy Baird, who gave this assignment to his students in an undergraduate geography course on sustainability (see http://www.pinktime.org/). For three different 75 minute classes during the semester, students were told to "skip class, do whatever they want, and give themselves a grade" (Baird, Kniola, Lewis, & Fowler, 2015, p. 148). Students were also told that their activities should relate to the course, which was possible because most things relate to sustainability. At the next class meeting, each person had 90 seconds to share what they did for their assignment. During the remainder of the 75-minute class, 30 minutes was spent in small group discussion and 15 minutes was spent in whole class discussion. After class, students sent the grade they wanted on the assignment to the professor by email. Students chose activities such as reading a book, exploring websites, watching videos, learning to play a song on the guitar, hiking a mountain, making cross-country skis and using them, networking with new people, among others. Across the three times that students completed this assignment during the course, some students tried different activities while others delved more deeply into their initial topics. This assignment allowed students to "embrace an expansive view of sustainability where their own interests and values, which are connected to real sustainability concerns, become the focus of their motivation, learning, and assessment" (Baird et al., 2015, p. 154). Thus, by empowering students, Dr. Baird was able to also use the usefulness and interest components of the MUSIC model to motivate students.

Empowerment Strategy 2

Incorporate learner-directed approaches.

Lectures don't provide students with any control over their learning (other than deciding whether they should attend the lecture and listen or not). Yet, lectures and classes where professors do most of the talking can be very motivating to students. Yes, you read that correctly: "*very* motivating to students." Are you surprised I wrote that? I mean it. I'm sure you've found some lectures to be very engaging and useful (consider the popularity of TED Talks). The problem is that when professors rely too much on lectures or they aren't good at lecturing, students can become bored, stop actively thinking, and become disengaged. Listening is hard work, even for good listeners; and therefore, teaching in ways that require students to listen a lot can easily lead to unengaged students even for the best, most well-intentioned students. Instructors can solve this problem by incorporating learner-directed approaches into their instruction.

I'm using the label "learner-directed approaches" to include any instructional approach in which students have some control over and "direct" some of their learning. These approaches are often contrasted with "teacher-directed" approaches in which teachers direct most of the learning (e.g., lecture, direct instruction). You may be familiar with the term "learner-centered" or "student-centered" approaches and I view these terms as synonymous with "learner-directed" approaches. I prefer the term "learner-directed" because all instruction should be "centered" around the learner, whereas the term "learner-directed" highlights the idea that these approaches empower students to "direct" their learning by having control over what and how they learn (Ormrod, 2012, p. 211).

Given this broad definition, the following approaches can be considered learner-directed: problem-based learning, project-based learning, inquiry approaches, case studies, collaborative and cooperative learning, team-based learning, inductive approaches, and discussions. Explaining each of these approaches is well beyond the scope of this book. Instead, I highlight a few of these approaches in this section to get you thinking about how you can implement them in ways that are consistent with the MUSIC model.

Example M.2.1 – Using Problem-Based or Project-Based Learning

Use problem-based learning (PBL) or project-based learning to engage students in real-world problems. PBL is typically defined as an instructional activity in which students work to solve a complex problem that exists in the real-world. *Project*-based approaches are similar to PBL except that the outcome is a product (the "product" is defined very broadly to include many different possibilities). As an example of a project-based approach, Aki Ishida, a professor in the School of Architecture + Design at Virginia Tech, assigned students a project to help them learn about the properties of concrete in her *Building Materials* course (Ishida, 2014-2015). The project required students "to work in teams of three or four to construct a concrete wall that allows light to pass through" (Ishida, 2014-2015, p. 12). Students were graded on design, execution, diligence, quality of photographs and drawings, and site management. Thus, students were given specific instructions with a specific grading rubric, yet were empowered by having the ability to make decisions about how to best achieve an effective solution.

The following explanation focuses on PBL, although it also applies to project-based learning. Four general principles have been identified as critical to the success of PBL approaches, including: creating goals appropriate for students, providing support for students, providing frequent opportunities for students to self-assess and revise, and providing opportunities for students to work together productively (Barron et al., 1998).

PBL is consistent with the MUSIC model because it provides students with autonomy to make decisions (empowerment), involves a real-world problem (usefulness and interest), and provides a structure in which students are supported by the instructor (success and caring). However, when implemented poorly, PBL can have a negative effect on students' MUSIC perceptions. To help you avoid these pitfalls, I provide a few suggestions based on PBL research with the MUSIC model. Many of these suggestions are based on research conducted in engineering courses by Jones, Epler, Mokri, Bryant, and Paretti (2013) and Mora, Anorbe-Diaz, Gonzalez-Marrero, Martin-Gutierrez, and Jones (2017).

You'll need to decide which aspects of the problem to give students control over, because having control and choices can lead to increases in students' empowerment and motivation. You should consider the pros and cons of giving students choices over:

- the problem they will solve,
- who they will work with to solve the problem (e.g., Will you place them in groups or let them choose their groups?),
- how they will interact within the groups,
- the types and amount of resources available to them to solve the problem, and
- who they can select as an advisor to help them throughout the problem-solving process (e.g., Can only the instructor advise, or can others advise, such as other faculty or more experienced students?).

Giving students more choices can increase their motivation to engage in the problem. However, if students are not provided with the resources necessary to make good decisions, their perceptions of success will drop and they will become less motivated. For example, if students are given choices about how to work with others in their groups, but don't have the interpersonal and communication skills necessary to work well with others (e.g., handling conflicts), the group won't function effectively and students won't believe that they can succeed in solving the problem together (which may also result in students viewing other students as uncaring). In this case, you'll need to provide information with suggestions about how they can work together effectively (e.g., lead a class discussion about or role play strategies for working effectively in groups).

Similarly, the instructor (or group advisor) must accurately assess the amount of assistance needed by students. If the instructor provides too much assistance or gives too many directives, students may feel less empowered and less motivated. However, if the instructor provides too much empowerment and not enough assistance, students may struggle to figure out what they need to do and how to solve the problem effectively. Furthermore, they may view the instructor as uncaring because s/he doesn't provide the needed assistance. The following quotation from a senior undergraduate engineering student demonstrates what can happen when the instructor provides a lot of empowerment, but perhaps not enough assistance.

'It empowers us because it's allowed us to take the project where we want to, and forces us to take this project as a real project. There are no real bounds to it. The

problem is that this project is so above our heads that we were pretty lost for the first few weeks and had zero guidance. It was a lot of hard work on our part to try to understand the material." (Jones, Epler, et al., 2013, p. 52)

This is a great example as to why you must consider how changes in one component of the MUSIC model will affect the other components. Here, too much empowerment without also supporting students' success and caring perceptions may lead students to struggle too much and disengage (see Figure 4.1). Of course, it's also possible that students will be motivated to continue to struggle and eventually figure it out on their own, leading to greater motivation. Either way, the instructor must be cognizant of the possibilities and assess how empowerment is affecting students' perceptions of success and overall motivation to work on the problem. An effective instructor would be ready to step in and provide more or less assistance as needed.

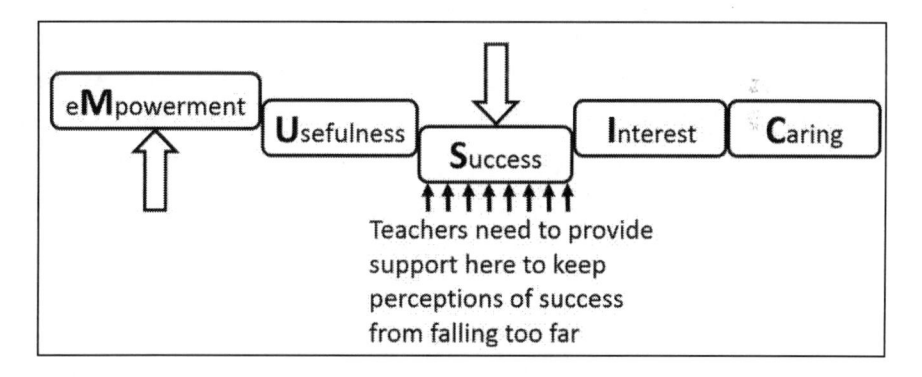

Figure 4.1. *Increases in empowerment perceptions shouldn't lead to decreases is success perceptions*

Also, the problem that you choose (or that students choose) is critically important to students' interest and perceptions of usefulness. If students perceive the problem to be interesting and useful to their future goals, they'll likely be motivated to engage in solving the problem; otherwise, not so much. Therefore, you should work to ensure that the problem is viewed as interesting and useful *by the students*. If they don't think that the problem is useful, but you do, help them understand why it's useful.

In sum, you should consider how much empowerment to give students with respect to the project (the selection, type, and scope of the project), the group in which they work (the selection of others, how the group functions, and how they interact), and their instructor/advisor (options for selecting an advisor and the role of the advisor) (see Figure 4.2).

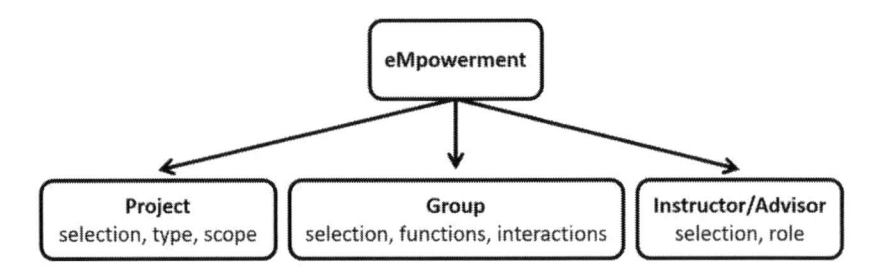

```
                    eMpowerment
         ┌──────────────┼──────────────┐
         ↓              ↓              ↓
     Project          Group      Instructor/Advisor
 selection, type,  selection,       selection, role
     scope       functions,
                 interactions
```

Figure 4.2. *Instructors need to decide how much empowerment to give students with respect to the project, group, and instructor/advisor.*

Example M.2.2 – Using Inquiry Approaches

Incorporate inquiry approaches into your course. "Inquiry approaches" (a.k.a., inquiry learning, inquiry-based learning) is a broad term that can refer to any type of teaching strategy in which students inquire by answering questions or solving problems. Inquiry approaches require students to use a variety of thinking and reasoning skills as they use evidence to support their answers. The examples provided here are simply examples, they're not intended to represent all types of inquiry approaches.

Eggen and Kauchak (2001, p. 242) describe a six-step inquiry model in which students identify a question, make hypotheses, gather data, assess hypotheses, generalize their findings, and analyze the inquiry process. Students are empowered because they have control during these steps to make decisions. The role of the instructor is to guide students as they work their way through these steps. Similar to PBL (discussed in the prior example), the motivational role of the instructor involves assessing when and how much assistance students need to be successful (see Figure 4.1). In fact, similar to PBL, inquiry approaches are consistent with the MUSIC model because they provide students with autonomy to make decisions (empowerment), may involve a real-world problem (usefulness and interest), and provide a structure in which students can be supported by the instructor (success and caring).

As an example, let's consider the use of an inquiry approach in an undergraduate neuroscience laboratory course, as described by Tu and Jones (2017). An inquiry approach was selected "to help students develop the essential skills to design experiments, collect useful data, analyze the results, and make further speculations" (Tu & Jones, 2017, p. 137). The inquiry approach involved students working in groups of two to four students after listening to a 40-minute lecture at the beginning of each three-hour class. The lecture served to reinforce the basic knowledge needed for the inquiry, but the instructor also asked students questions to get them thinking about the inquiry. During the lecture, the instructor also provided instructions for the inquiry and empowered students by explaining that it was their job to plan ahead, think about what they were going to do, and then talk to her only on an as-needed basis. During the inquiry, instead of giving students the answers when they made procedural mistakes or obtained unexpected results, she asked them to think critically and derive their own answers. Interestingly, in subsequent semesters when less-experienced teaching assistants taught the course, students' perceptions of empowerment decreased significantly (as measured on a quantitative scale). This decrease in empowerment could have occurred because, in contrast to how the instructor forced students to think about and develop their own answers, the teaching assistants were more likely to provide students with specific "correct" answers. This example demonstrates the key role of the instructor in empowering students within an inquiry approach. One implication is that if you use teaching assistants, they need to be taught how to interact with the students in ways that empower them, yet support their success.

Example M.2.3 – Using Case Studies

Use case studies in your course. Case studies have been used in business, law, and medical education for years and can be used in a variety of college courses (Barnes, Christensen, & Hansen, 1994). Case studies are stories that describe a realistic, complex event or situation that involves a problem or dilemma. The case should include enough information that it can be analyzed accurately by students. Cases are often open-ended because there's not only one correct answer. Cases can range in length from a paragraph to 25 pages or more (e.g., Harvard Law School, 2017). You might also find short videos that can be used loosely as case studies because they show a situation that can then be used to discuss course concepts.

The key teaching element is that the case must provide the opportunity for students to discuss concepts related to the course objectives. In larger classes, you will need to divide students into smaller groups to discuss the case. In smaller classes you can arrange the seating so that everyone can see and hear one another during the class discussion.

The Eberly Center for Teaching Excellence & Educational Innovation at Carnegie Mellon University (2015) provides a nice concise six-step process for implementing case studies, as summarized here: (1) "give students ample time to read and think about the case;" (2) "introduce the case briefly and provide some guidelines for how to approach it;" (3) assign students to groups and ensure that everyone is involved; (4) have the groups produce something (e.g., a decision, a rationale, an analysis) and present it to the rest of the class; (5) serve as a discussion leader by asking students for clarification, evidence, examples, and deeper analysis; and (6) synthesize the discussion at the end.

You can create your own cases, you can use existing cases, or, to empower students even more, you can ask them to develop a case. Some disciplines have developed detailed cases that you can use or buy, such as Harvard Law School (2017), Harvard Kennedy School of Government (2017), and the Institute for the Study of Diplomacy at Georgetown University (2017). For instance, here is a description of a case that you can buy and then use in courses in international relations and comparative politics.

> *"This case study examines the historical evolution of secularism in Turkey and analyzes the legality of veil bans in Turkey and in some Western European Countries. Through the lens of Leyla Sahin, who was not allowed to register for classes at the University of Istanbul in 1998 simply because she wore an Islamic veil, it sheds light on whether banning Muslim veils in public spaces falls within the realms of current regional and international human rights law."* (Institute for the Study of Diplomacy at Georgetown University; Case Studies Summaries, p. 100)

As an example of student-generated cases, in my graduate course on motivation, students create a case based on real-life in which someone was motivated or unmotivated in a particular situation (typically about two or three paragraphs in length). Students submit their case to me, I review it to ensure that it's sufficiently complex and relevant to the course concepts, and when it is, I post the case on the class online discussion board. I grade students' cases on pre-established criteria students receive ahead of time. The other students analyze the case and explain how the case is consistent or inconsistent with the concepts and theories in the course. They post their analysis in the online discussion board. Everyone in the class submits one case and analyzes all of the cases (or almost all, depending on the size of the class) and I grade their analysis based on pre-established criteria. Sometimes we discuss the cases in class and sometimes we don't, which is a little unusual for a tradition case study because usually there's discussion involved with case study teaching. However, there are no rules, do what works for your situation; sometimes I just don't have enough time in class to discuss the case solutions, but students still get feedback on their analysis from me online as part of their grade. In addition, once students submit their case analysis, they are automatically given access to view the other students' case analyses. Reading these analyses provides another opportunity for students to gain new insights and compare their analysis with those of their peers.

Empowerment Strategy 3

Explain to students the amount of control they have in the course.

You can help students to interpret the amount of control they have in your course by (a) explaining how they have control over some aspects of the course and (b) explaining why they don't have control over other aspects of the course. Although it may be obvious to you that they have control over many aspects of the course, students may not recognize this control, which could reduce their motivation in the course. Conversely, they won't have control over other aspects of the course. Why not? You probably have good rationales, so why not share those rationales with the students? Doing so can help them to understand that their lack of control is necessary to help them reach the course objectives most effectively.

Example M.3.1 – Explaining to Students How They Have Control

Explain to students how they have control over certain aspects of the course. Students almost always have control over some aspects related to a course, such as when and where they can study, the amount of time they spend studying, and the attitude they bring to the course. For instance, in one study, students in an online course reported that they had control over: the pace at which they worked, the amount of textbook reading they completed, whether or not to complete the practice test questions, where and when to take the online multiple choice exams, when to correspond with the instructor, and when to complete the course (Jones, Watson, Rakes, & Akalin, 2012).

In addition, after reading this chapter, you may also intentionally design your course to include some choices for students (see Empowerment Strategy 1). Explain to students that you intentionally designed the course with these choices to allow them to have control over some aspects of the course. Doing so may increase their perceptions of empowerment in the course and raise their level of motivation to engage in it.

Example M.3.2 – Providing Rationales for Rules

Provide students with your rationales for the course rules. Some aspects of the course, such as rules and directions, will be non-negotiable despite what students want or prefer. In these cases, students will feel less empowered and possibly believe that you are a controlling instructor. To minimize this possibility, you can provide your rationale for the rules. You can do this verbally when explaining the rules or in writing on the syllabus and assignments. By providing rationales, students are more likely to believe that you are not trying to be mean or a "control freak;" but rather, you have logical reasons for your requirements.

I recommend that you focus your rationales on learning, by conveying the message that the reason you do things is to help them meet the course objectives. After all, if that isn't the case, you have to ask yourself: Why am I requiring students to do that?

As an example, pretend that on the first day of class you explain to students that you have a class rule that typing on laptops is not allowed during lectures and presentations. Then you immediately provide the following rationale.

> *"The reason that I created this rule is that typing distracts students sitting next to you because clicking on the keyboard is noisy. The rules in this class are intended to help you learn, and you learn less effectively when you're distracted, such as when someone near you is making noise by typing. If you believe that you'll need to type during a lecture or presentation, please email me or see me this week and we can discuss it."*

Providing them with an explanation like this shows that you care and that the rule is intended to help everyone learn, not simply to control their behavior. I'm not suggesting that this particular rule is appropriate for your class, but if it is, you could continue your explanation by anticipating students' objections to the rule.

> *"Note taking can be an important strategy to help you learn. Because I don't allow typing in this class, I'm numbering all of the presentation*

slides and making them available on the class website prior to class (or handing them out during class). You can jot down some notes directly on the printouts or take notes and refer to the numbered slide in the presentation. I don't anticipate that you'll need to take a lot of notes in this class because the presentations are fairly short."

This type of explanation makes it clear that you've thought about the implications of your rule and that you're really concerned about their learning. If you want to add some more empowerment to this explanation, you could ask students to email you some suggestions for other possible ways in which you can help them take notes during class. Or, after explaining the rules on the first day of class, ask students to jot down their ideas on a piece of paper and hand them to you at the end of class.

Empowerment Strategy 4

Don't give rewards that may be perceived as controlling.

Students need feedback about their abilities in the class to stay motivated and to ensure that they're learning the appropriate knowledge and skills. Therefore, it's important to let students know how they're doing in relation to the objectives of the class. Rewards are one way to let students' know that they're doing well (or not doing well, if they don't receive a reward). The problem with rewards is that they can be perceived as controlling, which can reduce students' perceptions of empowerment and decrease their motivation. For this reason, rewards should be avoided when possible, and instead, students should be provided with feedback about their abilities (see Chapter 6, Strategy 4 for explanations as to how to provide effective feedback).

You may be wondering if rewards are ever appropriate. The research is pretty clear that rewards can be used effectively in two situations. First, rewards can be used to motivate students when they will not otherwise engage in an activity. In this case, students can be motivated by selecting a reward that's perceived as useful to their short- or long-term goals (thus, they are motivated by the usefulness component of the MUSIC model). These types of rewards are almost impossible to use with an entire class because it's almost impossible to imagine a class in which no one will do anything. Consequently, these rewards are generally negotiated with students individually and are more common at the K-12 level than at the college level. Ideally, the rewards will engage students to the extent that some of the other MUSIC model components "kick-in" and the rewards can be reduced. For example, after engaging in an activity, students begin to feel successful, become interested, and feel cared for in the learning environment, all of which can support their motivation in the course without the use of rewards.

Rewards can also be used effectively when they're not anticipated, but instead, received as an acknowledgement of something well done. For example, students who do well on an assignment are given a special recognition in the class or are allowed to do something special. In this case, the reward serves as notice that the student was successful, which can support students' motivation (see Chapter 6 for more information about success). These types of rewards only become problematic if they start to become anticipated *and* students begin to feel controlled by them (because they will feel less empowered).

"Rewards and punishments are the lowest form of education." – Zhuangzi (cited in BrainyQuote, 2015b)

Example M.4.1 – Avoiding Unnecessary Rewards

Avoid using rewards unnecessarily when they are not needed to motivate students. Because you're probably busy, you only want to implement instructional strategies that are worth your time and that increase students' motivation and learning. Therefore, as I noted previously, it is imperative that you only use rewards when they (a) motivate students to do something they wouldn't do otherwise, or (b) acknowledge students' accomplishments, in a manner that was not anticipated by the students.

As an example, there is an app that instructors can use to give students points when they stay off their phones during class (Daves, 2015). There may be many good reasons to use this app. My point here is not to evaluate or judge the app, but I do want to use it in one scenario.

Let's say that students in Professor Huffman's courses didn't use their phones much during his class. Then, his colleague told him about this app and he decided to use it because it was a cool use of technology that might motivate students through the reward of the points that students can obtain and use at campus restaurants. My recommendation to Dr. Huffman would be not to use the app because he's trying to solve a problem that doesn't exist. That is, he's using rewards unnecessarily. Most students don't use their phones in his class anyway. And, by using the app, he's potentially creating a situation in which students may feel less empowered because they feel manipulated and controlled by him. This example reminds us of the MUSIC model design cycle presented in Chapter 3 because you should only select strategies that solve a problem. If there's no problem, save your time and don't try to solve it.

Example M.4.2 – Reframing "Punishments" as Rewards

Reframe your "punishments" as rewards. Professors often design a syllabus to punish students who have not complied with certain requirements. This approach may be reasonable in many cases, however, it's definitely a controlling strategy. Sometimes, instead, it may be possible to reframe controlling punishments as empowering rewards. Reframing is a strategy used by effective politicians (Lakoff, 2004) and it can be used effectively by professors as well. Let me give you a couple of examples of what I mean by this.

Re-doing assignments policy. Professor Yanovitch teaches a lab section and genuinely wants his students to succeed in the course. Therefore, students must redo lab reports that are below a certain grade. Students may perceive this professor to be caring because he's willing to regrade subpar assignments to help them succeed. Or, they may view this policy as a controlling punishment. He could find out by assessing students' MUSIC perceptions. If he finds that some students believe that this policy is controlling, how can he reframe this requirement to make students feel more empowered? Here is one solution that seems to work based on the experience of "scienceprof" (retrieved from ChronicleVitae, 2016, July 29): "I used to require students to rewrite lab reports that were below a 'B,' which resulted in a lot of whining. Now I ALLOW students to rewrite, and I get a lot of gratitude." This is a simple example of how reframing an assignment by changing a few words can make students feel more empowered and less controlled by the instructor.

Attendance policy. Professor Keuler sincerely wants his students to attend class because he believes that students who attend class learn more and learn things that are not easy or practical to assess through the typical course assessments. If Dr. Keuler requires students to come to class, takes attendance, and punishes them (by reducing their grade) for missed classes, students may perceive him as controlling and resent his manipulative policy. Yet, if he doesn't take attendance, fewer students attend, and it's usually the students who need help the most. One solution is to keep the policy, but reframe it as: "I want to give you credit for what you learn in class that might not be assessed in other ways in this class. Therefore, you receive 1 point for each class you attend up to a maximum of 20 points." This way of framing it has a different feel than saying: "You must attend class or else you will lose 1 point for every class you miss." The end result is the same, but your approach is different. You might not believe that these subtle differences can make a difference in students' perceptions and I will admit that I don't have hard evidence to provide support for this exact attendance example. However, researchers have documented that when children receive task instructions that are less controlling, they have higher levels of motivation and enjoyment (Koestner, Ryan, Bernieri, & Holt, 1984).

Personally, I usually take attendance in classes to reward students for what they learn by coming to class (even graduate classes). But others have argued effectively that not taking attendance can be advantageous. For example, not taking attendance (a) empowers students to decide whether it's worth their time to come to class or not, (b) reduces disruptions caused by students who don't want to be there, and (c) provides feedback to the instructor about the quality of the class (i.e., if students don't attend, maybe your class isn't very good and you need to redesign it (Marshall, 2017; Sperber, 2005).

Final exam policy. Professor Valley's students are generally motivated in his class. Students who have put forth effort in prior semesters have done well and have reported that they've learned a lot in the class. To make the class more "motivating" this semester, Dr. Valley decides to use incentives by announcing that students who have a 95% average or above at the end of the course won't have to take the final exam. He wants to reward students who do well during the semester by allowing them to skip the final comprehensive exam. Although his intentions are good, his rationale for the reward is illogical. First, there's no evidence that motivation is a major problem for most students. Second, there's no evidence that students who are less motivated will be more motivated through this new reward system; instead, he should work towards understanding why some students aren't motivated. Third, and maybe most importantly, there's an implicit message in this reward system that the comprehensive final is really punishment for not learning what was supposed to be learned during the class and students will be relieved of this punishment if they do what they're supposed to do during the course. There are other interpretations, but this is a reasonable one.

Instead of using this "reward" system, Professor Zugel explains the final comprehensive exam in his course differently. He uses it as an opportunity for students to reflect on what they learned in the course and to synthesize, organize, and elaborate on information, all of which have been shown to increase students' learning (Ormrod & Jones, 2018). Therefore, everyone has to complete the final because it's important for everyone to learn as much as possible during the course. Students who do well during the course will still be rewarded with more knowledge and higher grades, and they'll be motivated to continue to learn the information until the class is over, not to "check-out" mentally before the end. Reframing the final exam in this way can send the message that learning is important and that the professor is interested in students' learning, as opposed to being interested in manipulating them into getting high grades for which they'll be alleviated from the pain of taking a final exam. This recommendation, in combination with others from the MUSIC model is what will motivate students, not unnecessary and illogical rewards. For this reason, Dr. Zugel's final exam policy is more consistent with the MUSIC model approach to motivation than Dr. Valley's policy.

Empowerment Strategy 5

Avoid controlling language and allow students to talk more.

Language is very important because it can either empower or disempower students, depending upon how it's perceived. Words such as "should" and "must" can elicit perceptions of disempowerment. Instead, try to use language that may be perceived as less controlling, yet is still clear and explicit.

"I don't like school, they boss us around." – Kindergarten student (personal communication)

Also, sometimes simply the use of too much language—talking too much—can disempower students. It's likely that students will feel less empowered if they're not allowed to share their voice in the class, either verbally or in some type of written medium (e.g., paper, blog, discussion board, email).

Example M.5.1 – Minimizing Controlling Language

Minimize the use of controlling language. Reeve (2009, p. 170) provides some nice examples of what you don't want to do as an instructor because these behaviors can be interpreted by students as controlling and disempowering.

> *Teachers who verbally push and pressure students toward specific predetermined products and solutions, right answers, and desired behaviors typically communicate through messages that are rigid, evaluative, and pressure inducing (e.g., "get started"; "no, do it this way"), and they often do so through the use of recurring directives (Assor et al., 2005), two-word commands (e.g., "hurry up," "stop that," "let's go"; Reeve et al., 2004), compliance hooks (e.g., "should," "must," "got to"; Ryan, 1982), and a pressuring tone in general (Noels, Clement, & Pelletier, 1999).*

Consider the difference between the statements by the following two professors.

Professor A: "You have to complete the assignment by the due date in the syllabus. If you don't, I will deduct 10% of the points for each week it's late."

Professor B: "The due date for the assignment is shown in the syllabus. If you choose to complete the assignment after the due date, you will lose 10% of the points for each week it is late."

I believe that Professor B is less controlling and more empowering than Professor A. Of course, it also depends on the tone of voice used by each professor. Will the students of Professor A be less motivated than the students of Professor B after this *one* comment? Probably not, but over time, the language of Professor B would create a more empowering class environment than the language of Professor A.

I want to be clear that both Professor A and B have the same amount of control over the class rule in the example above and Professor B is not more vague or lenient than Professor A. Professor B may simply come across as less manipulative and controlling to some students.

Let me give you another example that might be more convincing. These two professors are walking around their classrooms helping students who are working in groups of two to solve 10 problems that are due the next day (the students will finish them at home that night).

Professor A: "You shouldn't work together on all the parts of the problem or you'll never get finished by the due date tomorrow."

Professor B: "I notice that you're working together on all of the parts of the problem and that it's taking you much longer than other students who work on some parts independently. Do you think that you'll be able to finish all 10 problems working the way you're currently working?"

Professor A assumes that he knows the best way to solve the problems and that he needs to tell the students how to work. He's very direct and he may be correct in what he's saying. But Professor B makes more of an observation and has students reflect on their working habits. Doing so can help them to become more in control of their learning and make decisions for themselves, which can also feel empowering and help teach them to become better at self-regulating their learning. If Professor B is really concerned that the students won't finish on time, he might add (after listening to students' responses to his first question), "I'm just worried that you might not finish by tomorrow if you don't try another strategy because I've never seen anyone finish all this work in one day using your strategy." Now the students have the information they need to make an informed decision. If they fail to meet the deadline, it was their decision. And I doubt that these same students would be any more convinced to change their strategy after listening to the statement by Professor A.

Example M.5.2 – Talking Less

Use language only when you have something worthwhile to say; otherwise, keep your mouth shut. Students can get bored when you speak too much. Instead, provide other activities that allow you to talk less. However, it may not be easy for you to keep your mouth shut; the reason many people want to become professors is that they like to profess to others.

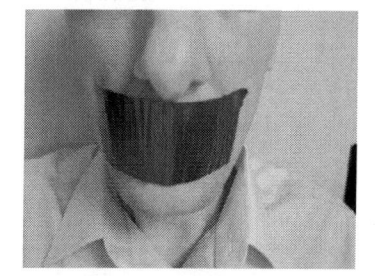

Of course, talking less in class raises other challenges for professors. As I'm sure you've experienced, when students speak, they may talk about topics unrelated to the course objectives and some students may monopolize the conversations. So, in many ways, your job is more difficult when you speak less than if you simply lecture. But by designing good activities ahead of time and being a good facilitator, you can teach effectively with less talking.

One of my favorite stories about talking less is when Joseph Finckel, an English professor at Asnuntuck Community College, lost his voice in the middle of a semester and taught his courses anyway (Finckel, 2015). Although his voice returned soon after, he continued teaching all of his courses (including developmental English and Shakespeare) for the remainder of the semester without saying a word. As Professor Finckel explained:

> *"My experience teaching without talking proved so beneficial to my students, so personally and professionally centering, and so impactful in terms of the intentionality of my classroom behavior that I now 'lose my voice' at least once every semester...I submit that nothing empowers learners as immediately and profoundly as does removing the professor's voice from the room"* (Finckel, 2015, second and third paragraphs).

Because of his positive experience with not talking, Professor Finckel intentionally loses his voice at least once each semester. If you want to lose your voice for a class, he recommends that you plan a discussion in which you ask students a series of questions (projected on a screen in front of the class), with each question building on the prior question (Finckel, 2015). Another option is to prepare an activity and give students a handout with detailed instructions. When you need to direct or focus students' learning, you can always write on the board, snap your fingers, clap, whistle, tap, or make other gestures.

Example M.5.3 – Allowing Students to Talk More

Allow students to talk more, which will help you talk less; or perhaps you can talk about the most important points and cut out extraneous talking. When students talk, they have control over what they say, which can meet their need for autonomy. You can use a variety of activities to allow students to talk more, including many of the strategies provided in this chapter. As examples, you can ask students to solve a case study, participate in an activity, create a project, solve a problem, or involve students in discussions (see the chapter on interest in this book). Notice that all of these examples ask students to *do* something (besides sit and listen to you). Think about how you can have them use their knowledge or find the knowledge they need to do something. Common approaches include problem-based learning, project-based learning, and inquiry approaches.

CHAPTER 5

Strategies to Leverage Usefulness

Problem

Students don't believe that the course content, assignments, or activities are useful for their future.

Solution

You need to ensure that students understand why the course content, assignments, and activities are <u>useful</u> for their short-term or long-term goals.

Overview of Usefulness

During your schooling, you probably remember asking your teacher (or thinking to yourself), "why do I need to learn this?" It's a good question, and you probably wanted to know the answer because you were more motivated when you knew *why* you were learning something. The same thing is true for your students. When we don't know why we're doing something, it can seem pointless because it doesn't seem to relate to our goals in life.

<u>Key Point:</u> Students tend to be more motivated when they understand how the course content, assignments, and activities are useful to their short-term or long-term goals. Students need to understand the relevance of what they're learning. Students have short-term goals (e.g., "I want to get at least an A- in my calculus class this semester") and long-term goals (e.g., "I want to become an architectural engineer").

It can be fairly easy to motivate students to engage in courses directly related to their major, as noted by this undergraduate student: "I put in a medium to high amount of effort in this course and do all the readings because I feel like the material is relevant to my major and my future." But even in these courses, instructors should design the course to make it clear to students how the content and skills taught are relevant to students' futures.

It may be more difficult to motivate students to engage in courses unrelated to their major because the content may seem unrelated to students' goals. The same may be true of students who are unsure of their goals or whose goals change over time. The purpose of this chapter is to provide strategies to help you motivate students when they don't immediately understand the usefulness of what they are learning.

"Nothing in education is so astonishing as the amount of ignorance it accumulates in the form of inert facts." – Henry Adams (cited in Bartlett, 2002, p. 570)

In this chapter, I present the following four strategies and provide several examples of each.

- U.1 Explain how the content is useful to students' lives.
- U.2 Ask students or someone else to share the reasons they find the course content useful.
- U.3 Design activities that allow students to see firsthand the usefulness of the content.
- U.4 Provide opportunities for students to set and reflect on their goals.

Relevant Theories

In this section, I provide very brief explanations of some of the theories that are most directly relevant to the usefulness strategies in the MUSIC model. These are not comprehensive explanations, so please look-up the citations if you are interested in more information.

- Utility value (Eccles et al., 1983). Utility value is one of the constructs in the value component of expectancy-value theory (Eccles et al., 1983) and it "refers to how a task fits into an individual's future plans" (Wigfield & Eccles, 2000, p. 72). Individuals are more likely to be motivated when they understand how a task fits into their future plans.
- Future time perspective theory (Lens, 1988; Lewin, 1942; Nuttin & Lens, 1985). Future time perspective researchers posit that humans understand themselves in relation to time and that this understanding is critical to explaining their

motivation and behavior. Thus, students' future time perspectives affect their motivation to engage in activities (see Kauffman & Husman, 2004).

- Instrumentality (Husman & Lens, 1999). Instrumentality, which is consistent with the future time perspective theory, is defined as "the perception that completion of a task will directly increase the probability of achieving a future goal" (Husman, Derryberry, Crowson, & Lomax, 2004, p. 64). Students are more likely to be motivated to engage in a task when they perceive that the task is connected to a valued future goal.

- Goal setting theories (Locke & Latham, 2002). Goal setting theories explain "that specific, high (hard) goals lead to a higher level of task performance than do easy goals or vague, abstract goals such as the exhortation to 'do one's best'" (Locke & Latham, 2006, p. 265). Therefore, *specific* goals help students to focus their attention and effort, which leads to higher performance. Students are more likely to be motivated and perform at higher levels when they have specific goals.

- Goal orientation theories (Ames, 1992; Elliot, 1999; Maehr & Midgley, 1991; Nicholls, 1984). Goal orientation researchers have identified several different types of goals. Students with mastery-approach goals want to *develop* their competence, whereas students with performance-approach goals want to *demonstrate* their competence to others. In contrast, students with performance-avoidance goals want to avoid appearing incompetent to others. Students are more likely to be motivated and perform at higher levels when they have mastery- or performance-approach goals than when they have performance-avoidance goals.

Usefulness Strategy 1

Explain how the content is useful to students' lives.

Students are more motivated when they perceive the content to be useful to their goals in life. Although you might think that it's obvious as to why the knowledge or skills students are learning in your course is useful, they may not. So make it obvious by explaining different reasons as to why what they're learning is useful to their goals in life. Some of the examples in this section describe how you can figure out their goals if you don't already know them.

Example U.1.1 – Relating Content to Students' Everyday Lives

Relate the content to students' everyday lives or issues they face. To learn about students' lives, it may be necessary to talk to them before or after class to gather ideas. Or, it may be necessary to survey students on the first day of class or online during the first week of class (obviously, there are many other possibilities as well).

As an example, consider a psychology professor who tells her students: "Today we're going to learn about *working memory*. Knowing how to use your working memory more effectively can help you remember and learn things better, and we're always remembering and learning new things throughout life." You can also give students examples from your own life and explain how the content is useful to you.

ENGAGE Engineering (funded by the National Science Foundation) has worked with teams from 72 engineering schools to implement strategies that focus on retaining undergraduate students (http://www.engageengineering.org/about-engage/). One of their three main strategies that they focus on is "Everyday Examples in Engineering." I encourage you to visit their website if you need examples in content related to math, science, or engineering because they have many lesson plans and demonstrations related to a variety of content and concepts (http://www.engageengineering.org/e3s/whyitworks).

Example U.1.2 – Explaining the Benefits for Their Future

Convey to students how the content can benefit them in the future. Even if the knowledge and skills students are learning in the course are not relevant to their present lives, they may be useful to students in the future in some way; otherwise, what's the purpose of the course? As an example from a research study, college students who wanted a career as a teacher were more motivated and engaged when they were told that learning about correlation coefficients could help them become better teachers in the future (Jang, 2008).

Here's another example that demonstrates how you can use this strategy slightly differently to motivate students to complete course readings. Before students complete an assigned reading, an education professor gives students a few different real-life scenarios that the students will likely encounter in their future careers as an educator. The instructor doesn't tell the students how to resolve the scenario problems, but instead, tells them that the answers are in the readings. Therefore, completing the readings will be useful to students in the short-term by improving their grade (assuming the instructor gives a graded assignment that requires students to explain their solution to the problem scenario) and useful to students in the long-term in their careers as an educator.

Example U.1.3 – Explaining the Purpose in Writing

Explain the purpose of each assignment in writing. For example, at the beginning of your assignments (directly after the title of the assignment and before the instructions), include a section titled "Purpose" and provide a few sentences about the purpose of the assignment. Here's a specific example.

> *"The purpose of this assignment is for you to reflect on the study strategies you are using in this course. It provides you with the opportunity to consider whether your study strategies are helping you to learn the concepts more effectively, make your study time more efficient, and help you to achieve a higher grade in this course."*

This purpose can then be followed by the specific instructions for the assignment.

Example U.1.4 – Explaining the Importance of Each Assignment

Explain how particular readings and assignments can help students succeed in the course. You may believe that all of the course readings and assignments are important; however, students may not share your belief. So explain how the course readings and assignments will help them to master the content, meet the course objectives, and achieve a higher grade in the course. This strategy could be particularly motivating to students who don't see the usefulness of the course, but who want to get a high grade because achieving this short-term goal will help them obtain their longer-term goals.

Example U.1.5 – Explaining Cross-Training for the Brain

Provide other ways of thinking about how the content is useful. If students don't believe your explanation as to why your course is useful, explain to them that learning in different subjects is like cross-training for the brain, which can keep your brain fit. As Rob Jenkins, an English professor, explains: "To be mentally fit, we have to push against resistance. But we also must encounter different types of resistance and respond to them with different parts of our brain. That's why math majors need to study literature and English majors have to sit through math classes and all of them need to take history and science and fine arts and so on. What we have traditionally referred to as the 'core curriculum' in reality is nothing less than cross-training for the brain" (Jenkins, 2015, paragraphs 11 and 12). I haven't checked the scientific validity of this metaphor, but it seems reasonable and appears to be consistent with studies by Carol Dweck and her colleagues that suggest that students are more motivated when they believe that intelligence is changeable (Dweck, 2006).

> *"It is well to read everything of something, and something of everything."* – Joseph Brodsky (cited in BrainyQuote, 2015a)

Example U.1.6 – Explaining Usefulness When it Doesn't Exist

Be creative (yet truthful) in explaining to students how your course is useful. It's rarely be the case that a course is not useful to students' futures in some way. But if you perceive your course to be one of those courses, you either need to redesign the course or your school's curriculum, or you need to think more broadly about the usefulness of your course. For example, your course may be useful because it improves students' abilities in reading, writing, logical thinking, reasoning, critical thinking, creativity, problem solving, organizing, or other abilities that can help students develop intellectually. These abilities may also be valued by students' future employers, and therefore, should be considered valuable to students. Try to make connections to these broader abilities more evident to students. Clearly this undergraduate student was able to make these types of connections: "Ultimately this class is a history class, so facts are not always incredibly useful, except to crush opponents in trivia. But the public speaking and persuasive writing elements are very beneficial."

If your course is really not useful for much at all, then there's still hope that you can motivate your students by using the other components of the MUSIC model. Usefulness is only one component of the model (see Figure 5.1). If students don't believe that it's useful, rely on the other components by empowering students to engage in interesting activities in ways in which they can succeed in a caring environment.

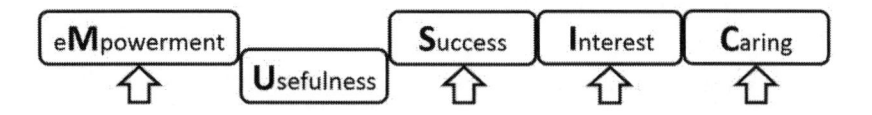

| e**M**powerment | **U**sefulness | **S**uccess | **I**nterest | **C**aring |

Figure 5.1. *When students don't perceive the course to be useful, you can use the other components of the MUSIC model to motivate students.*

Usefulness Strategy 2

Ask students or someone else to share the reasons they find the course content useful.

Instead of *you* explaining to students why the content is useful (as suggested in Usefulness Strategy 1), have students or others do the explaining. In some cases, students may be more likely than you to think of reasons as to why the content is useful to them, so give them the opportunity to do so. In other cases, students might be more willing to listen to or believe someone other than you, such as experts, people in their community, other individuals their age, or famous actors, athletes, or musicians.

Example U.2.1 – Allowing Students to Reflect on the Usefulness

Allow students to reflect on the usefulness of the course content. You can ask students to reflect at one or more times during the course. I ask students to reflect near the middle and end of my educational psychology course, in which students learn about educational psychology principles and strategies so that in the future they can apply them as teachers. Near the middle and end of the course, they complete an assignment in which they identify five of the most important ideas from the course that will be most useful to them as a teacher.

Example U.2.2 – Allowing Students to Search for Usefulness

Ask students to search for some ways in which the course content is useful. Create an assignment for which students go beyond what they already think they know about the usefulness of course content. You can suggest that students search the web, talk to experts in the field, or whatever ideas they have as long as they go beyond talking to other students in the class. Their ideas can relate to everyday events or career opportunities. You can ask students to share the ideas in class or to post their ideas in an online forum, blog, or wiki.

Example U.2.3 – Learning From Others About Usefulness

Allow students to hear reasons from one another as to why the course is useful. On the first day of a course, after discussing the syllabus (and anything else related to the content of the course), place students in groups of 3 or 4 and tell them to: (1) introduce themselves to one another, (2) discuss how the class relates to their short- and long-term goals, (3) discuss topics that interest them in the course, and (4) develop at least one question per person about anything they want to ask you. This activity has been shown to increase students' perceptions of the usefulness of the course, and it can also promote interest and foster caring relationships by requiring students to meet one another and to ask the professor questions (McGinley & Jones, 2014).

Example U.2.4 – Using Guest Presenters

Identify careers that require the use of the knowledge and skills in your course and invite individuals in those careers to give a guest presentation in your course. These presentations can be conducted in person or via video conferencing (e.g., Skype). Similarly, you can show online videos (e.g., youtube.com) with these types of presentations. It's fairly easy to find online videos with individuals from different careers discussing what they do and the knowledge and skills they need to perform their job. As another example, a physics professor had some of his colleagues at his university come to his introductory physics course to discuss their research (Ruff, 2013).

Usefulness Strategy 3

Design activities that allow students to see firsthand the usefulness of the content.

Many of the strategies in Usefulness Strategies 1 and 2 require students to listen to others to understand why the course content is useful. Another approach, which can be used with or without Usefulness Strategies 1 and 2, is to design activities that allow students to discern the importance of the course content through their participation in the activities.

Example U.3.1 – Making Connections to Their Lives

Give students an assignment that asks them to make connections between the course material and their lives. Doing so can force students to think seriously about the connections between the course and their lives because they are forced to write down their ideas.

As an example from a recent study, the instructor of an introductory psychology course gave an assignment to students after the first exam and then again after the second exam (the course included four exams spaced evenly throughout the course; Hulleman, Kosovich, Barron, & Daniel, 2017). The first assignment asked students to write one or two paragraphs about how the material in a course related to their life. Then after the second exam, they asked students to choose from a list of course topics that was personally useful and meaningful to them; and in one or two paragraphs, describe how learning about that topic was useful to their life at that time. Then, they were asked to write one or two more paragraphs on the same or different course topic about how learning about that topic could benefit them in the future (e.g., education, career, daily life) (Hulleman et al., 2017, p. 394). Compared to a control group, students who completed these two assignments were more likely to expect to do well in the course, find the course more useful, and perform higher on a future exam in the course.

Example U.3.2 – Interviewing a Professional

For an assignment, ask students to conduct a brief interview with a professional in the field in which they intend to work. The interview could be conducted by phone, video conferencing (e.g., Skype), email, or in person. Require students to ask the professional about which knowledge and skills are most important in her profession, which ones she learned during school, and which ones she wished she had learned during school.

An alternative is to require students to ask the professionals specific questions that you're fairly certain will lead to them understanding the usefulness. For example, if students in a science course don't see the usefulness of becoming good writers, you could ask them to ask a scientist how much time she spends writing and how important writing is to her job performance.

After the interview, you can place students in groups to share with one another what they learned from the professional or have students present their findings to the entire class. Another idea is to have students write a paragraph or two about what they learned from the professional in an online blog or discussion forum so that students can read about what other students learned from their interview.

> *"I put some effort into this class but only on assignments that I feel are relevant to my professional career."* (Undergraduate student's response as to why she puts forth effort in a course.)

Example U.3.3 – Using Course Content to Complete Important Tasks

Ask students to complete an assignment related to their goals that requires using the course content. For example, if students are interested in owning a business someday but don't see why they have to learn certain mathematics or writing skills, you could create an assignment that requires them to submit a proposal to a funding source with a budget. Through completing this assignment, they would quickly see the importance of being able to convey ideas in writing and using estimation and other mathematical skills to create a proposed budget.

Example U.3.4 – Connecting Content to the Real-World

Require students to create or contribute to a product that connects course content to the real-world. Instead of taking *your* time to search through things like the Internet, magazines, news outlets, and journals yourself, ask *students* to engage in this activity. For example, Antonio Izzo, a professor at Elon University in North Carolina, uses Flipboard (www.flipboard.com) in his microbiology courses by asking students to find course-related articles online and to include them in the Elon Microbiology Magazine (https://flipboard.com/@aizzo/elon-microbiology-magazine-kgvfl8npz). Flipboard allows individuals to do this easily by identifying content (e.g., articles) on the web and posting them in their magazine. Essentially, they create a link in their magazine to point to these articles on the web.

You could do something similar by creating a Flipboard magazine for your course and asking students to link to a certain number of articles during the semester without repeating any of the prior links (maybe each student could contribute four new links). Doing so requires students to read at least the headlines of the other articles in the magazine (and they may even read some of the articles!) and find additional course-related articles, which can help them connect course content to current issues. Students' participation can help them to see how the course content is related to the real-world. Students may also be more likely to take this assignment seriously because they're contributing to a product available for everyone in the world to view online. This activity requires little work on your part aside from keeping track of the number of times that students contributed to the magazine. And, you might learn some new things or be introduced to some new online articles.

As another example, Rob Jenkins, a professor of English at Georgia State University Perimeter College, teaches a first year composition course in which he tries to make his research paper assignment similar to what students will experience in the real-world. (Jenkins, 2017). He first asks students to think of a general field or subject area that is important to them and that they want to write about. Then he asks them to think about a specific problem within that area by thinking about it, doing some research, talking to someone in that area, etc. (e.g., parking problems on campus; salary disparity between NBA and WNBA players; out-of-control deer population). Next, students identify an audience that cares about the problem and who could do something about the problem; and, they decide who they are as the writer (e.g., an NBA executive). Students submit all this information in a proposal to him and if it's accepted, they write their paper on that topic to that audience in the role of the writer they specify. Professor Jenkins reports that "the result has been papers that are much more focused and meaningful—to them and to me—than they would have been otherwise" (Jenkins, 2017, para. 26).

Example U.3.5 – Sharing Work with an Audience

Share students' work with an audience. When students share their work with an audience, they're likely to view their work as useful and to want to do well. There are many ways to find an audience for students' work. One way is to publish students' work online, either through blogs, websites, or other means. Another way is to have students read an article and then write a press release about it for a newspaper.

A more unique way to share students' work is to compile their work into a book and self-publish it. In 2017, Wikipedia listed 29 different self-publishing companies (https://en.wikipedia.org/wiki/List_of_self-publishing_companies) from which you could choose. One example of a self-published book is *Desks to Destinations: 25 Students, 49 Countries, 175 Pages of Reflection* (Sojourners, 2014) that was created by a group of students and their instructor at Elon University based on their reflections during their travel abroad experiences. Because the book makes a profit by selling on amazon.com, they contribute the proceeds to a needs-based study abroad scholarship at their university. Thus, the book is useful for another reason as well: it provides scholarship money to students. In addition to being perceived as a useful project, imagine the feelings of success and accomplishment that students feel after the book is published.

Example U.3.6 – Using Online Virtual Worlds

Allow students to engage in an online virtual world to have almost real-world experiences. Second Life (http://secondlife.com) is the largest virtual world and it's being used to provide educational experiences that are impossible or more expensive in real life. Consider this list of possible uses of Second Life for instructional purposes, some of which I based on ideas from EDUCAUSE (2008) and Harrison (2009).

- Students could tour a replica of a city in the past, such as Berlin in 1920, and identify features of the city and inhabitants that are likely accurate and inaccurate.
- Students can design clothing that can be difficult to make in real life.
- Students can learn about stereotypes and biases by creating an avatar of a different ethnicity or gender than themselves.
- Because Second Life has a functioning economy, students can examine questions related to economies.
- Students can set-up a store in a mall and examine how people interact with their storefront, display cases, signs, etc.
- Students can investigate how people respond to advertisements or campaigns.
- Students can practice their language skills as they speak in foreign languages in foreign cities.
- Students can examine and critique artwork by others.
- Students can visit virtual planetariums.
- Students can discuss literature in buildings designed to be replicas of the actual buildings in the literature.
- Students can practice their teaching skills by teaching classes with students.
- Students can walk around a 3D molecule and ask questions and discuss it.

For more information, you may be interested in joining the Second Life Educators (SLED) email list at http://tinyurl.com/qfvv4.

Example U.3.7 – Administering a Test During the First Class

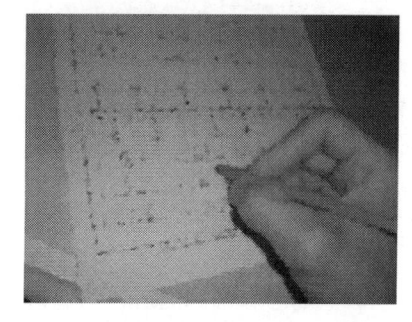

Give students a content test on the first day of class. Sometimes students don't realize what they don't know or may think that they know more than they do. In these cases, students might not be motivated to engage in course material because they believe they already know the content. When this happens, it can be useful to give students an ungraded content test on the first day of class. After seeing their poor score on the test, students will realize that they have more to learn about the content. With this awareness, students may be more motivated to learn the course content because they realize that it is useful. And if students do well on the test, you can use the results to help you modify the course content to better serve students (maybe they did already know the content!).

Example U.3.8 – Aligning Labs with Courses

Align lab sections of courses with the corresponding course so that material in the course matches with the labs each week. Labs and courses can complement each other and students can see the usefulness of course concepts if they see the application of the concepts in the lab. Sometimes it may be beneficial for students to complete the lab first because it may make them curious about what happened and arouse their curiosity and interest. Then during the course, they can find answers to the questions that arose in the lab.

Usefulness Strategy 4

Provide opportunities for students to set and reflect on their goals.

College students may not have clear goals or they may change their goals sometime during college. It's difficult for students to be motivated towards goals when they don't have goals or when their goals are unclear. Professors can help students reflect on their goals during a course. Obviously, some courses are better suited than others to help students with this. For example, some universities have courses specifically designed to provide students with experiences in one or more disciplines. But I would encourage all professors to consider how they might help students reflect on their goals and how the objectives of the course relate to those goals.

Higher education institutions can also provide opportunities for students to think about their goals outside of official coursework. For example, Harvard University offers a program for students (three 90-minute sessions) titled "Reflecting on Your Life" that are designed to "create an opportunity for freshmen to reflect – outside the classroom – on what matters to them and why" (The President and Fellows of Harvard College, 2015, para. 1).

> *"If you don't know where you're going, you might not get there."* – Yogi Berra (cited in Wikiquote, 2015c)

Example U.4.1 – Writing Down Goals

Ask students to write down their goals. Writing down goals makes the goals more concrete than simply talking about them. One way to do this is to have students list their long-term goals, and then under each long-term goal, list the short-term goals that they need to meet to make progress towards their long-term goals. You could do this near the beginning of a course, but you could also do it again near the end of the course. At that point, they could also reflect on their progress towards their goals and explain how the course helped them to shape their goals.

Understanding their short-term goals is important because students will be more motivated to act on their goals if their goals are proximal (fairly short-term and not in the distant future), specific, and of moderate difficulty (Locke & Latham, 2002). These proximal goals can then lead a path to students' longer-term goals. Professors and advisers can help students set realistic goals and to prioritize their goals so that they're more likely to achieve them.

> *"Goals are the fuel in the furnace of achievement. Think on paper and write them down!"* – Brian Tracy (cited in AZ Quotes, 2015a)

Example U.4.2 – Thinking about Values

Ask students to think about what they value in life. Sometimes students' have adopted goals without putting much thought into them. Maybe they've simply accepted goals to meet the expectations of their parents or society. To help students think more deeply about their values, ask them to list things that they value in life. These should be things that they believe are important to them (tell students that the list should range from about five to 15 items). Then, ask students to assign a percentage to each item they listed, with the percentage indicating the relative importance of the item. The percentages should add up to 100%. For example, a student might designate 50% importance to family and friends, 25% importance to schoolwork, and another 25% importance to hobbies. You can ask them to create a figure (e.g., pie chart) to show this graphically. You don't have to grade the figure or even collect it because it may be too personal for the students to share with you. But you can use this activity to help students think about their short- and long-term goals.

Richard Light (2015), a professor at Harvard University, explains a similar activity in which students are presented with 25 words (e.g., dignity, love, fame, and family) and are asked to circle five of the words that best describe their core values. Then students are asked: "How might you deal with a situation where your core values come into conflict with one another?" (Light, 2015, para. 11). For another activity, students are asked how they want to spend their time at college, then are asked to list how they actually spend their time, and finally, are asked how their commitments match their goals. This activity challenges students to think about how they can align their time commitments with their personal convictions.

Instructors at a large European business school conducted a similar, but more extensive, assignment that required students to consider their goals and values (Schippers, Scheepers, & Peterson, 2015). Researchers found that students who completed the goal-setting assignment in the first trimester of college had higher academic achievement and retention over time than students from prior years who had not been given the assignment. The assignment is too detailed to explain here, but if you're interested in goal-setting assignments, I encourage you to look up their study to see what was included in the assignment.

Example U.4.3 – Sharing Your Goals

Share your goals and how you have accomplished some of them and continue to strive to achieve others. In doing so, you will be providing a model for students in how to set and attain goals. Modeling may be useful for students who share similar interests to you, but modeling can also be useful to students whose interests are very different from yours. In sharing your goals, you can explain the *process* you went through to achieve some goals and the current processes you're using to achieve other goals. Talking about your failures can be useful too because it's evidence that overcoming failures is an important part of reaching your goals (this also relates to the success component of the MUSIC model).

You can share your goals during a face-to-face class. Sometimes there are natural places within a curriculum or lecture to discuss your goals because they relate to the content. At the University of Texas-Austin, Tricia Berry added an "occasional 15-minute cookie break in first- and second-year engineering classes for professors to talk about themselves and their work" (Loftus, 2011, para. 11). In fact, they've had more than 13,000 cookies delivered to 110 classes (http://www.engageengineering.org/fsi/cookie-connections)! If there's no time in class or you teach an online course, you can create a short video and allow students to view it outside of class time. You could even answer students' questions about your presentation in an online chat or discussion board.

CHAPTER 6

Strategies to Support Success

Problem

Students don't believe that they can achieve at a high level in some aspects of the coursework.

Solution

You need to ensure that students believe that they can <u>succeed</u> if they put forth the effort.

Overview of Success

How do you feel when you succeed at something really challenging? How about when you don't do as well as you expected or when you try something and fail completely (maybe even an epic fail!)? Do you try again? How about if you're unsure if you can succeed if you try again?

<u>Key Point:</u> Students are more motivated and more likely to persist in the face of challenges when they believe that they can succeed. It's important that students succeed in a course, but it's as important (and sometimes more important) that students *believe* that they can succeed. Of course students tend to believe they can succeed if they have succeeded at similar tasks in the past, so the "success breeds success" slogan is relevant here. However, it's also true that two students who score exactly the same on an exam can have different perceptions of their expected success on the next exam, which can affect their engagement in the class, assignments, and studying in preparation for the next exam. So part of the job of an instructor is to help students interpret their achievements in a course.

Although students need to believe that they can succeed, that doesn't mean that they should never fail. Failure is part of learning. Students who never fail, never learn how to overcome failure. So it's okay for students to fail, but you don't want that failure to persist to the extent that they believe they can't succeed. When failures are overcome, they can actually increase students' perceptions of their ability and of their confidence to succeed in the future.

> *"Even if you fall on your face, you're still moving forward."* – Victor Kiam (cited in iz Quotes, 2015d)

Researchers have identified four major contributors to students' success beliefs (Bandura, 1977; Usher & Pajares, 2008), as shown in Figure 6.1. The factor that usually affects students' success beliefs the most is their past performance in that activity. When students are asked in a math class how confident they are that they can complete a particular integral, students will think about how they have done in the past in solving integrals to estimate how well they'll do in the future. Students will also base their confidence on their observations of others, including you, a graduate teaching assistant, and others in the class. If others can do it, they might believe that they can do it too, especially when the others are similar to them. If other students of a similar gender, race, age, or education level do well at the activity, they will be more likely to believe that they can do well too, and vice versa. Students are also influenced by feedback from others, including their professors. If someone says, "I know you can do it!" students may be more likely to believe that they can do it. And finally, students are influenced by their emotional reactions to the activity. For example, if they get anxious and start sweating and shaking when presenting in front of their class, they might have less confidence in their public speaking abilities than if they are slightly anxious, but also excited and enjoy the experience.

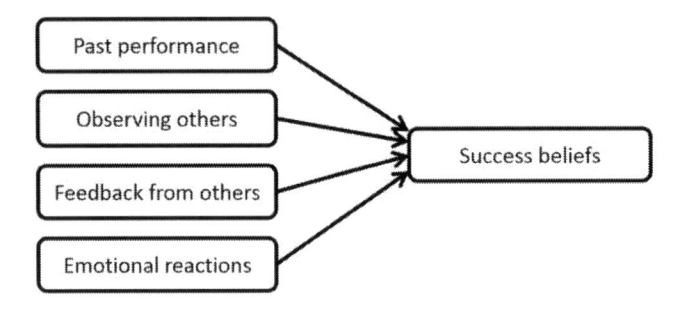

Figure 6.1. *Students' success beliefs are affected by their past performances, by observing others, by feedback from others, and by their emotional reactions.*

Please don't interpret the success component of the MUSIC model as meaning that the course activities should be easy. Students are most motivated to engage in activities when the challenge of the activities matches their ability levels. When an activity is too difficult, students can become anxious; however, when the activity is too easy, students can become bored (Csikszentmihalyi, 1990). Therefore, students are most motivated when the challenge meets their ability level (see Figure 6.2).

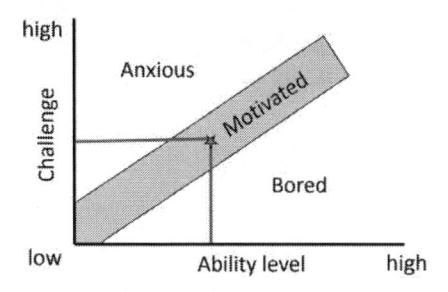

Figure 6.2. *Students' are motivated when challenge meet their ability level (based on Csikszentmihalyi, 1990, p. 74)*

This phenomenon can be evidenced when you hear a 4th grade student say: "I don't want to do that, that's 3rd grade work" (because it's too easy). Therefore, it's important to provide students with learning activities that challenge students to use their abilities. If the challenge is too difficult though, students become frustrated. And if they can't meet the challenge, over time, they will give up and not be motivated to engage in that activity, or closely related ones.

In this chapter, I present the following five strategies and provide several examples of each.

S.1 Help students believe they can succeed at course activities when they put forth the required effort.
S.2 Create an environment that promotes and supports successful learning.
S.3 Match the difficulty levels of class activities and assignments with the abilities of the students.
S.4 Provide students with honest, specific feedback about their level of competence at regular intervals.
S.5 Be explicit when describing your expectations and communicating to students.

Relevant Theories

Several motivation theories are based on the importance of appraising one's competence. In other words, how good we think we are at an activity or subject area affects whether we're motivated to engage in it or not. In this section, I provide very brief explanations of some of the theories that are most directly relevant to the success strategies in the MUSIC model. These are not comprehensive explanations, so please look-up the citations if you are interested in more information.

- Self-efficacy theory (Bandura, 1977, 1986, 1997). Self-efficacy is a construct within a broader theory entitled social cognitive theory (Bandura, 1986). "Perceived self-efficacy is defined as people's judgments of their capabilities to organize and execute courses of action required to attain designated types of performances" (Bandura, 1986, p. 391). In layman's terms, self-efficacy is the extent to which one is confident that s/he can perform a specific task. Students are more likely to be motivated for a task when they have a higher level of self-efficacy for the task.

- Expectancy for success (Atkinson, 1964; Eccles et al., 1983). Expectancy for success is a construct within expectancy-value theory. In an educational setting, expectancy for success is defined as a student's belief about how well s/he will do on an upcoming task (e.g., "I expect to do well in science this year"; Wigfield & Eccles, 2000, p. 70). Expectancy for success is similar to self-efficacy in many ways, although it is aligned with a different theoretical approach (expectancy-value theory) and is most commonly studied at the subject area level (e.g., mathematics), whereas self-efficacy is studied at the task level (e.g., double-digit addition problems). Students are more likely to be motivated in a subject area when they have higher expectancies of success for that subject area.

- Need for competence (Deci & Ryan, 1985, 2000). Need for competence is a construct within cognitive evaluation theory, which is a subtheory of self-determination theory. "The need for *competence* encompasses people's strivings to control outcomes and to experience effectance; in other words, to understand the instrumentalities that lead to desired outcomes and to be able to reliably effect those instrumentalities" (Deci & Ryan, 1991, p. 243). Students are more likely to be motivated when their need for competence is met.

- Self-concept theories (Marsh, 1990; Shavelson & Bolus, 1982). "In very broad terms, self-concept is a person's perception of himself" (Shavelson, Hubner, & Stanton, 1976, p. 411). "More specifically, academic self-concept refers to individuals' knowledge and perceptions about themselves in achievement situations" (Bong & Skaalvik, 2003, p. 6). Typically, academic self-concept refers to students' beliefs about their abilities in academic subjects (e.g., "I am good at mathematics"). Students are more likely to be motivated when they have a positive academic self-concept.

- Self-worth theory (Covington, 1992). "Self-worth Theory can be summarized in a nutshell: Individuals struggle to give their lives meaning by seeking the approval of others which involves being competent and able, and avoiding the implications of failure—that one is incompetent, hence unworthy" (Covington, 2009, p. 145). Students are more likely to be motivated when they have a positive self-worth.

- Attribution theory (Weiner, 1986, 2000). Attribution theory explains how individuals' attributions of prior events affect their future motivation (e.g., "I didn't study hard enough last night"). Students are more likely to be motivated when they attribute their successes and failures to internal, controllable factors (e.g., effort).

- Self-Theories of Intelligence (mindsets) (Dweck, 1999, 2006; Mueller & Dweck, 1998). Self-theories of intelligence focus on students' beliefs about whether their intelligence is changeable or fixed. Students are more likely to be motivated when they believe that their intelligence is changeable and not a fixed entity.

- Goal orientation theories (Ames, 1992; Elliot, 1999; Maehr & Midgley, 1991; Nicholls, 1984). Goal orientation researchers have identified several different types of goals. Students with mastery-approach goals want to *develop* their competence, whereas students with performance-approach goals want to *demonstrate* their competence to others. In contrast, students with performance-avoidance goals want to avoid appearing incompetent to others. Students are more likely to be motivated and perform at higher levels when they have mastery- or performance-approach goals than when they have performance-avoidance goals.

- Goal setting theories (Locke & Latham, 2002). Goal setting theories explain "that specific, high (hard) goals lead to a higher level of task performance than do easy goals or vague, abstract goals such as the exhortation to 'do one's best'" (Locke & Latham, 2006, p. 265). Therefore, the difficulty of the goals will determine the extent to which students believe that they can be successful. Students are more likely to be motivated and perform at higher levels when they have harder goals than when they have easy goals.

- Control theories. There are many different concepts and theories related to the concept of to control (e.g., locus of control, sense of control, helplessness). It is beyond the scope of this book to review all of these concepts; but if you're interested, Skinner (1996) wrote an article in which she reviewed over 100 terms used by psychologists to study control. You may be wondering why "control" theories are associated with the *success* strategies in the MUSIC model instead of the *empowerment* strategies, which deal directly with control. It's a little complicated for me to explain briefly, but I'll use learned helplessness as an example. If individuals consistently fail at a task, they will eventually believe that they can't do it (they can't *succeed*) and they will stop trying. Thus, they have lost their motivation to complete that task (i.e., they don't intend to try to do it anymore). Consequently, they feel as if they don't have any control over the outcome. This loss of control over the outcome, therefore, is a key variable in their lack of motivation, which is why perceptions of control are critical to motivation. The primary means through which individuals can become motivated again is by succeeding at the task and feeling as if they have some control over their success. Because success is critical to changing students' beliefs about control, the strategies related to control are included in the success component of the MUSIC model.

Success Strategy 1

Help students believe they can succeed at course activities when they put forth the required effort.

Students may or may not be motivated to engage in course activities if they believe that they can succeed at them. But it's almost always the case that students will *not* be motivated to engage in the activities if they *don't believe* that they can do so successfully. Professors can help students believe that they can succeed by attributing students' successes and failures to their effort and strategies. Students need to believe that course outcomes are due to their effort and use of effective strategies, and not believe that their failures are due to their lack of natural, genetic ability. When students attribute their failures to internal (i.e., genetic) and stable (i.e., unchanging) causes, they lack the motivation to engage because doing so is fruitless. Why would someone keep trying to do something if they believed that they didn't have the genetic ability to do it? Everyone has a need to feel competent at activities in life, which is why consistent failure is neither fun nor motivating.

"They can because they think they can." – Virgil (cited in Knowles, 2004, p. 812)

When students believe that they cannot succeed, they may start making excuses or engage in self-handicapping. Self-handicapping occurs when students behave in ways that undermine their success. For example, they may reduce their effort, misbehave, set unattainable high goals, take on too many responsibilities in their lives, procrastinate, cheat, and/or abuse alcohol or drugs (Ormrod & Jones, 2018, p. 167). Self-handicapping allows students to "save face" by giving them a justification for their inevitably poor performance. They can blame their lack of success on something besides their lack of ability. When you notice such behavior, it's probably time to meet with the student individually and discuss that: (1) you've noticed the behavior, (2) the behavior is affecting their performance, and (3) you are willing help them to improve their ability so that they can succeed in your course. Hopefully the example strategies provided in this section will help prevent students from reaching the point at which they need to engage in self-handicapping behaviors.

Example S.1.1 – Attributing Failures to Effort and Strategies

Help students attribute failures to a lack of effort or the use of ineffective strategies. When students are doing poorly in your class, they may come to you for help or you may need to contact them to discuss the reasons for their struggles in your course. Often, students who are struggling are simply not putting in the amount of time and effort needed. I find that most of them are able to correctly attribute their lower grades to their lack of effort and realize that increased effort could lead to higher grades. These students either will or will not put forth more effort, but either way, *you* often have little control over it.

Other students who are struggling are putting forth effort and can't figure out why they're not getting higher grades in your course. These students need your help. If you can verify that they're putting forth enough effort (simply ask them), then tell them that they're likely not using the most effective strategies. At this point, you can refer them to a "Tips" document (see Example S.2.2) to ensure that they're using some of the strategies in this document. If students continue to struggle, ask them to tell you exactly what they're doing to prepare for assignments and tests, and discuss ways that they can use strategies more effectively. Students who succeed by using more effective strategies can logically conclude that their success is due to their change in strategies and not their fixed abilities. This is very motivating because they know that they can do well though the use of effort and appropriate strategies, both of which are within their control.

Example S.1.2 – Giving Students a Muscle Analogy

Give students the analogy that the brain is like a muscle that gets stronger with exercise. Some students may believe that their abilities in a particular subject, such as math, are fixed and unchangeable; that is, they're "not a math person." Sharing the analogy that the brain is like a muscle may help them to reframe their views of learning in those subjects to believe that their abilities are changeable through effort (exercise). Maybe they will still believe that they learn the subject slower than other students, but that's okay because at least they believe there's hope if they put forth effort. These views can be reinforced if these students go on to put forth effort and achieve success through their effort and effective strategy use.

Example S.1.3 – Learning from Failure

Create a culture in which failure can be part of the learning process. When students believe that they always need to succeed, failure is disconcerting and anxiety provoking, a state that students don't want to be in. Consequently, some students may stop engaging in the activity to avoid these feelings. Instead, students need to believe that failure is okay and, in fact, part of the learning process.

You can share quotations such as "make mistakes faster" (attributed to Andy Grove, former CEO of Intel Corporation; AZ Quotes, 2017) because it implies that everyone has to make mistakes, and if you make them faster you will achieve successes faster as well.

Another quotation that is often used is the following one from a *Nike* TV ad from 1997.

> *"I've missed more than 9,000 shots in my career. I've lost almost 300 games. 26 times I've been trusted to take the game winning shot and missed. I've failed over and over and over again in my life. And that is why I succeed."*
> – Michael Jordan (Goldman & Papson, 1998, p. 49)

It's easy to say it's OK to fail, but if students don't have opportunities to fail, then it's really just empty words. So to back it up, find a way to give students time to make mistakes and learn from them before they have to perform. Allow them to learn by completing activities that improve their abilities in preparation for a "performance" (e.g., test, project). Figure 6.3 shows that learning is preparation for performance, but also that performance provides students with feedback they can use to learn from as they prepare for the next performance.

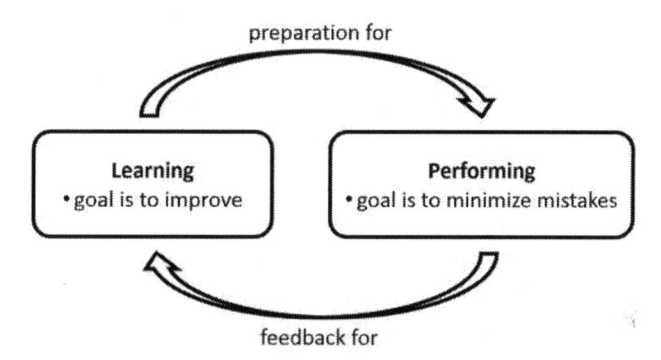

Figure 6.3. *Learning is preparation for performance and performance provides feedback for further learning*

You can create safe learning spaces by allowing students to practice difficult problems in a low-stakes environment. To help students believe that they can succeed in solving difficult problems, they need to successfully complete difficult problems. One way to do this is to give them a lot of practice problems that allow them to learn strategies that you and other students use to solve the problems. Providing a low-stakes environment can allow them to focus on the process instead of worrying about obtaining the correct answer (i.e., their performance). For example, you may give students credit for simply completing the problems or allow students to work together to solve them. Then, if you want to test their knowledge, you can always give a more formal graded test later.

"Man errs as long as he strives." – Johann Wolfgang von Goethe (cited in Bartlett, 2002, p. 365)

Example S.1.4 – Sharing Stories of Famous People's Struggles

Share stories in which someone famous overcame their struggles in the discipline represented in your course. Students may be more likely to believe that they can overcome struggles if they know that even people who were famous struggled. And relatedly, it's important for them to realize that learning and success requires work. Sometimes learning is hard, and that's okay, but they'll get through it with the proper effort and strategies.

In one study (Lin-Siegler, Ahn, Chen, Fang, & Luna-Lucero, 2016), researchers randomly gave high school students one of three different 800-word stories about three famous scientists: Albert Einstein, Marie Curie, and Michael Faraday. One of the stories, titled "Trying Over and Over Again Even When You Fail," was about the struggles these three scientists experienced while working on their scientific discoveries. Another story, titled "Overcoming the Challenges in Your Life," was about the difficulties these three scientists experienced in their personal lives. And the final story, titled "The Story of a Successful Scientist," was about these three scientists' achievements. The purpose of the study was "to confront students' beliefs that scientific achievement reflects ability rather than effort" and the two struggle stories "were designed to show students that even the most accomplished scientists are relatable people who often fail and struggle through difficulty prior to their triumphs" (Lin-Siegler et al., 2016, p. 315). Students who read the struggle stories received higher class grades in science than the students who read "The Story of a Successful Scientist" (which did not include the struggles faced by the three scientists).

You could share struggle stories of famous people in the discipline represented in your course (or even your own struggle stories) by telling them the stories during class, by providing written stories as handouts or posted online, by providing links to information about the famous people, or by thinking of other creative ways to share stories.

Example S.1.5 – Setting Reasonable Expectations

Set high, but reasonable expectations. High expectations can motivate students to achieve their best work. But unreasonably high expectations can lead to debilitating anxiety and a lack of motivation. To determine an appropriate workload for students in your course, it can be useful to review your colleagues' syllabi. How does the amount of work you expect from students compare to the amount of work other professors expect? It can also be useful to survey students about the course workload by asking them: How does the amount of work required in this course compare to the amount of work required in your other courses (1 = *much less*, 2 = *less*, 3 = *about the same*, 4 = *more*, 5 = *much more*)? You may want the amount of work in your course to be less, more, or about the same as other courses, depending on the goals of the course. But the important thing is to know how much you're expecting so that you can adjust the workload if needed.

The difficult, and often philosophical, question is: How do you balance what you know to be an appropriate course workload with the real demands students face outside of your course, including other courses, employment, family life, etc. If your students have difficulty keeping pace with the course, you may consider reducing the workload during certain weeks to allow students to catch-up. Or, give some assignments with flexible deadlines, so that students can better fit them into their schedules.

Example S.1.6 – Viewing Weaknesses as Opportunities

Remind students that their weaknesses are opportunities for improvement. Everyone has weaknesses. But instead of viewing their weaknesses as fatal flaws, they can view them as opportunities for improvement.

Example S.1.7 – Soliciting Testimonials from Former Struggling Students

Solicit testimonials from students who have completed the course. Select students who were once struggling, but overcame their struggles to have success in the course. You can show quotations from former students during class or create a handout or online document with quotations. Hearing that former students overcame initial struggles can give current students hope that they too can overcome their struggles.

A related strategy is to show current students examples of test (or assignment) scores from former students that were initially low, and then show them how their former students' scores improved over time.

Success Strategy 2
Create an environment that promotes and supports successful learning.

To build on Success Strategy 1 and to ensure that students really believe that they can succeed in your course, you need to create a culture and environment that promotes and supports successful learning. There are many ways to accomplish this general strategy. In this section, I provide a variety of concrete examples that can help students believe that they can succeed in your course.

Example S.2.1 – Teaching Students How to Study

Teach students how to study and learn the knowledge and skills in your course. Many students—even students at the "best" universities in the world—do not know how to study effectively or how to study the concepts in a particular course most effectively. When I was an instructor at Duke University, a student who had received a low grade in my course the prior semester met with me to find out what she could do to improve her grades in the future. I was astonished to find out that she never wrote down the due dates of her course assignments and tests. I assumed everyone in college knew how to set goals and adjust their study time accordingly. But this student from one of the top universities in the world taught me that you can't assume that students know how to study effectively. Even students who do perform well may use strategies that produce good results, but that are overly time consuming or that lead to superficial understanding.

Therefore, you'll likely need to spend some time teaching students how to study. If it's an upper-level course, you may be able to simply highlight some effective study strategies fairly briefly, especially ones that will help them learn the knowledge and skills related to your course. If it's a lower-level course and students haven't attended college very long, you may need to spend an entire 50 minutes discussing study strategies.

It's beyond the scope of this book to provide you with an explanation of effective study strategies, but I can recommend *Our Minds, Our Memories: Enhancing Thinking and Learning at All Ages* (Ormrod, 2011) if you're looking for an easy-to-read book to share with students. Basic study strategies include those that involve preparing for studying, setting goals, reviewing, and using strategies such as organizing (e.g., outlines, concept maps), summarizing, visualizing, and tying new information to existing knowledge. Two specific strategies that you might want to teach them (or provide them with links to) are the Cornell Note-taking System (http://lsc.cornell.edu/study-skills/cornell-note-taking-system/) and the PQ4R strategy (see Appendix A). But you don't have to reinvent the wheel; you may find videos online that teach students study strategies (e.g., http://lsc.cornell.edu/study-skills/study-skills-videos/how-to-study/).

Also consider that different subjects can require different ways of thinking, and therefore, different types of study strategies. You will need to make these strategies explicit to students if you want *all* students to have the best chance of succeeding, especially those who are new to your subject area.

Finally, remember that your students aren't you. You can share with them what you did, but don't expect them to be able to process information exactly like you did. Maybe you were faster or slower than them, or maybe you had practiced or not practiced certain strategies for many years in school before college. So be patient with them and teach them a variety of effective learning strategies. In the next example, I provide a specific recommendation for how to help students learn effectively in your specific course.

> *"The will to win is important, but the will to prepare is vital."* – Joe Paterno (AZ Quotes, 2015b)

Example S.2.2 – Providing "Tips for Success" Document

Help students learn study strategies that are effective in your course by providing them with a document that includes tips on how to succeed in the course. Students often don't know the best way to study or the best way to study the content in *your* course. You can help them learn these strategies by providing them with a document that includes various strategies. It not only helps the students, but it will also save you time from having to repeat yourself over and over with questions from struggling students. Then, when students ask you what they can do to improve their grades, you can ask, "Have you read the tips document?" If they haven't read it, you can tell them to read it; then, contact you again with any questions they may have about the document. If they've read the tips document, ask them if they've tried any of the tips provided in the document. This process will allow you to enter into a more in-depth conversation about the student's strategies much more quickly than if you had to inquire about their strategies from the beginning and teach them basic strategies.

I provide students with several different types of tips in a document that I title "Tips for Succeeding in [insert course abbreviation and number]". See Appendix A for an abbreviated example of a document I used in a class. First, I provide a section on how to learn and study from a textbook. Even students who do well in a course can benefit from reading other strategies or being reminded of other strategies that they can use to improve their learning from a textbook. The second section includes broader tips for studying, such as minimizing distractions, reviewing, avoiding procrastination, etc. In the third section, I provide tips for taking the multiple-choice quizzes that are part of the course. Many of the tips in this section might seem obvious, but over the years I've found that struggling students don't do them. In the fourth section, I provide any final tips that I've learned over time related to a particular course. I ensure that this document includes all of the things that I would otherwise say to multiple students each semester when they asked me, "How can I improve my grade?" This document has saved me a lot of time. And then when I do meet or email students, we have better conversations because they've already tried the basics and we can work towards better understanding exactly what they can do to improve their study strategies. Finally, you can ask current or former students for strategies to include.

Example S.2.3 – Giving Students Time to Take Notes

Give students time to take notes. When you're lecturing or when students are engaged in other activities and they need to take notes, watch them to ensure (a) that they're taking notes (and if not, remind them that notes are necessary to remember information later) and (b) that you're giving them enough time to take sufficient notes. Again, remember that your students aren't necessarily like you. If they are slower than you, you must accommodate them as long as it's not unreasonable.

Example S.2.4 – Handing-in Notes

If note taking is essential in your course, you can require students to hand-in their notes as an assignment. I'm sure you're thinking, "How am I going to grade their notes?" The simplest way is to give them full credit for handing in reasonable notes and no credit for not handing in reasonable notes. This assignment doesn't have to count as a large part of their grade, but it gives them motivation to take better notes and it allows you to give them feedback that they truly might need.

An added bonus for you is that you get to see if what you're doing in class is translating to what they're hearing, understanding, and writing. You may find that what you thought you were teaching isn't what they were hearing and understanding. If you want to get more nuanced with your grading, you can develop a rubric with criteria that you find most important.

Example S.2.5 – Creating Study Groups

Help students create voluntary study groups. Some students may wish to study with other classmates and some may not. But either way, you can help students create study groups by creating an online form (as a discussion or Google form or something else) in which students can sign-up online (or pass around a piece of paper in class). You can let students work out the times and locations or you could reserve some rooms around campus for students who wish to show up.

Example S.2.6 – Answering Questions Online

Create a discussion board online to allow students to ask you (and other students) questions. You can create a discussion board in your class management system or find a commercial site, such as google.groups.com, piazza.com, or tophat.com. Answering questions in class is effective, but answering questions online provides a few important advantages. First, it provides students with more time to think about their questions, which can lead to better questions than if they just ask something that pops into their heads during class. Second, it provides another means of communication that may be preferable to students who don't enjoy asking questions in class (maybe they're shy, introverted, or self-conscious). Third, writing online may be more accessible for students with disabilities or special needs. Fourth, it allows students to answer other students' questions, which can increase their perceptions of success and save you time. Fifth, it provides a written record of questions and answers that students can read later or that you can refer to when similar questions arise in the future. Sixth, it allows all students to ask questions if they want to, which is often impossible during class because there isn't enough time and/or the class is too large.

Example S.2.7 – Providing Opportunities for Early Success

Provide opportunities for students to succeed early in the class. You don't have to make the class *easier* at the beginning of a course, but the earlier in the course that students receive feedback, the earlier they can make adjustments to their studying.

And remember that the success opportunities don't have count towards students' grades. As an example, you can offer ungraded practice quizzes or short ungraded assignments that allow students to practice the knowledge and skills they're learning.

Example S.2.8 – Planning for the Possibility of Early Failures

Plan for the possibility that students will not do well early in the semester. One way to do this is to weight the earlier assignments (or tests) less than later assignments/tests. This is relevant to students' motivation because if some students get a 50% on the first assignment/test and it's worth 20% of their grade, the highest percentage those students can receive in the class is 90% (which may be the cutoff for receiving an A). Surely this would affect students' perceptions of success in the course. One possible solution is to give two smaller assignments/tests worth 10% instead of one larger assignment/test.

Example S.2.9 – Reflecting on and Selecting Better Strategies

Require students to list the strategies they've used so far, reflect on how they're working, and provide a list of other strategies they could be using. The purpose of this assignment is for students to reflect on their study strategies and to consider other possible strategies that they could use to improve the efficiency of their learning. Writing down their strategies forces them to reflect on what they're doing and consider how their strategies are working. I've had master's degree students tell me that throughout their undergraduate college experience, they never reflected on how their strategies were working. They just studied a lot or they didn't. This assignment is intended to be especially helpful to these types of students, although I'm convinced that it can be helpful to all students.

You also want to make it clear to students that they can come to you for ideas for other strategies if they're not achieving as well as they would like to achieve. From a motivation perspective, you want students to believe that they can succeed. See Appendix B for an example of an assignment that I give my students. I find that the assignment is easy to grade and that students complete it satisfactorily. The due date for the assignment needs to occur after students have had a chance to complete a couple assessments; otherwise they won't be able to discuss what they did or what they could do differently.

And best of all, I think you will be amazed how much insight you gain into how your students are engaging in your course. You can then use this information to help students in the future by editing your "Tips for Succeeding" document (see example S.2.2) and sharing ideas with students.

Example S.2.10 – Assigning Problems with Several Correct Answers

Assign problems with several correct answers because students will feel less pressure to find the one correct answer; and instead, focus on the knowledge and process needed to solve the problem. As an example in a first-year physics course, one professor used Fermi problems during class because they are, by definition, problems that require estimation, educated guesses, and don't have a precise answer (Ruff, 2013). Example problems include, "How many piano tuners are there in Chicago?" and "How many ping-pong balls can fit in this classroom?" Completing these problems in class gives students practice in starting and working through difficult problems. As the course progresses, students gain more confidence in their ability to solve such problems.

Example S.2.11 – Providing More Opportunities for Students to Improve

Provide more opportunities for students to improve if they want to improve their grade. Sometimes professors give students more opportunities by assigning extra credit assignments. Personally, I prefer not to give extra credit assignments because I don't want students to learn *extra* things, I want them to learn the knowledge and skills that relate to the course objectives. So if you give extra credit, I suggest that you relate it directly to the course objectives.

Another approach that basically achieves the same goal is to give students more assignments during the course. As explained by "scienceprof" (ChronicleVitae, 2016, July 29): "I used to give 10 quizzes and drop the two lowest. Now I give at least 10 quizzes, and keep the 8 highest. The students beg for more quizzes, so anytime I think they haven't 'gotten' something I throw in an extra quiz, with no complaints."

Example S.2.12 – Allowing Students to Re-Do Assignments and Tests

Allow students to re-do assignments and retake tests (see Appendix C for an example). By doing so, you're sending the message that it's okay if they struggle sometimes because they can go back and learn what they didn't understand the first time they tried to learn it.

"Mountainguy" (ChronicleVitae, 2016, July 29) notes how he allows students to re-do assignments in the following explanation.

> *"I let students re-write any assignment (except final essays) for a higher grade, provided that it was submitted on time. I then calculate their new assignment grade using the following formula: [.6 (original grade) + .4 (re-write grade)]. Students think I'm doing them a favor and rarely grade-grub about written work. Few of them take me up on the offer. It's too much work for them because they actually have to pay attention to what my comments say."*

I included mountainguy's idea here to get you thinking about how you can grade the resubmissions. For some reason mountainguy only counts the re-write as 40% of the students' final assignment grade. Why not count it as 100% and forget about the original grade? I don't have an answer, but this may or may not be a good idea; you need to decide what works for you in a way that will motivate students to meet the course objectives. Also, I'm a little concerned that most students don't do a revision. If the purpose is to help students learn, then I would want to know why they don't re-write their assignments. If mountainguy is correct that it's too much work for students to re-write, then either the course is too much work (which he has control over) or the students don't have enough time (which he doesn't have control over and that's the way it is). I would talk to students or survey them to find out what's going on here so that I could address the issue.

Allowing students to retake *tests* can be difficult to implement because creating good test questions is a difficult task. Here are a few things that might help you when you allow students to retake tests.

- You can allow students to retake all tests if you're able to create another test that is similar to the first one, yet different enough to be considered a different test. Because it can be time-consuming and difficult to create second parallel tests, you may opt to allow students to retake only a few tests.

- If you have (or can create) a large number of test items, you can randomly select some items for one test and other items for another test. This can be accomplished easily with most online classroom management systems (e.g., Blackboard) because you can have the computer select the questions randomly from a large pool of questions.

- Another option is to provide students with one or more ungraded practice tests before the graded test. This option is attractive because you can use the same ungraded test items in different semesters and simply change the graded test items.

- A final option is to not include students' lowest test grade (or however many you choose) as part of their final grade (i.e., drop their lowest test grade; or as I noted in another strategy, don't count all of them towards their grade). The problem with this option is that students aren't necessarily held accountable for learning the content that is not included as part of the grade.

Example S.2.13 – Administering a Collaborative Two-Stage Exam

Give students a collaborative two-stage exam in which students complete the exam once by themselves and then again with three other students. Logistically, use about 70% of the exam time for the first stage when students work alone. Then, ask students to turn in their exams and solve similar or the same problems during the second stage as they work with others. For more detailed implementation information and an example, see Rieger and Heiner (2014) and this video: http://blogs.ubc.ca/wpvc/two-stage-exams.

From a motivational perspective, there are a few possible advantages of a two-stage exam over a traditional exam. First, when students work together during the second stage, students are more likely to believe that they can succeed because they can receive assistance from their peers. Second, students receive specific feedback from their peers immediately after completing the exam, which can help them learn and correct any misconceptions or misunderstandings they may have had (thus increasing their perceptions of success for the future). Third, knowing they can work with others for part of the exam may reduce some anxiety and increase success perceptions as they prepare for the exam.

Many students view the two-stage exam positively, as documented in a study of students in a physics course for which 76% of students reported a positive opinion of two-stage exams, 14% reported neutral/other opinions, and 10% reported an overall negative opinion (Rieger & Helner, 2014). And from the perspective of instructors, Wieman, Rieger, and Heiner (2014) noted that "Witnessing the intense productive discussions in which nearly all students are engaged during the second stage has been the most convincing reason for most faculty for using the two-stage format" (p. 51-52). Finally, some studies have documented gains in students' learning over time as a result of participating in the two-stage exams (Gilley & Clarkston, 2014).

Example S.2.14 – Showing Examples from Former Students

Show students examples of completed assignments from former students to give them an idea of what's possible and what good assignments looks like. Of course, you wouldn't be able to show students answers from assignments that were exactly the same as the ones in the current course. But you can do this when you expect students' answers to vary substantially or when you modify the assignment from prior courses.

Example S.2.15 – Allowing Students to Share Experiences

Show students examples of students who have completed the course successfully or who are currently completing the course successfully. Beliefs about success can be changed by watching others. When students see that other students can or have succeeded (particularly students like them in terms of age, ethnicity, sex, background, abilities, etc.), they're more likely to believe that they can succeed.

> *"You can observe a lot by watching."* – Yogi Berra (cited in Wikiquote, 2015c)

You could bring in a former student as a guest speaker to discuss her experiences in the course and any struggles and successes she had and how she overcame them. You could also show comments from former students on end-of-course evaluations. If you don't have any questions related to this on your course evaluations, you could add some questions such as: "What did you do in this course when you were struggling? What helped you to succeed when you weren't doing as well as you wanted to do?"

To show role models more broadly, you could search YouTube for videos of individuals in your discipline discussing their experiences in the field or what they're doing now and how school prepared them for their current job. Or, create your own video at the end of your course by having some students talk about their experiences in the course and strategies they implemented to be successful. You can show these videos in your courses in the future or ask students to watch them as an assignment.

It can also be beneficial for students to hear from students in your current course. They may be interested in finding out what their classmates are doing to succeed. A few weeks after the start of the course, identify a few students who are doing well in the course and ask them to describe what they're doing to succeed in the class. (You may want to contact the students ahead of time to see if they're comfortable doing this and to give them time to reflect on what they want to say.) You can even do this in your online classes. Email a few students who are doing well to ask them if they will share their strategies and then email their responses out to the entire online class. An example of an email to the students who are doing well is provided in Appendix D.

Example S.2.16 – Giving Students Time to Work in Class

Give students time to work on assignments in class. You may be more likely to help students succeed if they can work on assignments during class and get help from you and other students. This is one of the ideas in what some people call a "flipped" classroom, in which students work on activities in class, but it can also be incorporated in other types of courses. For example, you may just select a few classes throughout the semester in which students work on assignments with the opportunity to ask you questions in real time.

As another example, you could create a hybrid course in which students complete some of the activities as they would in an online course, and offer other activities as you would in a traditional face-to-face class. For instance, if your class normally met on Tuesdays and Thursdays, you could have students complete the online part of the course as their Tuesday work and then meet face-to-face on Thursday. Because your classroom is still available on Tuesday and the students won't have any other courses during that time, students could come to class to work on assignments and you could be there to help them if needed.

Example S.2.17 – Giving the Test Questions Ahead of Time

Give students the test questions before the test. This strategy allows students to prepare for the questions and do well on the test if they take the time to prepare. If your questions are good, students will be learning the material that is related to the course objectives. Professor "profxfiles" explains one way to do this (ChronicleVitae, 2016, July 29): "A few days before each of my four exams in my gen-ed classes, I hand out a list of a dozen essay questions. Then I choose two for the test at random. That way, none of the students can claim to be 'surprised' by the questions, yet I give them such a broad and comprehensive list of questions that they would have to know all of the major concepts in the class in order to be fully prepared."

Example S.2.18 – Extending Assignment Deadlines

Extend some of the deadlines for the assignments. You probably don't want to extend all of your deadlines or they won't be deadlines anymore and students won't take them seriously. However, extending some deadlines to provide students with more time to do a better job completing their assignments can let students know that the focus of the class is on their successful learning. And likely, students will feel that they can be more successful.

But if you extend some deadlines and not others, some students might say: "It's not fair that you're not extending the deadline for this assignment when I'm super busy, but you extended it for the last assignment when I completed it on time." To avoid these inequities and support students when they need it, you could allow all students to extend the deadline of one or more assignments of their choosing. Ellen Boucher, a professor of history at Amherst College, used this strategy and let students in her courses take a two-day grace period on any paper with no questions asked (Boucher, 2016, September 2). She explains, "If, at the end of that [two-day grace] period, they are still having trouble completing the assignment, they must meet with me in person to go over an outline of their ideas and set a schedule for getting the paper done" (9th paragraph). Her experience in using this strategy has been very positive based on the quotation that follows.

> *"Since changing my policy, I've seen higher-quality work, less anxiety, and fewer cases of burnout. Most of my students do take the grace period occasionally throughout the semester, but the great majority complete their assignments by the end of the two days."* (10th paragraph)

Example S.2.19 – Asking Good Questions and Waiting

Ask good questions in class and give students time to think about the answers. Sometimes instructors are quick to either answer their own question, rephrase their question, or call on the first student with his or her hand in the air. Instead, after you ask a question, wait several seconds, even if it requires some students to sit there with their hands up for a while. Waiting gives more students time to think about your question, which can increase the chances that they'll actually think about it and participate in class.

Probably worse than not giving students sufficient wait time, is to ask generic, useless questions and then proceed rapidly before anyone can answer. I'm referring to questions such as: Does that make sense? and Does everyone understand that? Of course these are good questions, and if you can get all students to answer them that's great. But I've been in a lot of audiences in which the presenter asks the question then moves on in one second if one person in the front row nods his or her head. Others in the audience who are confused will surely not feel successful in this situation because they will think that everyone else understands but them (even though that's probably not true).

Example S.2.20 – Creating Materials for Students

Create written materials, audio recordings, or videos for explanations of content. You may want to explain a course concept to students in your own words, as opposed to relying solely on course readings or existing videos to provide the explanations. But that doesn't mean that your explanations have to occur face-to-face as a lecture. Creating written materials, audio recordings, or videos allows students to review the explanations repeatedly and may give them confidence that they can learn the content if they take the time to do so.

By "written materials" I'm referring to things such as a paper handout, an electronic document (e.g., Word document or PDF), or a website. In 2002, when I found students' attention waning during my lectures, I decided to write down my lecture, word for word, including any figures or visual materials to which I referred during the in-class lecture. I found that a several minute lecture fit onto one or two pages of text, which seemed relatively short. So instead of lecturing, I included the text in a course packet with other materials I provided to students. In doing this, I was able to use the class time for other, more engaging activities. But it also helped students feel that they could succeed because they could re-read the text if they were confused and could ask me specific questions about it. It also helped the students who missed class to feel that they could succeed because they didn't miss my "profound" lectures that were only available to those who attended class. Writing out lectures is useful for both face-to-face classes and online courses, as are videos in which you provide the lecture in a video instead of face-to-face.

Audio recording your lectures is another option because you can make the recordings available as podcasts on the Internet. You can create lectures separate from what you do in class (instead of writing it out as I suggested previously), or you can record your classes and make them available as podcasts. Podcasts can be downloaded from the Internet onto virtually any media player or computer, making them handy for students as they ride the bus, drive their car, or do some other task. However, with smart phones, tablets, and laptop computers, videos along with the audio can provide a more engaging visual experience for students. A disadvantage of videos is that they're more time-consuming to create than the audio alone.

Although videos can take a lot of time to produce, they don't have to, and there are several options available to you to make simple videos fairly quickly. In addition to the video, I recommend providing the video narration and video slides (if the video includes PowerPoint slides) as a PDF to students. Providing both a video and a text gives students options, depending on their preferences and time availability. Here are some options for creating videos; you can search YouTube to watch a video for instructions in how to create these types of videos.

- Use text and audio only (for examples, search for "Brett D Jones" on YouTube or go to http://www.youtube.com/c/BrettDJones). For simple videos that get the job done, you can use PowerPoint to create slides and then talk over the slides as you would do for a presentation. You can do all of this within PowerPoint or you can create the audio in a separate program and add it to the PowerPoint using free software such as Audacity (http://sourceforge.net/projects/audacity/). I prefer to create the audio separately because it allows me to edit the audio to fix mistakes or take out long pauses. An edited video is a shorter video, which students seem to appreciate. A strength of this type of video is that you can provide the students with the PowerPoint slides without any extra work because you've already created them for the video. Simply save them as a PDF and make them available to students. Another strength is that students can see some of the text, which can be useful if they misheard or couldn't hear something you said. A weakness is that they don't get to see your facial and bodily expressions, which can create interest and a personal connection to you.

- Aim the video camera at yourself and talk (for examples, search for "Plaid Avenger" on YouTube or go to https://www.youtube.com/user/Plaidcast). A strength of this type of video is that you can create excitement and students can see your expressions. Shooting the videos in different locations that relate to the content of the videos can also create interest. A weakness may be that it's more difficult to edit video than audio only (without video) and that everyone is not as animated and interesting as the Plaid Avenger! It's easy for students to rewind the video to watch parts of it again, but you have to create the text for the narration separately if you want to share the text with students.

- Use text and video. Obviously, there are many different variations of videos other than the two I've described so far; however, the two I've already described are more practical because they tend to take less time and resources and can be implemented fairly easily. Another option is simply to record face-to-face lectures (for examples, search for "MIT Introduction to Superposition" on YouTube). Other types of videos that incorporate audio, video, images, and animations can be very engaging, entertaining, and effective, but require a lot of time (for examples, search "Physics Girl" on YouTube; https://www.youtube.com/user/physicswoman; here's a good example, https://tinyurl.com/pcolor44). For this type of video, it may be best to simply search YouTube and include videos that *others* have developed because they can take longer for you to create yourself!

Example S.2.21 – Focusing on the Process Instead of the Product

Give some "low-risk" assignments that allow students to be creative, take risks, and possibly fail without negative effects on their course grade (and maybe even have a positive effect on their grade!). These types of assignments tend to focus on the process instead of the product. You can create rubrics to assess the attributes that are important and if students attain these attributes, they can still do well on the assignment even if their final product is unacceptable. For example, the rubric might include items such as: "The product was unique, unusual, or creative."

Example S.2.22 – Reviewing Knowledge and Skills

Review important knowledge and skills prior to assessments. Reviews can bolster students' success beliefs when they're successful. If they aren't successful, reviews can provide students with information about areas in which they need further study. This knowledge can help them feel that they can succeed if they put forth the effort to study more.

To review vocabulary or concepts, you can play a modified version of the old TV game show titled "Password" (http://www.tv.com/shows/password/). Before class, create a list of ten or more vocabulary words or concepts that you want students to review. Divide students into groups of two and give half of the list to Student 1 and the other half to Student 2. Student 1 looks at the first word on her list and provides one-word clues to Student 2, who tries to guess the word. When Student 2 guesses the word, Student 1 continues to the next word on her list. You keep time for the entire class and tell students to stop when time is up (decide the amount of time that works for the difficulty of your words, but maybe 20 seconds or so). The game continues with the roles reversed (Student 2 provides the clues and Student 1 guesses). Students get one point for each word they correctly identify, and the winner is the person with the most points. Obviously, there are many different versions that you could play, including one that is closer to the actual rules of the TV game show.

To review relationships among concepts, you can ask students to draw a concept map with concepts in circles and lines between the concepts to represent the connections. Prior to class, make a list of concepts that you can then show on a large screen in front of the class. Using a piece of paper or concept mapping software on their laptop, students can create a concept map either individually or with one or two other students. You can randomly call on some students to share their map with the class on the large screen if you have a document projector. Or, you can ask students to share their map with other students. Save time at the end for student questions and for you to explain misconceptions that you notice as you walk around the room looking at their maps.

To review problem solving (such as in a math or physics class), you can write problems on pieces of paper and hang them around the room. Ask students to walk around the room and solve the problems on their own smaller piece of paper. Of course this is no different than simply giving the students a list of problems and asking them to solve them, but it can be more engaging because they have to walk around and it can foster discussion between students who are standing near one another.

Example S.2.23 – Helping Students Avoid Procrastination

Help students to avoid procrastination. Procrastination is an often-cited reason for students not doing well. Students may not believe that they can do well on a test or assignment because they waited too long to start it. To avoid this situation, talk about procrastination and give them (or have other students give their peers) strategies for how they might deal with it. To be even more proactive, you can require students to complete parts of an assignment before the final assignment is due. To meet these sub-goals, students need to start working on the assignment earlier than they would normally. To ensure that they complete these sub-goals, give them a few nominal points for turning in the assignment. You don't have to do much more grading because you can simply check off the assignment as either completed or not. Or, have a 3-point rating system (0 = not completed, 1 = partially met requirements, 2 = met requirements).

'Procrastination is the thief of time." – Edward Young (cited in Wikiquote, 2015b)

Success Strategy 3

Match the difficulty levels of class activities and assignments with the abilities of the students.

Students are more motivated when the class activities and assignments are neither too difficult nor too easy. To match the difficulty of the activity or assignment with students' abilities, it's necessary to ascertain students' existing knowledge and skills related to your course objectives. What do they know and what don't they know? These questions may seem obvious, but knowing the answers is so critical to fostering their learning and keeping them motivated that they shouldn't be underestimated. Conduct assessments early in the course to help plan your instruction for the remainder of the course. Then, continually monitor the difficulty level of your activities throughout the course.

Different students likely have different tolerances for frustration. If you're working fairly closely with individual students, you may be able to judge their tolerance for frustration and adjust the challenge of the activities appropriately. To make things more complicated, I've found that tolerance for frustration can also vary for an individual at different times, depending on how stressed they are in life, how much sleep they've had, etc.

Example S.3.1 – Providing Shorter Activities

Divide complex learning activities into shorter activities that can be more easily comprehended. Of course, sometimes you may want students to work on ill-structured problems that are complex and messy (even wicked!). In that case, however, make the objective explicit to students so that it's clear that the purpose of the activities is to challenge them to become better at solving these types of ill-structured problems in the particular content area.

Example S.3.2 – Addressing Prerequisites

Ensure that students have the necessary prerequisites to learn the new knowledge and skills. A week or more before the course begins, you can email all of the students with any basic knowledge and skills that they're expected to know at the beginning of the course. Additionally, you can include any resources (such as websites and readings) and ideas you have that will help them to obtain or review these knowledge and skills.

Students can have difficulties reading college-level texts and articles, including the top students at "elite" universities (because the jargon and concepts in a discipline can be difficult to understand regardless of their reading abilities). To help students succeed at reading, professor Peter Doolittle and his colleagues recommend using *reciprocal teaching* because it can teach students reading comprehension strategies, as well as how and when to use the strategies (Doolittle, Hicks, Triplett, Nichols, & Young, 2006). It's beyond the scope of this book to describe reciprocal teaching in detail, but I encourage you to read the Doolittle et al. article (available online) for more details and case studies of reciprocal teaching in action.

Example S.3.3 – Ordering Activities

Order activities from easiest to most difficult. Allowing students to work on easier (but not too easy) assignments, or steps within assignments, builds their confidence and motivates them to continue to more difficult challenges. This is an important principle in videogame design. Many games start at an easier Level 1 and then continue to more difficult levels as players gain confidence and skills along the way. It's one of the reasons that videogames are so engaging.

Example S.3.4 – Using Competition

Use competition among students to challenge them. But realize that it's not the competition itself that motivates students, because competition can be very demotivating to some students. Competition is motivating when students see it as a challenge AND they believe they can succeed at the challenge. Competition can be demotivating to students who don't believe they have a chance to succeed at the challenge. One way to increase students' perceptions of success is to place them in groups to complete the challenge. Students are more likely to feel that they can succeed when they're working with others who may have strengths that complement their weaknesses.

Example S.3.5 – Allowing Flexible Pace of Work

Allow students to work at their own pace when possible. Doing so can empower students, but it can also help them feel more relaxed and allow them to adjust the difficulty level of the tasks as needed. For example, they can slow down and re-read parts that are confusing to them instead of feeling rushed to move on.

Success Strategy 4

Provide students with honest, specific feedback about their level of competence at regular intervals.

To stay motivated, students need to believe that they're competent at the course activities in which they're participating. Providing feedback informs students about their competence level and allows them to determine whether or not their learning strategies are working to help them meet the course objectives.

Provide assessments (such as assignments, quizzes, etc.) <u>regularly</u> as a means to give students feedback. And remember that not all assessments have to be graded. Don't wait too long after the start of a course to give the first assessment. The first few assessments in a course will help to set expectations and allow students to adjust their learning strategies accordingly before it's too late in the course to make any significant improvements. You can imagine students thinking to themselves any of the following thoughts after the first assessment or two.

- "I thought I understood these concepts, but I guess I don't! I'll have to study more, or maybe I need to use different study strategies."
- "Oh, that's what the professor wants me to learn. I didn't think those types of things were important. Now I see what she wants."
- "My study strategies are working well, if I keep doing what I'm doing I'll be able to do well in this class."
- "This course is going to be more difficult than I thought, I'm going to have to put forth more effort than I have been if I want to get an A."

All of these realizations are good because they show that the students are aware of their ability level as it relates to the course objectives. You want students to have this awareness early in a course so that they have the opportunity to feel that they can succeed or find ways to help them feel that they can succeed.

In addition to frequent feedback, it's critical to <u>provide *specific* feedback</u>. Feedback such as "Great job" or "Needs work" is not nearly as helpful to students as, "The second and third sentences of this paragraph are confusing, please provide more explanation to clarify the concepts to the reader." Generally, the more specific the feedback is, the more useful it is to students. Often it's difficult to provide specific feedback about everything, so prioritize your feedback to ensure that you provide feedback related to the most important points.

And finally, you need to <u>be honest</u> in your appraisal of their knowledge and skills in your feedback to students. Trying to protect students from the truth won't help them become more knowledgeable or skillful. Don't try to be nice to protect students. However, there are many ways to present the truth to someone and you should be careful in how you present your feedback. Being honest doesn't give you permission to be mean or derogatory. Insulting the competence of students is a sure way to demotivate them. Instead, treat them with respect and help them get better, that's your job.

Example S.4.1 – Administering Frequent Graded and Ungraded Tests

Administer frequent quizzes, tests, or assignments to provide students with feedback about their abilities. Frequent testing provides feedback that students can use to judge their ability and their likelihood of success in the course. Another benefit of frequent testing is that it can improve learning (Foss & Pirozzolo, 2017; Zaromb & Roediger, 2010), by means of what is often called "the testing effect" when the same or similar questions are asked over time (Myers, 1914).

To help students when they're first learning something in class or in a textbook, give them several test questions (multiple-choice, true/false, short answer, etc.) to test their knowledge. These tests may be ungraded to provide students with feedback in a way that promotes learning over performance. Ideally, you should provide rationales for the correct and incorrect answers. Then, after they've practiced with ungraded tests, give them a test that counts towards their grade with questions that are the same as or that test concepts similar to those in the ungraded tests.

Some textbooks contain guides for professors that include multiple-choice items. For an ungraded assessment, you can give students access to some or all of these questions at the beginning of the course so that they can conduct self-assessments throughout the course after they have completed the associated readings and assignments. If you create online videos to explain course content, you can embed quizzes in the videos by asking students questions, telling them to pause the video to consider their answer, and then continuing with the video to hear your explanations of the answers (see www.youtube.com/c/brettdjones for examples). Students tell me that they find these types of quizzes useful.

Obviously, graded quizzes take more of your time than ungraded quizzes, so you need strategies to keep the amount of grading manageable or you'll be less likely to incorporate them because they're too time consuming. One strategy is to put the quizzes online in a program that grades the quizzes automatically and sends their quiz score directly to a gradebook. Most course management systems (e.g., Blackboard) have this capability. One decision you'll have to make is whether or not to allow students to use resources (such as notes, books, etc.) during the quiz. You basically have two choices if they're completing the quizzes on their own outside of class time where it's impossible to monitor their use of resources.

1. You can explicitly explain in your syllabus and in class that the use of resources is not allowed during the online quizzes and that it is considered cheating if they use resources. State this in writing. In addition, you can require them to agree to the university "honor code" by making a statement at the beginning or end of the quiz such that, "In completing this quiz, you agree that you have not received any assistance from other resources as stated on the syllabus." Of course, if students want to cheat, this will not stop them; however, it makes most reasonable students at least consider their actions. And, importantly, it gives you more evidence that you told students about the expectations if you need to report the student for cheating to a university honor court. My colleagues and I have reported students to our university honor system and one of the questions that's always asked is: Was it clear to the student that s/he was not allowed to use outside resources during the quiz. Including statements on your syllabus and on the quiz can make it clear that the answer to this question is "yes"!

    Some online course management systems also include an option that requires students to turn on their computer camera during an online test and it also locks-down their computer so that they can only access the test (and not other programs or documents). This possibility provides another means to ensure that students are completing their own test.

2. In contrast, you can allow students to use resources during online quizzes. In doing so, you may need to adjust the types of questions you ask or set time limits. Setting time limits requires students to study prior to the quiz because you can design the questions and time limit in a way such that students will not have time to simply look for the answers during the quiz. In my courses I generally give students 90 seconds per question plus an additional 5 minutes at the end to review their answers (e.g., 35 minutes to complete 20 multiple-choice items). When I give students less time than this, some students complain that it's not enough time. This amount of

time seems reasonable for everyone and I don't receive any complaints about the amount of time allotted. Most course management systems have a feature that allows you to use timed quizzes in which the student is cut-off at the time limit and their score is calculated at that time. These systems also allow you to see how long each student took to complete the quizzes. This allows you to monitor how long students are taking and you can adjust your time limits in the future if needed.

Example S.4.2 – Explaining Answers

Explain the answers to quiz/test questions that were answered incorrectly by students. You can provide explanations in class orally and/or you can ask students to identify questions for which they want explanations. You can use an electronic "clicker" system or twitter to ask students to provide quiz/test items for which they want an explanation. To avoid having to repeat your explanations in multiple course sections or to students who were unable to attend your class, you can create a video to show your explanation.

Another option is to place students in groups and have them review the test/quiz questions with each other. One student can take the lead in explaining each question and they can rotate the student leader for each question. If you want to hold students accountable, you can ask them commonly misunderstood questions again on a final comprehensive exam. Or, for small classes, you can give each student a follow-up exam with questions that only they got wrong on a prior test.

For a "high-tech" method to provide feedback, use a screencast with audio narration (if you're unfamiliar with options, search online and you will find free options, such as screencast-o-matic at http://www.screencast-o-matic.com and Jing at https://www.techsmith.com/jing.html; also Voisi is an option). Screencasting allows students to hear your verbal feedback and see a video of whatever you're doing on your computer monitor (such as pointing with the cursor, highlighting text, typing, etc.). You record the voice and the video at the same time and then you can save it as a file on your desktop or in the cloud so that students can access it through a URL. I've used it before and students love it. It's most useful if you want to show them something at a particular location in a document and explain something about it. It's like giving face-to-face feedback to students, but you do it asynchronously. They click on the URL or open the file you email them to listen and see what you recorded. (Note: Although I called this a high-tech alternative, it has been around for several years and you can find research related to students' perceptions of it.)

Example S.4.3 – Providing Timely Feedback

Assess students' knowledge, skills, and/or attitudes before or during class and provide feedback as soon as possible. Here, I provide a few of the many ways in which you can accomplish this. Whatever you do, the key points are (a) to provide the feedback in a timely manner and (b) to remember that the best kind of feedback is the feedback that students will pay attention to and use. If your students aren't reading all the feedback you're giving them, give them the feedback without a grade and have them guess their grade based on your feedback. Then, later that day or the next day, give them their grades (e.g., post them on the class management system, send them emails)

One strategy to provide timely feedback is to ask students to post questions in an online discussion board at least a few hours before class starts. Then, you can read through the questions, select a few to answer, and provide the answers during class. You can encourage students to write down questions during class and post them online prior to the next class if their questions are not answered during class (of course you can collect questions on paper during or at the end of a class as well). Using this procedure, neither the students nor you have to spend time answering questions online, which some students and professors find burdensome (although it can be very useful in the context of some classes).

Another strategy is to have a problem or question on the large classroom screen as students enter the classroom and then ask students to answer it during the first two minutes of class. Then you can explain the answer immediately. This can serve as a review of the topics from the prior class, or you can use a problem or question that students posted online prior to class.

A third strategy is to ask multiple-choice questions during class and have students raise their hands to select one of the options. A fun alternative is to label each corner of the classroom as A, B, C, or D (sometimes this activity is called "Four Corners"; see Figure 6.4).

```
┌─────────────────────┐
│ A                 B │
│                     │
│     Classroom       │
│                     │
│ D                 C │
└─────────────────────┘
```

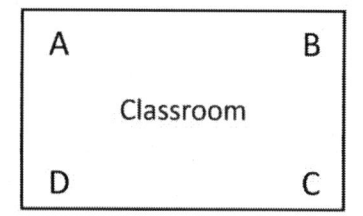

Figure 6.4. *A visual representation of the "Four Corners" activity*

Then, after asking a multiple-choice question (with up to four possible answers), ask students to walk to the corner of the classroom with the letter that matches their answer to the question. Similarly, you can create a continuous scale on a wall by labeling one end of the wall as *strongly disagree* and the other end as *strongly agree.* Then, after asking a question about their attitude or belief about something, you can ask them to stand along the wall according to their attitude or belief. Both of these activities provide a nice visual as a frequency distribution. Once students are in place, you can ask students at the different locations to explain their answer. These answers can lead to good conversations about the problem or topic.

Alternatively, you can use "clickers" (i.e., audience response systems), Twitter, or other web-based polling software (e.g., https://www.surveymonkey.com, https://polldaddy.com, https://www.polleverywhere.com) that allows students to use their phones, tablets, or computers to participate. You can use the results to provide feedback about their responses (e.g., "Based on your answers to this question, many of you seem to have a common misunderstanding about this concept, so let me explain it further.").

Instead of *you* asking students questions, another idea is to stop during any point during a class and ask students to write down a confusing point from the day's class (sometimes called the "Muddiest Point" activity). Instead of writing their point on paper, you can have them tweet it or write it on a class discussion board or blog if they have laptops for class. You can collect these confusing points or have students read some of them aloud. You can address them immediately or during the next class.

Professor Vinod Lohani used a more sophisticated software program called DyKnow (http://www.dyknow.com) in his Engineering Exploration course for first-year students at Virginia Tech. Students brought their tablet PCs to his class and logged-in to the DyKnow session with him (Lohani, 2014-2015). DyKnow allowed Dr. Lohani to upload a set of PowerPoint slides and then write on the slides during class as they were projected on a screen in front of the class. Students also received the slides and the associated writing on their tablet PCs in real time. In addition, in less than a minute, Dr. Lohani was able to poll students about their perceived level of understanding at various points during the class (i.e., "I understand well"; "I understand a little"; "I do not understand"; or "no response"). These levels of understanding were displayed in DyKnow as a pie chart that showed the percentage of students answering each of the four response options. The coolest part was that he was able to give students a problem, have them sketch a diagram necessary to solve the problem, and then randomly retrieve a few sketches from students' tablets to show on the screen in front of the class. He was then able to make annotations on the students' diagrams to illustrate correct and incorrect aspects of the diagrams. You can do something similar without using DyKnow by having students draw their diagrams on a piece of paper, collecting all of the papers, selecting a few randomly, and using a document projector to show the students' responses on a large screen in front of the class.

Example S.4.4 – Having Students Submit Assignments Electronically

Require students to submit their assignments electronically to speed-up your grading process. I recommend that you ask students to submit their assignments in a Word document so that you can use the "tracked changes" and "comments" features to provide specific feedback. Of course, professors have been providing feedback on written assessments for centuries, but providing electronic feedback is better for a few reasons: you can provide more feedback more efficiently (if you can type faster than you can write), your feedback will be easier to read, you can locate your feedback exactly where it needs to be in their paper, it's easier to edit your own feedback without crossing-out hand-written changes, and, given all this, you may provide more feedback.

You can also speed-up your feedback process by creating several possible responses to students' assignments and using the "copy and paste" features to paste them into students' documents. Providing written feedback on students' assignments is arguably the most time consuming aspect of providing students with feedback and the likely reason professors don't provide more graded assignments. Therefore, it's critical to implement a system that will allow you to give this feedback efficiently or you won't continue doing it in the future. For most assignments there are a limited number of responses that you will provide to students. Identify these responses, type them into a Word document, and copy and paste them into the feedback you're providing to students. Then, you can personalize them as needed for each particular student.

Here's an example. You ask students to write 1,000 words in response to a question related to the course content. You realize that there are basically four types of feedback that you're giving students, summarized as (1) exceeded expectations, (2) met expectations, (3) could meet expectations with a little more of something, and (4) did not meet expectations in many or any ways. Given these four categories, you can write a few sentences related to each. Then, when grading, copy the appropriate sentences into the student's document and add another sentence or two as needed to provide feedback more specific to his particular response. Of course you will need to address outlier students individually. Identifying four categories of responses doesn't limit you to giving only four different grades, your grades can vary. But this method cuts down on the amount of time it takes to grade because you're simply tailoring your responses instead of recreating them each time. If you've never done this before, I bet you will be surprised how few categories of responses are needed for most assignments.

Example S.4.5 – Using Online Discussions

Use online discussions to provide students with feedback related to their questions. Or, generate important questions yourself and allow students to discuss them online. Online discussions can be fairly manageable in small classes, but how can this be accomplished in larger courses? William "Terry" Fisher, a professor at Harvard Law School, has used online discussion groups in his online introductory course on copyright (titled *CopyrightX*; Garlock, 2015). In addition to lectures and readings, he engages students through Socratic discussions and writing assignments. Students participate in online discussions in a group with 24 other students that is led by a Harvard Law School student. The students and their leader log-in synchronously to an Adobe conferencing system for 90 minutes each week to debate law cases.

Example S.4.6 – Sending Short Feedback Emails

Send students short emails with feedback. There are at least three types of feedback emails that you can send. One type of feedback email can be sent to students who are doing poorly in your course. You want to start monitoring students for low grades no later than when about a quarter of the course is complete, and you may want to start monitoring grades before then. You'll get a more accurate assessment after the first two or three graded assignments (assuming that you have several assignments). At that point, contact all of your students whose grades are low by sending them a short email similar to this one.

> Hi Morgan,
>
> I'm writing because I see that you are in the C- range for your grade in this course and wanted to offer some unsolicited advice in case it might help you. It's still possible for you to improve your grade, but you will need to start working on it soon or you will run out of time in the course to improve substantially. Generally, I find that when students aren't doing well, they're just too busy to put in the time to learn the material. I don't know if this applies to you or not, but it may. However, there may be other study strategies that you can use too, especially if you're spending time completing the readings and assignments. If you want to discuss some options and strategies that may help you to improve, please contact me and we can discuss some possibilities.
>
> Thanks,
> Brett Jones

Of course, you will have to modify this email to make it fit with your course, but hopefully it gives you an idea of what I mean. The main purposes of this email are to let students know that they're not doing well and that you're willing to help them if they want help. The email also shows that you care about their learning, which is another important component of the MUSIC model (the caring component). Sending follow-up emails to these students after they begin to succeed can also help to encourage them ("I noticed that you got an A- on the last quiz, it appears that your new strategies are working. Keep up the good work!").

A second type of feedback email is one that is sent to students who are doing well in the course ("I noticed that you're doing well in the course, keep up the good work!") or to students who did something particularly well in the course ("I liked your explanation in class today, it showed that you really understand that concept. Keep up the good work!"). A handwritten note (instead of an email) given to a student before or after class can also be appropriate.

A third type of feedback email is one that is sent to the entire class. These emails can be used for a variety of purposes, such as: (1) identifying areas of strengths and weaknesses ("Many of you are struggling with the quizzes. Please remember that there are several resources available to help you, including…"); (2) alerting students to potential areas of difficulty ("Students in prior courses have struggled with Chapter 3, so I have created several explanations of the concepts and solved problems in the online document. I hope that this document will help to clarify any misconceptions that you may have."); and (3) weekly reminders of due dates for assignments and tests.

Short emails are easy to send and they can have a significant positive effect on students' beliefs about success, so why not use them?!?

Example S.4.7 – Using Peer Feedback Outside of Class

Require students to provide feedback to each other *outside* of class time. There are several advantages to using peer feedback. First, students have to *think* when they provide feedback, which can lead to increased learning. Second, a student's ability level is closer to their peers' ability level than yours, which can help them better understand and respond to other students' problems. Third, peer feedback allows students to receive other perspectives than yours on their work. Fourth, it increases the amount of feedback students receive without creating more work for you.

One simple example is to ask students to provide feedback on the writing of three other students in the class. Obviously, students can write on each other's hard copy papers. Alternatively, students can share Word processing documents and use the "track changes" and "comment" features to give each other feedback. Other possibilities include writing and giving feedback on modifiable webpages (such as wikis; www.wikispaces.com) or sharing files in the cloud (such as Google drive; https://www.google.com/drive/). Wikis allow users to identify when changes were made and who made them.

Another possibility is to ask students to use a technology like VoiceThread (http://voicethread.com) that allows users to add voice or text annotations to visual media. It's the same as providing a comment on a website, except that the comment can be a voice or text and it can be attached to visual media, such as a video, a slide presentation, or a collection of photos. It can be a very effective way for students to give feedback on an image of a project product, a video, artwork, etc. You can find some examples at http://voicethread4education.wikispaces.com/College.

Another high-tech method is to use *Perusall*, which is a website that allows students to annotate readings online and asynchronously respond to other students' comments and questions (available for free at https://perusall.com/). This program was developed at Harvard University and is used by some faculty there. Perusall allows students to give each other feedback, and the website claims that it creates an enjoyable experience by allowing students to engage in collective activities. I assume that students' motivation and engagement increases because they can support each other's *success* in a *caring* environment.

Example S.4.8 – Using Peer Feedback in Class

Allow students to provide feedback to each other *during* class time. Although the strategies in the previous example could also be used during class, feedback during class generally has to be shorter to fit within the class time.

You can use a version of the "Gallery Walk" to have students give feedback to one another. Before class, identify about five different problems or questions that have a few different correct answers (alternatively, you can give a statement that requires students to list a few things, such as "List the top three things that people can do to lower their cholesterol level."). Write down each of the five problems or questions at the top of separate, large pieces of chart paper and hang them around the classroom (see Figure 6.5).

Figure 6.5. *A visual representation of this version of the "Gallery Walk"*

Divide students into groups ranging from two to six students per group and ask each group to stand in front of one of the pieces of hanging chart paper (if the class has more than 30 students, you can still use five problems/questions, simply duplicate the questions as many times as needed). Students work together to answer the problem/question on their piece of paper and write their answer directly on the chart paper (alternatively, they can write their answer on a smaller "sticky" note and place the note on the hanging chart paper). After students have had time to answer the question, each group of students rotates to the next piece of chart paper and repeats the process. But in addition, they comment on the answer provided by the prior group, either on the paper or on a smaller "sticky" note. Continue this process until all groups have written on all five pieces of chart paper. Then, allow the students to circulate through the pieces of paper one more time to read all of the comments. During this activity, you should also read all of the answers and comments to decide whether you need to provide any further explanations at the end of the activity. At the end, you can ask students to explain their answers and ask them whether they have any further questions. If it's impossible to complete this activity in your classroom because of space limitations (for instance, if you have a large class), you can still do this activity by writing the problems/questions on regular-sized pieces of paper and asking students to pass the pieces of paper to the other groups. So instead of the groups moving from paper to paper, the papers move from group to group.

As another example, professors in the physics department at Harvard University used peer instruction to teach introductory physics courses (Crouch & Mazur, 2001). The part of their peer instruction that's most relevant to receiving feedback is that after students received a short presentation from the professor, they were asked to answer a question related to the main concept in the presentation. After considering their answer for one or two minutes, the professor polled students about the correct answer. Next, students discussed their answers with a few other students sitting near them by explaining their reasoning process in answering the question. After two to four minutes, the instructor polled the students for their answers, which may have changed based on the discussion. Then, the instructor explained the answer to prevent any misconceptions. This type of peer instruction may work best for problems that students initially answer differently. If almost everyone gets the answer correct or incorrect, it may be better for the instructor to provide some additional explanation (when answers are mostly incorrect) or to move on to the next concept more quickly (when answers are mostly correct).

Example S.4.9 – Requiring Self-Evaluations

Require students to provide feedback to themselves by conducting self-evaluations. Students' perceptions of success can increase when you ask them to judge the amount of progress they made towards performance tasks related to the course objectives. Of course, if students are unsuccessful and the self-evaluations are low, then students' perceptions of success won't increase, but it may motivate them to find more effective strategies that will help them become more successful.

One strategy is to give students a rubric and have them evaluate their own work using the rubric. Then, you can grade not only their work, but also how accurately they evaluated their own work. Because they know you will be rating their accuracy, they will spend more time trying to accurately assess their own work. Ideally, as students assess their work, they find weaknesses and actually improve their work before they submit it to you. Thus, this self-evaluation motivates them to produce higher-quality work and increases their success perceptions.

As another example of a self-evaluation, students in an undergraduate *Introduction to Computers in Education* course were asked to judge the amount of progress they had made in learning to perform tasks in a Hypercard unit on a 7-point scale from 1 (*none*) to 7 (*quite a lot*) (Schunk, & Ertmer, 1999). When students conducted these judgements weekly for a few weeks, they increased their perceptions that they could be successful. That is, simply asking students to rate themselves on their progress can increase their success perceptions. It seems that students need to remind themselves that they're making progress each week.

Success Strategy 5

Be explicit when describing your expectations and communicating to students.

Students don't know whether or not they can *succeed* unless they know what's expected of them. Therefore, it's important that course expectations are clear and explicit. Put everything in writing somewhere, such as on the syllabus, on assignments, etc. If you give all of your expectations in class orally, some students will miss your explanations and others won't hear it the way you intended or won't be listening. So write everything down and refer students to it when needed. Wherever you write it, make it available by email, course website, and any other place that is convenient for students. Sometimes students enroll in courses late and miss classes, so having a system in place for students to find the needed documents will make their lives and yours easier because you can refer them to that place.

Remind students of the expectations as the course progresses. It's easy to think that once students hear and read about the expectations on the syllabus at the beginning of the semester, they don't need to be reminded of them any more (after all, you spent part of the first day of class talking about them). However, the reality is that they need to be reminded during the semester, especially if it's something new that they haven't done in the class previously. I know you're not their parents, but just accept it and keep reminding them; it's part of being a good professor!

Failing to provide students with expectations or failing to remind them about the expectations can lower students' motivation and effort, as demonstrated by this undergraduate student's comment: "I only put a little amount of effort into the course because I am still unclear as to what the expectations are and have trouble following the assignments."

Example S.5.1 – Using Summary Tables

Create summary tables in your syllabus that include all assignments, dates, and point values. You might include at least two tables on your syllabus: one table that lists the number of assignments and total point values for each type of assignment, and another table that shows when each assignment is due. Appendix E shows an example of each of these tables. The important thing is that all of the relevant information is available to students. In addition to this summary information, provide as much detail as possible on your syllabus. For assignments that include fairly long directions, create separate documents and refer to them on the syllabus. Make all assignments and directions available at the beginning of the course if possible. Sometimes, if it's the first time you've taught the course this can be difficult, if not impossible, but provide as much information as possible.

Example S.5.2 – Quizzing Students About the Syllabus

Quiz students on the syllabus material. You can either grade the quiz or not. Some professors include a few syllabus questions on the first course quiz along with questions related to the other content for that quiz. I've seen this method used in both undergraduate and graduate courses. If you don't want to include the quiz score in students' grade, you can quiz them at the end of the first class or during the second class meeting after you've explained the syllabus and they've had time to read it. Or, don't explain the quiz and just give them a quiz on the material; that way, you save class time and it's more likely that they've read the syllabus. You might even want students to work in pairs to complete an ungraded quiz. Anyway you do it, the purpose of the syllabus quiz is to ensure that students have read and understand the information on the syllabus so they're aware of the course expectations.

Example S.5.3 – Setting Appropriate Expectations

Address students' inaccurate preconceived notions of your course on the first day and set appropriate expectations. After the first time you teach a course, you should have a good idea of how students' preconceived notions of the course aligned with the reality of the course. You can find out by asking them on a course evaluation at the end of the course or by speaking to them informally throughout the course. Students may believe that your course is difficult, or that it will require little work to get a good grade, or something else. But it's best to address these preconceived notions on the first day of class so that they can drop the course if these notions don't align with your expectations.

Kelli Marshall, a professor at DePaul University, addressed students' preconceived notions of her *Introduction to Film* course on the first day of class by projecting five questions on the large classroom screen: (1) "Are you taking FILM 1310 because you think it will be an easy 'A'?" (2) "Do you have problems getting to early morning classes?" (3) "Do you think films are created solely for the purpose of entertainment?" (4) "Do you have concerns about spending a minimum 2–3 hours/wk on course content alone? (This doesn't include studying for exams.)" and (5) "Finally, are you completely opposed to the use of a social networking platform like Twitter in/outside the classroom?" (Marshall, 2015, para. 10). She asked students to answer these questions honestly on a piece of scrap paper. Then she told students that if they answered no to most of the questions that they were in the right class. Otherwise, she recommended that they select another arts elective course. This is a very direct way to set expectations and change any inaccurate preconceived notions.

Example S.5.4 – Explaining a Participation Grade

If you choose to include a grade for participation, explain it clearly on the syllabus; otherwise, students may assume that participation is synonymous with attendance. If that's the case, then it would be clearer to change it from "participation" grade to "attendance" grade. If that's not the case, then think seriously about how you're going to assess a participation grade fairly in a manner that is understandable to students and that will not require so much of your time that it distracts from your primary teaching goals.

One possible solution, used by Denise Knight (2008), is to ask students to rate their own participation. A few weeks after the start of the semester, she suggests giving students the following question.

> "Please check the statement below that best corresponds to your honest assessment of your contribution to class discussion thus far:
>
> _____ I contribute several times during every class discussion. (A)
> _____ I contribute at least once during virtually every class discussion. (B)
> _____ I often contribute to class discussion. (C)
> _____ I occasionally contribute to class discussion. (D)
> _____ I rarely contribute to class discussion. (E)" (Knight, 2008, para. 3)

Then, she allows students to provide a brief rationale for their grade along with any other comments they choose. She reads the forms, offers a brief response, and returns the forms the following class. She explains that she gains valuable insight into why there are discrepancies between students' evaluation and hers. And, she claims that it can enhance both the amount and quality of participation. This is likely due to the fact that students have a clearer understanding of the expectations (which can increase perceptions of success), they feel more empowered (they are in control of their participation), and they feel more cared for because they know that the instructor is paying attention to their participation and wants them to participate (this would have to be conveyed to the students in your feedback).

Example S.5.5 – Using Explicit Language

Use direct, explicit language when giving directions and asking students to do something. Consider the following two possible statements that a professor could make as he talks to one of the five groups of students in his course. The professor wants the students to continue to the next problem because the class is almost finished for the day.

> Statement A: "Please take one more minute to finish your discussion of this topic and then go on to the next problem."

> Statement B: "Don't you think it's time to go on to the next problem?"

Statement A is better than Statement B because it's specific and leaves little room for interpretation. Statement B is *can* be interpreted by students as meaning: "The professor wants us to go on to the next problem, so we'd better listen to him." But some researchers have found differences between how students of different cultures can interpret statements such as this (Delpit, 2006). For example, a student could hear Statement B and think to himself, "nope, it's not time to go on, we need to finish this one." This example demonstrates the importance of using language precisely.

CHAPTER 7

Strategies to Trigger Interest

Problem

Students don't believe that the instructional methods or coursework are interesting or enjoyable.

Solution

You need to ensure that students are <u>interested</u> in the content and instructional activities.

Overview of Interest

Have you ever been involved in an activity when something else caught your attention and you became curious or interested in the other thing? Or maybe you were surfing the web and you found something interesting, and before you knew it, you had clicked on several different links and had read a few websites or watched a few videos on a particular topic. Maybe you got excited or angry about what you found, which led you to investigate it further. Or perhaps you simply enjoyed engaging in the activity. These are examples of situational interest.

<u>Key Point:</u> Students are more motivated to engage in an activity when they're interested in the activity. I'm sure this is obvious to you, but what can be less obvious is what you can do in a college course to trigger students' interest. Strategies that are part of the interest component of the MUSIC model are those that attract students' attention, pique students' curiosity, or stimulate emotional arousal in students. Professors have a lot of control over *situational* interest in a class because situational interest is a short-term interest that arises spontaneously in a particular situation (Schraw, Flowerday, & Lehman, 2001). In contrast, *individual* interests are those longer-term interests in topics or activities that students already have when they

come to class. When students have an individual interest in a topic, they value the topic, they generally have quite a bit of knowledge about it, and they like it (Hidi & Renninger, 2006). For instance, students might have a *situational* interest in watching a video about sharks for 30 minutes during class, but might not have an *individual* interest in marine biology which leads them to study for years to pursue a career as a marine biologist. The strategies in this chapter are intended to trigger students' *situational* interest.

Situational interest is important for teachers to consider because humans have a need for arousal and don't like to be bored. Furthermore, humans are curious and want to discover new things and resolve uncertainties (Hidi, 2016; Hsee & Ruan, 2016; Jepma, Verdonschot, Steenbergen, Rombouts, & Nieuwenhuis, 2012). Your students are no different; and therefore, the strategies in this chapter are intended to help you think about the ways in which you can design a course to incorporate elements that will interest your students.

"All men by nature desire to know." – Aristotle (cited in Wikiquote, 2015a)

Interestingly (pun intended), there is theoretical and empirical evidence to suggest that using the MUSIC model strategies in a class can increase students' *individual* interest in the discipline related to the class topics (Osborne & Jones, 2011). For example, students' perceptions of the MUSIC model components in a first-year university engineering course have been shown to affect students' longer-term individual interests (Jones, Osborne, Paretti, & Matusovich, 2014). Similarly, a middle school student who perceives his science course as being consistent with the MUSIC model principles is more likely to consider a science-related career (Jones, Ruff, & Osborne, 2015). So by incorporating the MUSIC model principles, you may not only trigger students' situational interest, but you may also foster students' longer-term individual interests.

In this chapter, I present the following four strategies and provide several examples of each.

    I.1   Design instruction that catches and holds students' attention.
    I.2   Use activities that pique students' curiosity about the content.
    I.3   Stimulate emotional arousal in students to avoid boredom.
    I.4   Design curriculum with a consideration of students' individual interests.

Relevant Theories

In this section, I provide a very brief explanation of the primary theories that are most directly relevant to the interest strategies in the MUSIC model. These are not comprehensive explanations, so please look-up the citations if you are interested in more information.

- Interest Theories (Hidi & Renninger, 2006; Krapp, 2005; Schraw & Lehman, 2001). Interest arises from a combination of situational interest and individual interest. "*Situational interest* is a temporary state aroused by specific features of a situation, task, or object" (Schiefele, 2009, pp. 197-198). In contrast, "*individual interest* is conceptualized as a relatively stable affective-evaluative orientation toward certain subject areas or objects" (Schiefele, 2009, pp. 198). Students are more likely to be motivated when they are interested in the object, activity, or topic of study.

- Arousal (Duffy, 1957). Arousal (a.k.a., activation, degree of excitation) has been called "the intensity aspect of behavior" (Duffy, 1957, p. 265) and has been assessed using physiological measures (e.g., skin conductance, muscle tension, pulse rate, respiration, the electroencephalogram [EEG]). Students are more likely to be motivated when they experience an optimal level of arousal.

- Intrinsic Motivation (Deci, 1975; Ryan & Deci, 2000). Intrinsic motivation is a construct most commonly studied within the broader framework of self-determination theory. "Intrinsic motivation is defined as the doing of an activity for its inherent satisfactions rather than for some separable consequence. When intrinsically motivated a person is moved to act for the fun or challenge entailed rather than because of external prods, pressures, or rewards" (Ryan & Deci, 2000, p. 56). Students are more intrinsically motivated to engage in an activity when it meets their needs for autonomy and competence, and when the activity is novel, challenging, or holds aesthetic value for the students (Ryan & Deci, 2000, pp. 59-60).

- Flow (Csikszentmihalyi, 1990). Flow is a construct with the theory of optimal experience and is defined as "the state in which people are so involved in an activity that nothing else seems to matter; the experience itself is so enjoyable that people will do it even at great cost, for the sheer sake of doing it" (Csikszentmihalyi, 1990, p. 4). Flow can be viewed as peak intrinsic motivation. Students are more likely to be motivated when they experience flow.

- Intrinsic or Interest Value (Eccles et al., 1983; Wigfield & Eccles, 2000). Interest value is part of the value component of expectancy-value theory (Eccles et al.,

1983). "*Intrinsic or interest value* is the inherent, immediate enjoyment one gets from engaging in an activity" (Eccles et al., 1983, p. 89). Students are more likely to be motivated when they have a higher level of intrinsic or interest value.

- Domain Identification (Osborne & Jones, 2011). "Domain identification is the degree to which an individual values a domain as an important part of the self" (Jones, Ruff, & Osborne, 2015, pp. 332-333). A domain can be thought of as a subject area, such as mathematics or engineering. Students are more likely to be motivated in a domain when their level of domain identification is higher.

- Theories related to emotions (Pekrun, 2009). Although there is no one specific "theory of emotion," researchers have documented the strong connections between students' emotions and their motivation (Pekrun, 2009). Students are motivated in different ways by their emotions.

- Neuroscientific research. Neuroscientists have investigated the neurobiological mechanisms underlying human motivation. Some of the findings most relevant to the interest component of the MUSIC model are those explicating the role of novelty and curiosity in human motivation (e.g., Jepma et al., 2012; for a review, see Hidi, 2016).

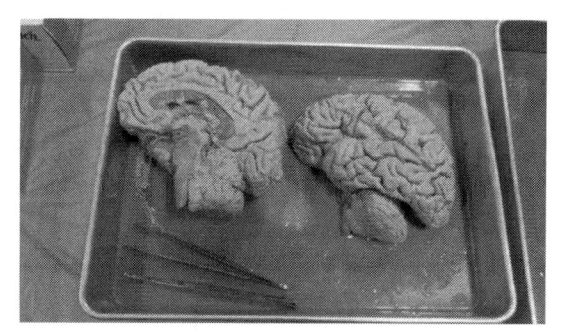

Interest Strategy 1

Design instruction that catches and holds students' attention.

The examples in this section demonstrate a few different ways that you can increase your chances of catching and holding students' attention. Attention is necessary for students' engagement in class activities. When students don't pay attention, the information doesn't enter their memory system and they have no chance of learning or remembering it. Figure 7.1 shows that information must be attended to in order to be remembered; however, even some information that is attended to isn't remembered. Unfortunately, humans aren't always good at controlling their attention, which includes distributing attention, sustaining attention, holding detailed information in their minds, and rapidly switching between competing goals (Gazzaley & Rosen, 2016).

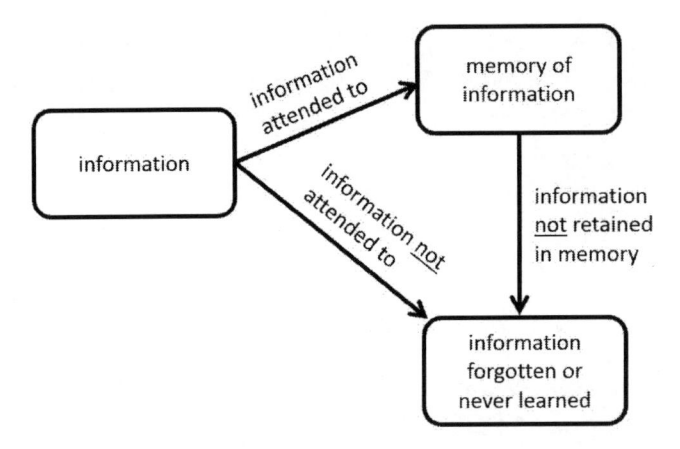

```
                    information
                    attended to
                                    ┌──────────────┐
                                    │  memory of   │
    ┌──────────────┐                │  information │
    │              │───────────────▶└──────────────┘
    │ information  │                       │
    │              │───┐                   │ information
    └──────────────┘    \                  │ not retained
                information               │ in memory
                attended to not            ▼
                    \               ┌──────────────┐
                     \              │  information │
                      ─────────────▶│  forgotten or│
                                    │ never learned│
                                    └──────────────┘
```

Figure 7.1. *Oversimplified (but still helpful) diagram of how information can enter memory or not*

To help us pay attention, we also need to block out irrelevant distractions. Therefore, some of the strategies in this section explain how to help students remove potential distractions. Unfortunately, our ability to block out distractions lessens as we get older (Gazzaley & Rosen, 2016); therefore, strategies to combat distractions are especially important when you're teaching older adults.

It's beyond the scope of this book to discuss strategies that can be used to remember information, but some common strategies are to make the information meaningful (by connecting it to something that students already know), to organize the information, to use visual imagery, to use elaboration (embellish on the information), and to repeat the information (Ormrod & Jones, 2018).

Example I.1.1 – Using Novelty

Use novelty to attract students' attention. Novel activities are ones students haven't encountered before or with which they've had limited experience. Novelty not only attracts students' attention and gets them interested, it can also help them to remember the information better (Tulving & Kroll, 1995).

As an example of novelty, Eann Patterson (a professor at Michigan State University) fried sausages in a pan during class until their casting burst to illustrate Mohr's circle for stress (Loftus, 2011). As another example, when I teach preservice teachers about the topic of *creativity* I play jazz background music and improvise on my saxophone for a few minutes. Then I follow it with a discussion about the extent to which I was creative during my improvisation. It always attracts students' attention because it's quite novel in that none of their other professors have played a saxophone in class (even music education students find it novel in this context of a non-music class).

Example I.1.2 – Avoiding Multitasking

Help students to avoid multitasking. Students can't pay close attention to you and the class activities if they're simultaneously attending to something else. People often think that they're good at multitasking, but research has shown that this is not true (Gazzaley & Rosen, 2016). It may be helpful to explain to students that humans are not good at multitasking (you can find examples of this online, for example, http://davecrenshaw.com/myth-of-multitasking-exercise/).

You might even tell them or show them the results of studies documenting these findings. In one study, students who multitasked on a laptop during a lecture performed lower on a test of the material. But in addition, the students who were in view of the other students' laptop screens also performed worse on the test (Sana, Weston, & Cepeda, 2013). Therefore, when students are multitasking on their laptops during class, they are actually impairing the learning of other students in the class who can see their screens.

If this is an issue in your class, you might want to implement a class rule that laptops, tablets, and phones are not allowed in class or are turned off unless you require them for an activity. Professors who have implemented this rule have reported to me that students' attention and engagement increased during class and that students generally appreciated the rule, especially those who were distracted by others who were typing or searching the web. Dr. Darren Rosenblum, a law professor at Pace University, found that after he banned laptops in his classes, students' engagement increased. He also noted: "With constant eye contact, I could see and feel when they understood me, and when they did not. Energized by the connection, we moved faster, further and deeper into the material" (Rosenblum, 2017, para. 7).

If you ban electronic devices, be sure to have and convey an honest rationale for this rule (as I discussed in Chapter 4 on empowerment). Possible rationales are that students will be more fully engaged during class and learn more without the distraction of electronics. Or, that others in the class find their use of electronics distracting, and thus, their use of electronics interferes with other students' attention and learning.

Interestingly, Hartanto and Yang (2016) found that when participants in an experimental research study were asked to have their smartphones taken away for the duration of the study, their level of anxiety increased, which had detrimental effects on their cognitive abilities. It's unclear to what extent these findings may transfer to real classrooms, but the implications are worth considering. It's possible that students are now so addicted to their smartphones and computers that turning them off or taking them away causes anxiety that has more detrimental effects than simply letting them keep their electronic devices.

A nice compromise that helps students avoid multitasking, yet allows them to keep their electronics, is to set specific times for them to text, check email, tweet, check Instagram, or whatever it is they do. You can tell them that every 30 minutes, you will stop class and they will have 3 minutes to check their electronic devices or stand up and stretch. Professor Gary Green at the University of Georgia reported that this strategy decreased the use of personal electronics significantly (if not entirely) in his large class (Green & Watson, 2015).

> *"To do two things at once is to do neither."* – Publilius Syrus (cited in Bartlett, 2002, p. 102)

Example I.1.3 – Limiting Distractions

Limit distractions during class. Many things can distract students during class. Pay attention during class and note anything that could be potentially distracting to students and try to eliminate or reduce the distractions. Some distractions are external to the class, such as a lawnmower or someone bouncing a basketball. For these types of distractions, take a moment during class to shut doors and windows to minimize the noise. Although you and some students may be able to block out the external noise, others may not be able to do so. Other distractions are internal to the class. For example, if you ask students to read a passage of text, ask the other students not to talk at all during that time. For some students, hearing other students talk, even quietly, may distract them from paying attention to what they're reading.

Example I.1.4 – Adding Theatrical Elements

Add some theatrical elements to your presentation. Because actors are good at gaining the attention of the audience members, it can be useful to borrow some of their strategies for your teaching. It's beyond the scope of this book to describe these strategies (and it's not my expertise!), but I want to encourage you to think about your classroom persona. Some professors prefer to be their authentic self, some prefer to take on another persona as an actor, and others are somewhere between these two extremes (see Figure 7.2).

```
┌──────────────┐      ┌──────────────┐                        ┌──────────────┐
│  Be your     │      │ Be yourself, │                        │  Be an actor │
│authentic self│      │but act a little│                      │              │
└──────────────┘      └──────────────┘                        └──────────────┘
◄──────────────────────────────────────────────────────────────────────────►
```

Figure 7.2. *A continuum of personas ranging from being your authentic self to being an actor*

As an example of a professor who acts, John Boyer is a professor of geography at Virginia Tech who has taught a face-to-face class live with over 3,000 students in the audience and he takes on a role called *The Plaid Avenger* (http://www.plaidavenger.com). He is entertaining and successful at filling a large auditorium with thousands of students (yes thousands!) every class meeting. His persona entertains and keeps the attention of students. Maybe his persona is actually very close to his authentic self, but that's not likely the case for most professors. In my classes of up to 30 students, I prefer to be my authentic self, although I try to implement some elements of acting to enliven my authentically boring self! You need to find what works for you, but don't be afraid to incorporate some theatrical elements into your teaching.

> "Good teaching is one-fourth preparation and three-fourths pure theatre." – Gail Godwin (cited in iz Quotes, 2015b)

Example I.1.5 – Calling on Students Randomly

Ask a question and call on a student randomly. Students will be more likely to pay attention if they know that they may be called on to answer a question. There are many ways to accomplish this, including writing students' names (or printing labels with students' names) on index or playing cards and then shuffling the cards and going through them one by one for each question. You can also number students and put numbers on the cards so that you can use the same cards in multiple courses. Or, use a random number generator to select students (https://www.random.org).

Because calling on students randomly may raise some students' anxiety, you might allow students to raise their hands if they want to answer. But make sure to wait at least a few seconds after asking a question to allow students to think about it and respond. Doing so can engage students who are shy or who need more time to think. You can practice this by not calling on the first few students who raise their hand.

Example I.1.6 – Involving Students in Discussions

Be creative in your strategies to involve students in discussions. Instead of asking a question to the entire class and waiting for one person to answer, try some of the strategies listed here.

- Hand out a sheet of paper to all students and ask them to respond to your question in writing on the paper. Then tell them to crumple the paper into a ball and throw it gently across the room. Have everyone pick up a paper ball, read the response, add their response to that paper, crumple the paper back into a ball, and throw it again. Repeat this process as many times as you like. Then, ask a couple students to read all the responses on their final sheet of paper, which then can lead to further discussion or clarifications. Professor Gary Green at the University of Georgia has noted that this strategy increased the energy level in his classes and students enjoyed it (Green & Watson, 2015).

- Ask students a question and ask them to tweet their responses. Show the tweets on a large screen in front of the class, read some of them, and use them to continue the discussion.

- Use the "think-pair-share" strategy in which you ask students a question and give them the required time to think about it. Then ask them to talk to one or more students next to them about it. Finally, call on a few groups of students randomly and ask them to share their answers with the entire class. This strategy can provide a safe environment in which students can fail without feeling stupid in front of the entire class, which can enhance success perceptions. This activity also provides students with some empowerment by allowing them to think of their own answers and not simply requiring them to repeat something that was learned previously (although certainly you can use this activity to review material).

- Use "clickers" (i.e., audience response systems) in class to have students respond to multiple-choice questions. For example, in a class at Harvard University, physics professor Dr. Eric Mazur shows students how ions affect the motion of pollen and then asks them to vote (using clickers) on whether it's the positive ions, negative ions, or both that make the pollen move (Mazur, 2012).

- Ask students a question that doesn't force them to show their ignorance, such as: What questions would your parents (or family or friends) have about this topic/content? The idea is to solicit "dumb" questions that students won't feel dumb for asking. Then you can answer them, which will likely help some students in the class who also had the same question. You could ask this question to the entire class, or ask this question and use any of the suggestions provided previously (i.e., crumple paper into a ball, tweet, think-pair-share, or clickers).

Example I.1.7 – Engaging Students in Mindfulness and Patience

Engage students in mindfulness, contemplation, and patience. "Mindfulness is paying attention to your life, here and now, with kindness and curiosity" (Saltzman, n.d., p. 1). By using mindful techniques, professors can help students to focus on course activities.

For example, to nourish self-awareness and presence, Tobin Hart, a professor of psychology at the University of West Georgia describes the following "Where are you now?" activity that he implements.

> *"Take a few moments and just relax. Take a few deep breaths. Close your eyes if you are comfortable doing so, and tune into where you are right in this moment. Are you thinking about the day ahead? Rehashing some past*

experience? Caught in an emotional hangover about a situation with a friend or family member? How much of you is in your body? In your head? Floating outside you? Do you feel out in front of you? Stuck in a painful nook? Just be aware for a few moments; just noticing where you are and how that feels." After a few moments you might ask, *"Now take two minutes and share your awareness with the person next to you (or in your notebook).'"* (Hart, 2004, p. 10)

If you're interested in this type of mindful activity, I would encourage you to read more about mindfulness and contemplation (see http://www.mindfuleducation.org and http://www.contemplativemind.org).

Mindfulness is related to patience. Jennifer Roberts, professor of the humanities at Harvard University, suggests that professors need to teach students how to be patient (Roberts, 2013). She does this in her art history courses by requiring students to write a research paper based on a work of art. But before they begin their paper, they're required to look at the painting for three hours and write down their observations, questions, and speculations as they arise. She has found that this assignment allows students to notice the details, orders, and relationships in works of art that take time to perceive. As Professor Roberts (2013) explains:

> *"The art historian David Joselit has described paintings as deep reservoirs of temporal experience — time batteries — exorbitant stockpiles' of experience and information. I would suggest that the same holds true for anything a student might want to study at Harvard University—a star, a sonnet, a chromosome. There are infinite depths of information at any point in the students' education. They just need to take the time to unlock that wealth. And that's why, for me, this lesson about art, vision, and time goes far beyond art history. It serves as a master lesson in the value of critical attention, patient investigation, and skepticism about immediate surface appearances. I can think of few skills that are more important in academic or civic life in the twenty-first century."* (ninth paragraph)

For more details, please read her article or watch her video at http://harvardmagazine.com/2013/11/the-power-of-patience.

Example I.1.8 – Limiting Online Distractions

Tell students about software and apps they can use to limit online distractions in online courses. When students are completing coursework online, it can be tempting to check email, Instagram, YouTube, etc. (you may have the same problem yourself, I do!). Time management tools can be used to track how you use your computer, track the websites you visit, and block yourself from distracting sites (for example, *RescueTime*, https://www.rescuetime.com/, *SelfControl*, https://tinyurl.com/scontrol22). In fact, there's evidence that when students in a MOOC (Massive Open Online Course) used some time management tools, they spent more time on the course and were more likely to complete the course than students who didn't use the tools (Patterson, 2015). There may not be any way to *require* students to use the software or apps, but you can make them aware of these tools and encourage them to use the tools if they find themselves becoming distracted during the course.

Example I.1.9 – Avoiding Narcissism and Aggrandizement

Find a balance between sharing personal information and becoming a show-off. In Chapter 8, I discuss the importance of sharing information about yourself and being a real person in the course so that your students can relate to you. Some students will find some of this information interesting and they'll be curious to learn more about you. However, learning about you and learning *everything* about you are two different things. When stories and anecdotes about yourself become too frequent, students will lose interest in listening to you. Students are in class to learn, not to hear about your difficulties over the past weekend or about how great you are at this or that. Sprinkle your class with information about yourself to appear relatable, but don't overdo it. I'm not sure exactly how much you need to share, but try to get some cues from your students and stop sharing if you students stop paying attention to you.

Interest Strategy 2

Use activities that pique students' curiosity about the content.

One way to pique students' curiosities is to present information or ideas that are discrepant from their current beliefs or conceptions. There are usually topics in any content area in which many individuals have misconceptions and you can use these misconceptions to get students curious to find out why their beliefs and conceptions are different from those presented in the course. For example, how do clouds stay aloft in the sky if the average cumulus cloud weighs a million pounds? Discrepancies can cause cognitive conflict, which can create unpleasant feeling, which can then motivate students to want to resolve the discrepancy (Berlyne, 1960; Jepma et al., 2012; Piaget, 1932). You can resolve the discrepancies by: having students read about the phenomenon, conducting demonstrations, providing explanations, etc. Several examples in this section describe ways in which you can create discrepancies, such as by using surprising information, contradiction, and controversy.

> *"The whole art of teaching is only the art of awakening the natural curiosity of young minds for the purpose of satisfying it afterwards."* – Anatole France (cited in Bartlett, 2002, p. 586)

Example I.2.1 – Incorporating Learner-Directed Approaches

Use learner-directed approaches, such as those provided in Empowerment Strategy 2 in Chapter 4 of this book (e.g., problem-based learning, project-based learning, inquiry approaches, case studies). Learner-directed approaches don't always present discrepancies, but they usually require students to find an answer or solve a problem, which can pique students' curiosity about the content and trigger their interest.

One way to do this is to ask students to answer a question that makes students curious to find the answer. For example, Dr. Richard Helm, an Associate Professor in the Department of Biochemistry at Virginia Tech, asked students: What is the difference between white and dark turkey meat? It's a question that most people in America might wonder, especially around Thanksgiving time. Dr. Helm asked students in his General Biochemistry course to answer this question by using large data sets to analyze the proteins that give turkey its color and the lipids in the turkey tissues (Painter, 2017). (If you're curious, "the concentrations of glycolysis proteins in breast were higher [than in the turkey thigh and leg] because this muscle is used for flight in birds, a process that relies heavily on glycolysis" [Painter, 2017, para. 9]).

Example I.2.2 – Providing Surprising Information

Provide surprising information, which is something that students would not expect. For example, when teaching about the dangers of talking on the phone when driving, a professor could ask: Did you know that people who drive while using a hands-free phone drive no better than those who drive under the influence of alcohol? This would likely be seen as surprising because they might think that the problem with driving while talking on the phone is holding the phone, which limits physical movement or response. Thus, students would likely be curious to think about other explanations for why hands-free phone driving is dangerous.

Example I.2.3 – Introducing Contradictions

Introduce a contradiction in which at least two situations or ideas appear to be in opposition to one another. Such contradictions can make students curious to determine whether there's an explanation for the contradiction. For example, when teaching about memory, a psychology professor might tell his students: "My father can remember stories from when he was 8 years old, but he can't even remember what he had for lunch the day before. How can that be?" This apparent contradiction may make students curious and can be resolved by finding out that we have different types of memory systems within our minds.

Example I.2.4 – Presenting Controversies

Present a controversy and ask students to consider the different sides of the controversy. One way to do this is to conduct a debate during class. You can empower students by letting them choose which side of the controversy they wish to debate. However, it can be more fun to assign them to sides randomly. Or even better, trick them by having them select a side and then assign them to the opposite side of the controversy. A reason to trick them like this is that they might learn more and be more likely to consider other beliefs if they have to argue a controversy from the position that they don't currently believe. These debates can also be conducted online in discussion boards.

Example I.2.5 – Teaching Concepts From Example to Definition

When teaching a concept (e.g., democracy, momentum, falcon, haiku), provide students with examples and non-examples of the concept and ask them to generate aspects of the concept definition. Be sure to label the examples as "examples" and non-examples as "non-examples" so that students can compare the similarities and differences. For example, to teach the concept of haiku, you could present 5 examples of haikus and 3 non-examples that are similar, yet differ in critical ways (all three lines have five syllables instead of the middle line having seven syllabus as it does for a haiku). Then, ask students to generate aspects of a definition that could be used to define the examples. Aspects of the definition would include statements such as: it is a type of poem or verse; it has three lines that (usually) contain five, seven, and five syllables (in that order); and it usually involves nature.

Teaching concepts from example to definition includes a few motivational aspects that are not present when the instructor simply gives a definition and then provides the examples and non-examples. First, the example to definition approach can pique students' curiosity and cause them to ask, "What are the differences?" Second, it has the feel of a game and taps into their need to feel competent and figure it out, possibly before others in the class. Third, it may provide a sense of empowerment by giving students control over figuring out the solution and it allows the instructor to talk less. Fourth, students can work together to discuss a solution (or they can work independently), which can foster interest and/or caring through peer-to-peer interactions.

Example I.2.6 – Including Interesting Information

Include interesting information about the content. This may seem obvious, but interesting information can get lost or become non-existent as professors struggle to cover content material during a course. To guard against this, you need to really think about what's interesting about the content. What questions do individuals in the content area seek to understand? Why are you interested in this content? What are current topics and issues related to this content? What might be interesting to your particular students? Answering these types of questions can help you think about ways to make the content more interesting.

Sharing information from recent professional conferences in the discipline and discussing hot topics in the field can be ways to share interesting information. Another way is to have students identify and share interesting news stories related to the content. Or, have students review the program from a recent conference in your field (often the conference programs are online) and ask them to identify titles of papers or presentations that they find interesting and would like to know more about. Give them a few points on an assignment or extra credit points for submitting a few titles and a paragraph explaining why they find these titles interesting.

Although you will want to include interesting information throughout your course, it may be especially critical on the first day to share some of the bigger, interesting ideas in the discipline. This is a great opportunity to get students motivated and set the stage for an interesting course. Don't get bogged down in covering only the technical aspects of the syllabus on the first day; instead, leave time to discuss some interesting ideas that will get students excited about your course.

Example I.2.7 – Including Non-Typical Sources

Include materials from non-typical sources. In addition to requiring students to read textbooks and journal articles, consider including course-related readings from other sources, such as song lyrics, poems, TV shows, movies, magazines, newspapers, blogs, etc. Short YouTube videos are also a great way to expose students to different aspects of course content.

Example I.2.8 – Using Stories

Use stories to explain a concept or to provide an example or analogy. Stories are another way to gain students' attention and pique their curiosity. Stories aren't only powerful as motivators, but they can also help students learn the content more effectively. First, you can tell stories related to the course content. Willingham (2004) suggests using stories at the beginning of a class or at times when students begin to lose focus, such as in the middle or end of a class. You may get some of your material for stories by searching the

Internet or reading biographies of famous individuals in your field. In fact, you can create an entire lesson around a real-life story by describing how an individual in your field solved a problem in your discipline. Instead of simply explaining how the individual first solved the problem, spend a little more time and provide some context and enhance the story by finding out other information related to conditions that led to the individual solving the problem. This may be hard for you to imagine, so you may want to take a look at a video of a course titled *Principles of Chemical Science* which shows an MIT professor telling a story about how the nucleus was discovered during her class (http://videolectures.net/mit5111f05_ceyer_lec02/). Her story lasts the entire class, and through it, she explains many concepts that relate directly to the course objectives.

Second, you can require students to read short biographies of individuals in your field to demonstrate their thinking or their passion for the field (Willingham, 2004). As another example, in my course for students who want to become K-12 teachers, I use a book that's a diary of a first-year elementary school teacher. I ask students to read it and identify strategies that the teacher used that are consistent or inconsistent with the theories and research presented in the course readings. Many students tell me that it is their favorite assignment in the course because it's interesting and useful.

Example I.2.9 – Identifying Interesting Information

After instruction, survey students about which aspects of the instructional activities interested them. This information might be useful to you in designing instruction for the remainder of your current course, but more likely, it will be most useful to you the next time you teach the course. Things that interest students in one course will usually interest students the next time you teach the course. So use the information from one class to make revisions as needed when you teach it again in the future.

Formal or informal interviews can also be used to accomplish the same thing. Before or after class, ask students what they enjoyed and what interested them the most about a lesson. You can also ask the entire class during class time by asking them to raise their hands if they were interested in something and then ask some students to elaborate on their responses. A nice follow-up question is: What do you still want to know about the topic? You can use these answers as you design your next lesson or your lesson on that topic the next time you teach the course.

Example I.2.10 – Getting Students to Wonder About an Image

Show an interesting image on the screen in front of the classroom as students enter class. The image could be a picture or it could be a figure, diagram, or something else related to your class topic for the day. You can also add a couple questions to the image to get students thinking and talking. Dr. Peter Newbury, Director of the Centre for Teaching and Learning at the University of British Columbia Okanagan, recommends adding two questions to the image: (1) What do you notice? and (2) What do you wonder? (Newbury, 2013). He finds these questions useful because all students can notice something and wonder about something; and therefore, it doesn't exclude anyone's perspectives. He also notes that it provides a means for students to practice interpreting graphs and figures, to talk about the topic/content/discipline, and to become more actively engaged in the class.

Interest Strategy 3

Stimulate emotional arousal in students to avoid boredom.

An optimal level of arousal can be motivating to students. When students experience too much arousal, they may feel a high level of anxiety that's sometimes referred to as debilitating anxiety, which can have negative effects on their motivation and learning. And when they experience too little arousal, they may be bored, which can also be detrimental because it can lead to inattention. Therefore, it's usually best to provide a moderate level of arousal.

Although researchers are currently very interested in the role of emotions in motivation and learning, it's not clear what the implications of emotions are for instructors other than the obvious. For example, fostering positive emotions in students, such as enjoyment and excitement, would make sense for a lot of reasons. Yet, sometimes it may be beneficial for students to feel frustrated, and even angry, if it motivates them to do something worthwhile. Consider a student who dislikes the writing style of William Faulkner so much that he's motivated to critique it (Bergin, 1999). In sum, triggering students' emotions and getting them to generate emotions about the content and activities may be interesting and motivating to students.

> *"A teacher who can arouse a feeling for one single good action, for one single good poem, accomplishes more than he who fills our memory with rows on rows of natural objects, classified with name and form."* – Johann Wolfgang von Goethe (cited in Bartlett, 2002, p. 364)

Example I.3.1 – Showing Enthusiasm

Show enthusiasm for the course content and activities. If you're not excited about the course, it's going to be hard for the students to get excited about it. Students tell me that there's nothing worse than boring professors who are unenthusiastic about their own course. The same holds true for videos that you create and appear in. Jeffrey Young (2013) interviewed students about their experiences in MOOCs (Massive Open Online Courses) and he reported the following.

> *"There's one thing that makes a great course—it's passion,' says Mr. Lepin. It is a sentiment that most everyone I spoke with seems to share."* (Young, 2013, para. 23)

Some days you may not be excited about being in class (maybe you're tired or you're facing some difficult personal issues at home). On those days, you'll have to feign your enthusiasm. You don't have to be a cheerleader that acts overly enthusiastic, but you don't want to be dull, lifeless, and unenthused because students may start to feel similarly about you and your course.

Probably the most basic way to show enthusiasm is to use your voice effectively by changing your volume level a little once and a while, and avoiding a monotone voice. As this undergraduate student explained, "I lose interest in class because the voice of instructor is monotone and quite slow." I discuss the pace of instruction in the next strategy.

Example I.3.2 – Noticing the Pace of Lessons

Be conscious of the pace of the lesson, in both face-to-face classes and online courses. Because an optimal level of arousal is motivating to students, you don't want the pace to be too slow or too fast. In face-to-face classes, you can watch students' faces and behaviors to see when your pace is off target. If the pace is too slow, students will fidget, look annoyed, sigh loudly, search the web, text on their phones, etc. If it's too fast, they might write notes furiously, look anxious, or simply stop trying to keep up with your fast pace.

It's harder to get a feel for the pace of online courses, which is why it can be important to ask students to complete online questionnaires about the instruction every few weeks. Ask them about the pace and other things that can help you discern their level of interest.

The pace of the speech and presentation is also important in online videos. Results from a survey of undergraduate and graduate students from around the world indicated that "the most common response for what makes a compelling video is a charismatic or compelling speaker. The students wanted someone who was animated, easy to understand, and interested in the topic that she or he was discussing" (Leonard, n.d., p. 3). Again, you want to maintain a pace that keeps moving, but isn't too fast. You can check out the pace of my voice and text on my videos that are on my YouTube channel. I don't have any illusion that my videos are great or that my pacing is perfect. But students give me good feedback about the pace, although some say that it's a little fast in some places which requires them to go back and listen to some sections again. I err on the side of talking too fast knowing that they can rewind and re-watch if needed. To maintain a constant pace and stay on topic, I write-out a script for my videos because I'm not a skilled orator. I find that it forces me to focus on the important points and reduces the length of my videos considerably, which students tell me they appreciate.

Example I.3.3 – Limiting Listening Time

Organize your class meetings to avoid long periods in which students are required to listen. How long is too long? It depends on your audience and the quality of your presentation. For college students, it may be about 15 minutes, but it really depends on the type of presentation, the usefulness of the information, the time of day, the time of year (the first day of the course or near the end of the course), etc.

When I plan to lecture or have a lecture with discussion, I try to start the class period with it because students are usually attentive at the beginning. Although sometimes, I'll ask them to discuss a content topic at the beginning to get them warmed up to the classroom and the ideas we're going to cover in that class period. I try not to lecture at the end of a class period except to have a short summary or wrap-up when needed. I can't cite research to support this practice, but it works well for my students. The key is that you try something, pay attention to how it works, and then modify it as needed. Figure 7.3 shows a timeline of how I try to think about organizing instruction in my almost 3-hour course periods for graduate students.

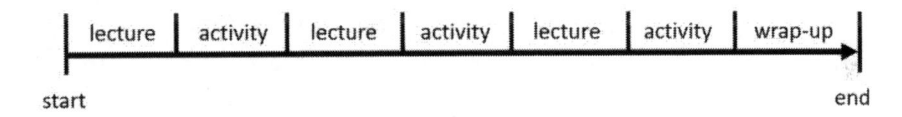

| lecture | activity | lecture | activity | lecture | activity | wrap-up |

start   end

Figure 7.3. *Pattern of instructional approaches during one class period from beginning to end*

Of course, you don't have to design your courses as strictly as shown in the figure, and the number of lectures and activities isn't precise in the figure (I just wanted you to see the general pattern). Sometimes I string a few different activities one after the other or include only a few lectures. The key point is that as students proceed through the class they experience a variety of different things to help them pay attention and remain interested.

Example I.3.4 – Varying Instructional Activities Across the Course

Vary instructional activities over the course to maintain students' interest and avoid boredom. Students are likely to get tired of anything, even something great, if it's used over and over again. My rule of thumb is to not use any assignment more than 4 or 5 times in a row in a course without making some modifications to it or inserting another assignment between. For example, you probably don't want to require students to complete a one-page summary of their readings every week for 15 weeks, even if it's a really good assignment. Students tend to lose interest in completing the assignments when an assignment is required regularly and often. One option could be to require this assignment for five weeks in a row and then give another one page assignment for which they have to answer two short questions, or take a quiz, or something else that allows them to show their understanding. Then switch back to requiring the one-page summary assignment again if you want to. The key is simply to ensure some variety if you want to maintain students' motivation and engagement on assignments, as noted by the following undergraduate student.

> "Doing the same thing every single night (read ____, watch ____, complete the concept quiz) is lame, because we do the exact same work every night and then go through the exact same schedule during class (powerpoint outline with interactive questions, classwork, leave)."

This doesn't mean that professors shouldn't have regular course procedures, such as how to submit an assignment. Procedures and rules should generally be the same throughout the course. However, instructional activities (e.g., assignments and assessments) should vary to maintain students' interest and avoid boredom.

Think about the order of all of the activities and assignments that you plan to implement during one particular lesson and then across several weeks. Is there variety across the activities and assignments? Consider what your students are thinking when they're sitting in the class. Will the activities and assignments keep them interested? If not, is there a way to re-order the activities or to change some of them to increase students' interest?

Also think about varying the out-of-class activities and assignments you require. For example, if you require students to read a textbook every week, you could consider mixing it up once and a while by having students watch videos or learn the content some other way instead of reading the textbook. Maybe you could include articles from current magazines or newspapers, or provide links to websites with the relevant information.

Example I.3.5 – Using Role Playing

Use role playing as a way to activate students' interest and emotions. Role playing not only requires participants and observers to actively engage, but also places them in a realistic context, which can lead them to solving problems, exploring their own and others' feelings, and/or exploring their attitudes about issues. Role-playing can be divided into nine phases: (1)

introducing the problem and explaining the roles, (2) selecting the participants, (3) setting the stage by outlining the scene, (4) preparing the audience to understand their role, (5) beginning the role play, (6) discussing the role play and evaluating it, (7) reenacting the role play as many times as needed, (8) discussing and evaluating the reenactment, and (9) sharing experiences and possibly generalizing the ideas to other situations (Joyce, Weil, & Calhoun, 2004; Shaftel & Shaftel, 1967). It's beyond the scope of this book to delve into the details of role playing, so if you're interested, I suggest referring to the books referenced in the prior sentence or finding other resources.

As an example of role playing in a course about the Korean War, Dr. Dahpon Ho, an Assistant Professor of History at the University of Rochester, divided his class into one group representing North Korea and another group representing South Korea. Over eight weeks, the students spent the beginning of each class role playing by plotting strategies, issuing propaganda, holding parades, conducting rocket tests, and re-enacting the funeral of a North Korean leader (Gose, 2017). Dr. Ho notes that "Students have to feel that they're part of the historical community. If history is fossilized, it will perish" (Gose, 2017, para. 9).

Example I.3.6 – Creating a Pleasant Learning Environment

Create a pleasant learning environment. Although "pleasant" is subjective, I offer a few ideas that might work for you.

- Examine the physical space each class meeting and adjust it to make it as pleasant as possible. Remove unattractive or distracting items from the walls that might have been left over from the prior class. Adjust the lighting, window treatments, and chairs as needed. Pick up trash left behind by others. You might think these tasks are beyond your PhD education, but they aren't if you want to create a pleasant environment for your students.

- Use humor to elicit positive emotions and create a class in which learning can be seen as enjoyable. There's little research to suggest that humor directly increases learning, which is why humor is discussed here as a means to elicit emotions. These emotions may then lead to students paying more attention to the content or feeling more comfortable in the class, which can lead to increased engagement and learning. Note that humor needs to be used cautiously and appropriately. An inappropriate or belittling joke can seriously harm the learning environment by making students feel uncomfortable or unwelcome. As a general rule, don't use sarcasm unless you're very, very, very skilled at it because it can be interpreted in different ways by different students and can convey implicit messages. And even if you think you're skilled at it, students may not agree or may interpret your sarcasm differently than you intended.

- Play music before class and during breaks. You may select music that conveys something about your interests or background. Sometimes students will offer to bring in music, which can create another way to connect to some students. (I recommend telling them to only bring music that could be played on the radio so you don't offend anyone with inappropriate lyrics.)

"I put in a good amount of effort because the teacher makes the concepts fun." (Undergraduate student's response as to why she puts forth effort in a course.)

Example I.3.7 – Decreasing Debilitating Anxiety

Decrease debilitating anxiety because it can have negative effects on students' motivation and learning. Some anxiety and arousal is good for learning, but too much can stress out students and cause them to experience debilitating anxiety.

Anxiety is often inversely related to students' feelings that they can succeed. When students have low perceptions of success ("I don't think I can succeed.") they tend to have higher anxiety ("I'm stressed out about this course."). Therefore, one way to reduce anxiety is to increase students' perceptions of success by using some of the strategies in Chapter 6 (Strategies to Support Success) of this book.

Ask students to list what's causing them to worry about the course and review the list to determine whether or not there's any way to reduce some of their worries. You can have students write their list on a paper anonymously and hand it to you in class, write it on a discussion board, email it to you, etc. You can use this feedback to consider changes to the course and recommend strategies to them to reduce their anxiety if possible.

Interest Strategy 4

Design curriculum with a consideration of students' individual interests.

Students can be more situationally interested when the topics and activities align with their existing individual interests. For example, if a student has an individual interest in architecture, the instructor of a math course could use building design as part of the examples to activate the student's individual interest. Although it may appear obvious that this strategy would work, sometimes it doesn't work because students with a higher individual interest in the topic also know a lot about it and are bored with instruction that includes simple topics in their knowledge area. Nonetheless, researchers have found that prior knowledge is positively related to interest (Schraw et al., 2001).

Example I.4.1 – Determining Individual Interests

Before instruction, survey students to determine their individual interests. A fairly well-known way to do this is to ask students about their background, interests, and hobbies. Then, during the course, you can relate course content to their interests or provide examples related to their interests. It definitely gets their attention when you call out a student's name and say something like, "I know Jack likes wrestling so he's probably very familiar with..." (and then you relate something in wrestling to the course content). You can also use this information to create small talk with students before or after class, such as, "Jasmine, I remember that you like to read fiction, have you read any good books lately?" Questions such as this can be a nice way to talk to students more informally and may increase students' perceptions of caring; however, they rarely lead to information that is useful in designing instruction (although it may make students more comfortable to tell you or ask you about information that is useful in designing instruction).

In addition to giving students broad survey questions (such as, "What things interest you?" or "What are your hobbies?"), think about specific questions that can help you in designing instruction. Before developing the questionnaire, think about your lesson objectives in the course and write questions that can help you make decisions about your lessons. For example, if you plan on showing students how to solve a problem the following week, you might think of a few different problems that accomplish your instructional objectives similarly. Then you could ask students which topic they prefer, either in class (by a show of hands or on a piece of paper) or in a short online questionnaire.

To take this a step further, send out an email message to students the week before class starts and ask whether anyone would be willing to meet with you for 30 minutes to discuss some ideas you had about the course. During this time, you could run your ideas by them and get their feedback. They might have some great ideas to make the content more interesting. You can also ask them why they enrolled in the course or what they think might be interesting in the course. Answers to these questions could help you determine how their expectations align with your plans and give you new ideas.

CHAPTER 8

Strategies to Foster Caring

Problem

Students don't believe that the instructor or others in the course care about whether they succeed in the course or care about their well-being.

Solution

You need to ensure that students believe that others in the learning environment, such as you and other students, <u>care</u> about their learning and about them personally.

Overview of Caring

Can you remember a time when you did something because your friends were doing it and you wanted to be with your friends? Or, you might have chosen to engage in activities that you wouldn't normally have engaged in because you wanted to spend time with a loved one, such as a parent, child, or significant other. Conversely, have you ever not done something because doing so would require you to interact with others you don't want to interact with? Throughout life, we have a need for secure and satisfying relationships (Baumeister & Leary, 1995), which can motivate us to engage in activities that allow us to experience quality relationships (or to avoid activities that require us to engage in aversive or hostile relationships).

<u>Key Point:</u> Students are generally more motivated and engaged in classes and school when they feel cared for and connected to others in the learning environment. Some researchers have distinguished between *academic* caring (the professor cares that students learn the content and meet the course objectives) and *personal* caring (the professor cares about students' well-being). As one student noted, "If we don't seem motivated it might be because you don't seem to care how we actually feel" (Matos, 2017). Because these two types of caring are often highly correlated (Jones & Skaggs,

2016; Jones & Wilkins, 2013), it's likely that strategies to foster one of these types of caring will also foster the other type of caring. Therefore, in this chapter, I discuss strategies that can be used to foster caring in general, without distinguishing between strategies for academic caring and strategies for personal caring.

You might wonder whether caring is really important in college courses. After all, these students are grown adults, why do they need to feel cared for? Well, researchers have consistently shown that when college students feel cared for (e.g., respected, listened to) they're more motived in their classes. And when students feel cared for and feel that they belong, they also achieve higher GPAs (Donachie, 2017).

Even college football players need caring! I know sports is different from academics, but I want to share a sports example that applies to educational environments as well. Shortly after Larry Fedora became the new football coach at the University of North Carolina, he found out that his players didn't think that the coaching staff believed in them (Adelson, 2015). Although Fedora did care about his players, he wasn't being perceived as caring by his players. So coach Fedora asked one of his star players, Ryan Switzer, what to do and here is what Ryan told him.

> *"I told him, 'Look at the relationship we have, where I can just come in and talk," Switzer said. "If you can get the other 100 or so guys on the team to feel that way, they'll run through a brick wall for you. That's how I am. I would do anything for you because I know you care about me. I know how much you want to see me succeed and I know you feel that way about everybody, but if you showed them that, there would be no limit to what they would do for you and how they would play. And he's certainly done that. He and the other coaches have done a 360 in terms of how they've made these 19-to-22-year-old kids feel. That's been a very big, monumental step for our team and our program."* (Adelson, 2015, para. 9)

Wouldn't it be great if college students would run through a brick wall for their professors!

A main idea for promoting caring in courses is that professors should show students they care about their learning. Another big idea is that students should feel welcomed and comfortable participating in the class and interacting with other students. Certainly, however, there are times when students should feel uncomfortable because their abilities and beliefs are being challenged (because this might lead them to reconsider or change their beliefs). Although professors often have little control over who is enrolled in their course, they have a lot of control over establishing the class culture and climate through the use of effective rules, procedures, and communications. Establishing an appropriate class culture and climate can provide the emotional support that students need to succeed in the class. And when students care about each other, students may draw motivation from each other when their own motivation is lower, as explained by this undergraduate student: "I don't put too much effort into this course, however I don't underestimate it either. It is an elective for me but I will not let group mates down because I am not motivated." In other words, this student is motivated because he cares for the other students in his group and doesn't want to let them down.

In this chapter, I present the following five strategies and provide several examples of each. There's no guarantee that students will run through a brick wall for you if you use them, but I'm sure they *won't* run through any walls for you if you don't use them.

C.1 Be approachable and relatable to students.
C.2 Ensure that students feel respected by you and the other students, both online and face-to-face.
C.3 Show students that you care about whether or not they achieve the course objectives.
C.4 Consider accommodating students when they experience extraordinary events, such as an illness or a death in the family.
C.5 Help students to fit into the culture of the class, major, college, or university.

Relevant Theories

In this section, I provide a very brief explanation of the primary theories that are most directly relevant to the caring strategies in the MUSIC model. These are not comprehensive explanations, so please look-up the citations if you are interested in more information.

- Caring Theories (Johnson, Johnson, & Anderson, 1983; Noddings, 1984, 1992; Wentzel, 1999). A caring relation is defined as "a connection or encounter between two human beings—a carer and a recipient of care, or cared-for" in which "both parties must contribute to it in characteristic ways" (Noddings, 1992, p. 15). Students are more likely to be motivated when they perceive a caring relationship between themselves and the teacher and other students in the educational environment.

- Need to belong (Baumeister & Leary, 1995). "The belongingness hypothesis is that human beings have a pervasive drive to form and maintain at least a minimum quantity of lasting, positive, and significant interpersonal relationships" (Baumeister & Leary, 1995, p. 497). Students are more likely to be motivated when their need for belongingness is met in the educational environment.

- <u>Belonging</u> (Goodenow, 1993). Belonging is defined "as students' sense of being accepted, valued, included, and encouraged by others (teacher and peers) in the academic classroom setting and of feeling oneself to be an important part of the life and activity of the class" (Goodenow, 1993, p. 25). Students are more likely to be motivated when their perceived belonging in the educational environment is high.

- <u>Need for relatedness</u> (Deci & Ryan, 1985, 2000). Need for relatedness is a construct within cognitive evaluation theory, which is a subtheory of self-determination theory. Individuals have a basic psychological need for relatedness, which "encompasses a person's strivings to relate to and care for others, to feel that those others are relating authentically to one's self, and to feel a satisfying and coherent involvement with the social world more generally" (Deci & Ryan, 1991, p. 243). Students are more likely to be motivated when their need for relatedness is met.

- <u>Attachment Theories</u> (Ainsworth, 1979; Bowlby, 1969). Attachment theory explains that the primary relationship between children and their caregiver creates children's mental representations of themselves and others. Children then use these mental representations as they interpret and judge other people's actions as they form new relationships. Children who receive predictable and sensitive responses to their needs develop representations that are associated with secure attachments. In educational settings, children's attachment style is assumed to affect their expectations in their relationships with their teachers. Students who have secure attachments with their caregiver are more likely to have similar attachments with their teacher, which then leads to more positive motivation-related beliefs and behaviors in school. (Please note that this is a very simplified explanation of this theory and, in many ways, it inadequately describes the complexity of the theory.)

Caring Strategy 1
Be approachable and relatable to students.

Professors need to be approachable and relatable to students so that students feel comfortable asking questions and receiving feedback, both of which are critical to the motivation and learning processes. I've heard more than once from undergraduates that it took them a while to see their professors as "real people." The strategies in this section provide a few examples of how to make yourself "real"!

Remember that it's the *perception* that you're approachable that's important, you don't actually have to interact with every student to be perceived as approachable. Students will judge your approachability, in part, by how they see you interacting with other students in the course. Being available by email is a common way to be accessible. Some professors have told me that they give students their cell phone number and that students don't call unnecessarily (who really wants to call their professor anyway?!?). But at the end of the course, students often report that the professor was always available and approachable, even if they never contacted the professor. Again, it's the perception that matters: they could have called if they wanted to.

> *"I learned most, not from those who taught me but from those who talked with me."*
> – Saint Augustine (cited in AZ Quotes, 2015c)

Example C.1.1 – Showing You're Approachable

Do the obvious things to show that you're approachable. I wasn't going to include these in this book, but what's obvious to some professors may not be obvious to others, so here are a few strategies related to approachability.

- Say hello to students before class as they enter the classroom and goodbye after class as they leave the classroom.

- Smile and make eye contact with students (or alter this as necessary based on the cultural norms of your students).

- Come to class a little early and stay a little late to initiate "small talk" with students. Ask them about their major or what other courses they're enrolled in. Ask them about where they grew up or what they want to do when they graduate. Often, this small talk can lead to students asking substantive questions about the course content. For example, a student might ask, "By the way, I was wondering about something in the reading for this week." This strategy requires you to be prepared for class before you enter the classroom so that you can arrange the room and set-up the needed technology immediately, and then, you have time to mingle with the students. Even if you don't get to talk to everyone in your class, that's okay because other students will see that you care enough to talk to some students and will be more likely to perceive you as a caring professor.

- Email students in online courses to show that you are available and approachable. As one student in an online course explained at the end of the semester: "I did feel that I could e-mail the instructor if I needed to, but an occasional e-mail from him just to say hello or check-in would make me feel much more engaged."

- Learn students' names. Based on my experience, it's possible to learn the names of 20 to 30 students in the first or second week of class with some effort (and I don't have a great memory!). A colleague of mine told me he learned the names of the 50 students in his class. But you need to use some strategies to learn this many names because it doesn't happen magically. In large classes, learn as many names as you can, learning 25 names is better than learning only a few and students might think that you know everyone's name even if you only know 25 names because you use them in class. For specific strategies to help you learn students' names, see Appendix F.

- Really listen to students when they talk to you, regardless of whether it's before, during, or after class.

Example C.1.2 – Adding Flexibility to Your Office Hours

Hold office hours at a variety of times and locations. Showing students that you're willing to meet with them when they are available, as opposed to when it is convenient for you, can demonstrate that you're trying to be approachable. I don't know the best times for your students, but maybe later in the day at 4:00 pm is better if students have morning and early afternoon classes. And don't be limited to your office, look for other on-campus locations, such as the dining hall, student union, or library. Students may be more relaxed in those locations than in your office and you may be able to save time in your schedule by combining your lunch with a student meeting.

Example C.1.3 – Being Friendly, But Not Friends

Be friendly, but don't try to be friends with students. It's your job to help them achieve their goals successfully, not to be their friend. In a student-professor relationship, the professor has more power than the student. In a true friendship, both individuals have a similar amount of power (at least theoretically!). Therefore, it's unrealistic and impossible for you to form true friendships with students while you remain their professor.

And in case you were wondering, I've heard several undergraduate students say that they don't want to be friends with their professors on Facebook, Instagram, Snapchat, etc. They often post personal information on social media sites and don't want to share that type of information with their professors. In my limited experience, graduate students seem to be more open to being friends on social media depending on the type of relationship you have with them. You can still create a Facebook or Instagram page for your class if that's useful to you, but I don't recommend trying to become social media "friends" with students. Some professors specifically tell students that they don't accept friend invitations from students until after they graduate. Implement any rule you like, but try to be consistent across students to avoid showing favoritism towards some students.

Example C.1.4 – Responding Promptly

Respond to students' inquiries promptly. Note on your syllabus how long students can expect to wait to hear back from you. You can include a statement such as, "If you don't hear from me within 24 hours after emailing me, please send your message again because I try to respond promptly." I think that responding within 24 hours (not including weekends) is reasonable, and certainly no more than 48 hours unless you're traveling or have other extenuating circumstances.

Example C.1.5 –Students Describing Themselves

Require students to provide a one-paragraph description about themselves. This activity can be especially important for students in an online course. In fact, some of my online students have thanked me for caring enough to allow them to share this information. Here are some example instructions to give to students for this assignment.

> *Write a paragraph and include things that will help me understand your background and knowledge, such as: your interests, the degree you are seeking, why you are working towards this degree or taking courses, any experiences related to the content of this course, your future plans, etc. Don't provide any personal information that you are not comfortable providing.*

You can assign this assignment as students' first graded assignment in the course and give them a few nominal points towards their final grade for completing it. It's easy to grade because either they completed it or they didn't. To make it a little more personal, you can respond online, by email, or on their paper copy with a few sentences, such as: "I hope that you find this course useful" and "I look forward to working with you this semester." You may also want to make some type of connection to something specific they wrote. For example, if they tell you that they're in the college marching band you could tell them that you too enjoyed playing in band.

In addition to creating a connection between you and the student, you can use this information as you design activities in your classes (e.g., you can select examples related to their interests).

Ming Li, a professor at Sias International University in China, uses this assignment in her class, but with an added element. Dr. Li collects students' paper copy of this assignment and then places all of their papers in a binder. At the next class meeting, she brings the binder to class, shows it to her students, and tells them that this is their class book. She explains that she keeps it with her so that she can learn about them and remember who they are. Clearly, she demonstrates that she cares about her students.

Example C.1.6 – Using Personal Anecdotes

Use personal anecdotes when appropriate. You don't need to tell them your life's story, but during a course there are usually times when you can share short anecdotes of things from your life that somehow fit with your content. Short anecdotes *unrelated* to the course content are also acceptable as long as they're short and appropriate.

> *"I developed a rule of thumb in graduate school. If a professor didn't mention something personal at least a single time—a reference to a child, an anecdote about a colleague—then it was a pretty good bet that I had nothing to learn from him. It's not that I needed my teachers to be confessional; I just needed them to be present."* – William Deresiewicz (2014, August 14, para. 12)

Example C.1.7 – Showing Similarities Between You and the Students

Show students that you are similar to them in some ways. I got this idea from an intervention study that was conducted with high school students. The premise of the study was that if teachers and students saw themselves as similar to one another, they would be more likely to like each other and develop closer relationships (Gehlbach et al., 2016). The intervention required teachers and students to write down answers to questions such as: (a) What is the most important quality in a friend?, (b) Which class format is best for student learning?, and (c) What would you do if the principal announced that you had the day off? (Gehlbach et al., 2016, p. 345). Then the researchers compiled the responses and gave the teacher and students a list of five things that they had in common with each other. Finally, the teacher and students were asked to look over the list and to do a few things, including identifying one thing that surprised them the most. The researchers found that this activity resulted in (a) better relationships between teachers and students and (b) students earning higher course grades compared to students who did not participate in the intervention.

I don't expect that you will be able to replicate this intervention in your class. However, it may inspire you to think about strategies you could use to increase students' perceptions of the similarities between you and them (and vice versa), with the ultimate goal of creating stronger relationships between you and them. For example, it may be possible to share some of your interests as you discuss content-related topics in class. Or, maybe you could use your hobbies and interests as part of an activity. Sharing personal anecdotes and interests briefly (without getting sidetracked on lengthy personal stories) throughout the course is an easy way to accomplish this.

Example C.1.8 – Teaching Students How to Interact with Professors

Teach students how to interact with professors. Because students have different expectations of the role of a college professor, they must be taught what to expect in your course. You can provide some ground rules and explanations on your syllabus or during your first class, by including statements such as: "I want you to contact me when you have problems in this course. It is my job to help you succeed, so please contact me by…"

A great resource that provides information to students about why and how to talk to their professors is provided by ENGAGE Engineering at their

"Talk to Me Tips for Students" website (https://tinyurl.com/talkto22). Individual professors may want to use this information, but also consider how your program, department, or college might share this information with students more systematically, perhaps at an orientation for new or first-year students.

Example C.1.9 – Trying to Appear Smart

Don't try to appear "smart." It can be common, especially for beginning and young professors, to feel the need to show students that they deserve to be in charge of a class by reminding students how smart they are. My advice is to avoid doing this for a few reasons. First, most students care about themselves and their learning, not about you and your credentials. They assume that you have the basic credentials or you wouldn't have been hired to teach the class. So reminding them how smart you are just makes you appear arrogant and insecure, which can make you appear less approachable. Focus on the students, not yourself. Second, your "smartness" will become apparent to students as the course progresses in your regular instruction and communications with students. If you know what you're doing, students will see that and respect you for it; it's not something you need to go out of your way to demonstrate. Third, students don't like professors who think they know it all (who does!?!). Being honest with students and admitting when you don't know something is refreshing to students and they're more likely to believe you when you have something important to say. To take this a step further, you can make it clear that just because you're an expert in the field doesn't mean that you can't learn more from students. You might say, "I'm here to learn from you as well." And admit that you don't know it all.

"Those people who think they know everything are a great annoyance to those of us who do." – Isaac Asimov (cited in iz Quotes, 2015c)

For students who want to know about your credentials, make your CV (curriculum vitae) available to them on your university biography webpage and provide the link to it on your syllabus. Interested and concerned students can examine it and others can ignore it.

Caring Strategy 2

Ensure that students feel respected by you and the other students, both online and face-to-face.

In all you do, day in and day out, the most important thing you can do as a professor is to respect your students if you want to motivate and engage them. Students are human beings and deserve to be treated the same way that you, as a professor, expect to be treated. Some days you may want to yell at, belittle, or dismiss students' concerns as insignificant, but you can't allow yourself to do so if you want to be an effective, motivating teacher. You communicate respect or disrespect in everything you do as a professor, such as in written and oral feedback, in informal conversations before and after class, in email correspondence, and in your lectures, presentations, and class discussions.

> *"He that will have his son have a respect for him and his orders, must himself have a great reverence for his son."* – John Locke (cited in Bartlett, 2002, p. 286)

Some students don't need to feel respected to be motivated in your course. They may want to get an A or believe that the content is useful to their future goals; and as a result, they study and learn no matter what you do. In one study, I asked students what could be changed in the course to increase their perception that the instructor cared about them and one undergraduate student wrote only: "Why the fu$% does that matter?" This comment demonstrates that some students may not need, expect, or want to feel cared for by the instructor; but in general, those students are the exceptions. And even for those students, you'll be a much more effective professor if you gain their respect by respecting them, because they're more likely to be motivated if they feel respected.

When students feel that their professor respects them and listens to them by making an effort to understand their perspectives, they're also more likely to listen to their professor's perspectives and feedback. This is critical because professor feedback can help them learn more knowledge and skills.

> *"Because I like the instructor, and my peers also like the instructor, I aim to do well in the class. I don't want to blow off this course because I respect the professor."* (undergraduate student)

When students feel respected, they're also more likely to feel that the class is a safe place for them to share their thoughts and ideas. When students feel that a classmate or the professor will disrespect them or their ideas, many will be less likely to engage deeply in discussions and ask questions that they really want to know the answers to, which can hinder their learning. As one undergraduate student explained, "I think Dr. X has already established an environment of mutual respect. I would not hesitate to approach him if I had a question."

Example C.2.1 – Developing Ground Rules

Develop the ground rules for student-to-student and student-to-professor interactions during a class. Always make the ground rules clear and always put them in writing, either on the syllabus, a handout, a course website, or somewhere that students can find them. Just talking about rules is not enough because students can forget after a few weeks and some students likely will not be in attendance during the talk. Figure 8.1 shows some rules that may be useful in your courses. Rules should be specific enough that students know what they mean, but broad enough to apply across a variety of situations. In addition to the rules, you might also want to share some of your beliefs about interactions and disagreements. I provide a few possibilities in Figure 8.1.

Ground Rules for Respectful and Equitable Interactions
1. Be verbal and engaged, but do not monopolize most of the time during discussions.
2. Treat others with respect and expect others to treat you similarly.
3. Ask questions when you are confused about what someone said or what is being learned because it's likely that others are confused too.
4. Speak for yourself, not for others.
5. Encourage others to participate in discussions.

Beliefs That I Hold True
- Disagreements can provide opportunities to learn.
- Sometimes two well-informed individuals will disagree.
- Others may have different interaction styles than me.

Figure 8.1. *Examples of rules and beliefs that can be used in a course*

In a college course, it might seem silly and childish to write down class rules for interactions, but it's not. I find the rules most useful for my graduate students who typically range in age from 22 to 70 years old, so I always discuss these ground rules with them on the first day of class. Some students like to talk a lot and a few tend to monopolize the class discussions. When this happens, it's important to talk to the students individually outside of class time and explain to them that you love their ideas and enthusiasm, but that they're monopolizing class conversations. I find that most of these students are unaware that they're dominating class discussions, and that by alerting them of their extensive talking, they're much more conscious of the extent of their participation in the future. Being able to point to the class rules is helpful during these conversations.

Instead of *telling* students your ground rules, you can allow them to participate in creating them, which can empower them. There are a few ways to do this. You can have students raise their hands, call on students, and create a list as a whole class. Or, you can have students work in groups, ask each group to develop a list of rules, and then compare lists across groups as a way to develop a class list. Or, you can create the list online via a discussion board, wiki, etc. For any of these approaches, you should create your rules first and then make sure that the students come-up with all of the rules on your list (without showing them your list). If they don't list all of your rules, ask them to consider some possible additions to fill-in the gaps. This isn't being dishonest, it's simply ensuring that you have the rules you need. Sometimes students simply don't think of the variety of rules needed.

Example C.2.2 – Soliciting Student Feedback

Allow students to give you feedback about your instruction and instructional materials. By doing so, you can show that you respect students' opinions and are willing to listen to them, especially if you implement some of their ideas.

Here are some of the many ways to solicit student feedback. Create an online survey that students can complete anonymously and send them the link to the survey every couple weeks. You could ask one or more broad question such as: What suggestions do you have for improving the course? Or, you could ask questions related to specific course activities. Other ideas for questions are provided in the *User Guide for Assessing the Components of the MUSIC® Model of Motivation* (Jones, 2017; available at www.theMUSICmodel.com). You can also give a handout in class with these types of questions and collect them at the end of class. Or, ask students to complete an "exit slip" before they leave where they take out a piece of paper and tell you anything they want you to know about the course (or ask them more specifically to list suggestions for improving the course).

Example C.2.3 – Providing Time for Students to Introduce Themselves

Incorporate activities that help students get to know one another. In some courses, many or all students already know one another, while in other courses almost none of the students know each another. Here are a few strategies you can use to help students get to know one another.

- In smaller courses, give each student some *Play-Doh* and ask them to make two different objects that depict something important in their life or something interesting to them. In an undergraduate Spanish language course, students created objects such as a dog, a house, a snowboard, and a tennis racket (Jones, Llacer-Arrastia, & Newbill, 2009). Next, ask students, one at a time, to share why they created their objects. Through this activity, students share some personal information that allows others to get to know them better.

- Ask students to bring to class an object that is important to them or that shows an interest of theirs. This activity can also be used online through photos or videos.

- Search online for icebreaker games. There are so many icebreakers that I don't want to take the space here describing them when you can search online quickly for ones that you think will work best for your students.

Example C.2.4 – Respecting Students' Out-of-Class Responsibilities

Recognize and respect the fact that students have lives outside of your class. Some students, especially non-traditional students, have many responsibilities (e.g., jobs, families) that can overwhelm them when combined with the work of a college course. Believing that a college course should be the most important thing in someone's busy life is simply not realistic, and it's not really fair for professors to impose their values on others. Just because students don't do well doesn't mean that they aren't trying or don't want to do well.

Professor Matos (2017) explained how some of her students admitted that other responsibilities got in the way of their school success by causing them to miss some classes or turn in work late, unfinished or not at all. But she also found that as bad as students reported that it was to do poorly in a class, what was even worse was when their professors *hated* them for doing poorly.

"More than one student reported slinking away from a course entirely after some relatively innocuous flaw, out of fear of facing a professor's outraged disappointment. Instead they suggested that we begin a corrective statement— either actually or at least mentally—with something like, 'I'm not mad at you, but...[you missed the deadline].'" (Matos, 2017, 11th para.)

What great advice! The suggestion that professors focus on the deadline and not their feelings reaffirms the course rules and expectations, but doesn't judge students for their behavior. In similar situations, you could say something like, "It's your life, you have to do what's best for you. Don't try to make me happy. It doesn't matter to me what you decide, but I'm here to help you succeed, so please let me know how I can help." Saying this doesn't mean that you're going to change your expectations or rules, but you may design the rules for cases like this so that if students need to make-up work after deadlines, they can. By focusing on their learning, and caring enough to allow them to succeed (even if only at a B or C level, they may be thrilled with that), you have done a lot to help motivate them to put forth effort.

Caring Strategy 3

Show students that you care about whether or not they achieve the course objectives.

There are many ways to show students that you care about their learning. Obvious recommendations include spending time to design a "good" course and being available to help students who have questions. When I've asked students in my research studies and in my own classes how they know that the professor was caring, they will often report that the professor took the time to design a good course and then list examples that are consistent with the MUSIC Model of Motivation (such as giving them choices, demonstrating the usefulness of the course, providing interesting experiences, etc.). Therefore, effectively implementing some of the strategies in this book will likely help you to be perceived as more caring!

Example C.3.1 – Telling Students You Care

Tell students that you care about their learning. This example is almost too obvious for me to write, but it's easy to overlook the obvious. Tell them at appropriate places during the course that you care about their learning and that you want them to do well.

Example C.3.2 – Addressing Students' Concerns Promptly

Address students' concerns during class, as they arise. Although it can be difficult to stop a class lesson to address students' concerns, it can be a very powerful indicator that you care about their learning if you make time to address their questions and concerns during class (Larsen, 2015). You may not have time to answer every student's question during class, but you can address some of them and then ask students to email you, write down their questions, or talk to you at another time if they have further questions. If the questions slow you down too much, you might say something like, "I know we're not staying exactly in line with the syllabus schedule, but it's more important to me that you learn the concepts correctly than to simply rush through them. I will send you a revised schedule this week." If you get too far behind, you'll have to make adjustments to your expectations or focus on the most important content during class and let the students obtain the other content through other means (for example, readings, videos, etc.). I realize that some courses have specific content that *needs* to be covered, and in these cases, it is important to create other opportunities for students to learn, such as in study groups or optional course meetings (face-to-face or online).

Example C.3.3 – Responding to Students' Concerns

Assess students' perceptions about the course and adjust the course as needed to address concerns that affect their learning. For example, I know professors who administer the MUSIC Inventory (provided in Chapter 3) during the middle of their course, show students the results, and then discuss changes they will make in the course to address the results. Responding to students' concerns in this way can show students that you care about their learning and will likely also increase their perceptions of empowerment and success. This comment by an undergraduate student demonstrates how students can feel a lack of caring when instructors don't respond to students' concerns or struggles: "The reason I don't think she cares is because our class average on tests is very low and I don't think she cares, and she hasn't changed anything in her teaching format."

Example C.3.4 – Scheduling a Meeting with Every Student

Schedule a meeting with every student in your class. Although most instructors probably schedule some office hours each week, students don't always attend. Yet, at least one research study documented that when students attend office hours, they earn higher grades (Guerrero & Rod, 2013). David Gooblar, a professor at the University of Iowa, suggests that instead of simply holding office hours as optional, instructors should *require* students to meet with them (Gooblar, 2015). He notes that required meetings can save instructors time in small courses in which students write papers because instructors can give face-to-face feedback on their papers instead of providing written feedback. Face-to-face feedback also increases the likelihood that students will understand and use the feedback. He suggests ending each meeting by giving students a brief to-do list.

But whether or not you assign papers, you can use these required meetings to talk about students' progress in the course on another assignment or in more general terms, which will show students that you care about their learning. I suspect that if students feel more comfortable with you after the meeting, they will be more likely to ask you questions or meet with you again in the future. Of course, the opposite is also true: If you come across like an uncaring arrogant jerk, students will surely not want to meet with you again!

Example C.3.5– Meeting with Groups of Students

Designate times to meet with groups of students to discuss course content. Groups of students are more likely than an individual student to generate more questions and they may feel more comfortable asking and hearing answers to questions in a group. Schedule the small group meetings at times that make sense in the semester, perhaps before certain assignments or tests, to provide students with feedback about what they know and still need to learn. Allow students to select their own groups or assign students to groups. Be creative in naming these meetings, maybe calling them "chats," "conversations," or "dialogues."

Example C.3.6 – Using Peer Mentors

Use peer mentors to provide academic and social support. I'm using the term *peer mentors* broadly to include other students who may be the same age/level or not, in the same course or not, and in the same major or not. All of these variations can provide different advantages and disadvantages, so do what works best for your situation. For example, in a university course for first-year students, a biochemistry professor had undergraduate peer mentors (junior- and senior-level biochemistry majors) facilitate some of the class sessions as small group discussions (Ruff, 2013). The peer mentors helped students map out the courses they planned to take during their next few years in college. The peer mentors also helped to guide the students through some of the course assignments. The professor reported that the peer mentors provided good tips for the students, which surely helped to create a caring environment for these first-year students.

Example C.3.7 – Focusing on Making a Difference

Focus on making a difference and sharing ideas. By focusing on making a difference in students' lives and sharing ideas, students will pick-up on your enthusiasm and the fact that you care about their learning. This is related to my prior example about not trying to be smart. Teaching is not about you, it's about the students. Consider this quote from a blog entry by Garr Reynolds.

> *"When I wrote the first edition of Presentation Zen back in 2007, I said that presentations are better when they're prepared and delivered in the spirit of truly wanting to make a difference and a belief in the power of sharing ideas. The secret to this spirit or approach is contribution. This is a key part of Presentation Zen. It's not about showing off. It's not about impressing. It's not about winning (or losing)."* (Reynolds, 2015, June 23)

Example C.3.8 – Explaining Differences Between High School and College

If you teach students who are in their first year of college, explain to them the differences between high school and college. As a college professor, you might not believe that it's your job to explain these differences to incoming high school students, but it is. Many students will likely not know what professors expect of students and others may have heard from their counselors, parents, or other students, but they need to hear it from you. Even if they've heard it before, hearing it again from you will reinforce that it's true (or not) and show that you care about their success.

Caring Strategy 4

Consider accommodating students when they experience extraordinary events, such as an illness or a death in the family.

It's easy to be inflexible and to say to a student, "I can't make special accommodations for you because it wouldn't be fair to everyone else in the class." I've said this before to some students and they understand it. So it's true that, in general, I recommend that you remain consistent with your expectations set forth in the syllabus. However, there are times when it's reasonable to make accommodations, such as when something happens in their life that prevents them from learning the course material. Remember that your focus is on their learning. If you show a student that you're willing to give her some type of accommodation (such as extending a deadline) because it can lead to an increase her learning, that sends a strong message that you're serious about the course and her obtaining the knowledge and skills in it. Your message can then motivate her to want to learn.

Ask students to give you their accommodation request in writing so that it's clear what they're asking for (unless it's a sensitive issue for the student, in which case a verbal explanation may be better). Then give your accommodation to the student *in writing*. It should be written down to ensure there's no confusion at that time or at a later time.

I assume that students are telling me the truth unless they give me a reason to suspect otherwise. I'm not naïve, I'm sure students have lied to me in the past. But by taking this attitude, I show that I *care,* and that's more important to me than being lied to by some small percentage of the students. But I wasn't born yesterday. If I feel that I'm being taken advantage of, I let the student know and don't allow the behavior to continue. I find that this happens rarely.

Example C.4.1 – Focusing on Learning

Keep the focus on learning when making decisions about students turning in assignments late. Sometimes students provide reasonable excuses as to why they were unable to turn-in an assignment on time, such as their grandmother died or they had a two-day hospital visit. If you don't plan to discuss the assignment answers in class, there's no harm in extending the assignment deadline. Doing so shows that you value their learning the knowledge and skills needed for the assignment. Of course it may prevent you from grading all the assignments immediately after they were due or having all the assignments completed by a certain date, but welcome to teaching, that's what good teachers do. If you can't keep up with your grading, that's a different issue that you need to address, either by making more time for grading or giving assignments that require less grading on your part (such as by incorporating peer grading or requiring different types of assignments).

As another idea, you can allow all students to turn in one assignment a few days late without any penalty. If you don't like my advice, you may want to use some of these humorous email replies to students who have said that their grandmother died: https://chroniclevitae.com/news/886-dear-student-should-your-granny-die-before-the-midterm.

Example C.4.2 – Creating an Effective Attendance Policy

Have an attendance policy that helps you and doesn't create unnecessary work for you. I decided long ago that I didn't like seeing students' doctor's notes (honestly, I thought that they could fake those anyway by changing the dates on them). And I didn't like figuring out whether their excuse rose to the level of a *good* excuse or not, because most of their excuses seemed pretty good to me and I didn't have the time or energy to decide. Instead, I allow students to miss up to two weeks of a 15 week course without any grade deduction. Therefore, they can miss two classes if the class meets once a week or six classes if it meets three times a week. If they miss more than that, I start deducting points each time they miss a class. I find this policy effective and easy to manage. And it promotes my philosophy that what I do in class is important (which is why they need to attend) without having to constantly monitor their every action. This also gives them some empowerment because it allows them to decide if and when they want to miss some classes.

- My plane arrived late
- My car broke down
- I had lice
- I had an allergic reaction
- I had jury duty
- I got food poisoning (or maybe it was the alcohol)

Caring Strategy 5

Help students fit into the culture of the class, major, college, or university.

Full-time students enroll in a variety of courses in addition to yours. It can be daunting for students to navigate through these courses towards a degree, especially if they're unsure of their interests or if their life goals change as they progress through school. Colleges generally use advisors to help students understand their course and career choices; yet, instructors play a critical role—if not the central role—in students' views of what it means to be a student and professional in a particular discipline or major.

I'm stating the obvious here to remind you that, as an instructor, you shape students' beliefs about your discipline and how they see themselves fitting into it (or not fitting into it). So while it can be easy to think that your only job is to help students meet the course objectives, you're also always shaping their beliefs about the broader context, such as their beliefs about the discipline, the related major or degree, your department, your college, etc.

The purpose of this section is not to provide a comprehensive approach to helping students fit into a discipline, major, academic department, or college. Rather, the goal is to acknowledge that instructors who follow the MUSIC model consider how their course fosters students' development and belonging within these broader contexts.

Example C.5.1 – Making Connections to other Content Areas

Connect your course content to content in other areas and disciplines. Although academic departments are often structured in what have been labeled as "silos" (because they're separate from one another), the terms *interdisciplinary* and *transdisciplinary* have become hot buzzwords in higher education to emphasize the importance of the interconnections among and beyond disciplines. Students must piece together and integrate their experiences in college to form their views and definition of self. Instructors can help students in this process by making explicit connections to other content areas and disciplines. The more connections that students notice, the more likely it is that they'll understand how the content is related to their own lives. Of course, this strategy relates directly to the usefulness component of the MUSIC model as well because it can help students understand how the course is related to their goals, which can help to motivate them.

As an example in the discipline of engineering, Dartmouth College "places a high priority in integrating liberal art skills with engineering, to help [students] understand and communicate the problems they will face as engineers" (Cheng, 2016, para. 7). This is likely one of the reasons that "in the class of 2016, Dartmouth College became the first national research University to graduate more women (54%) than men in its engineering department" (Cheng, 2016, para. 6).

Example C.5.2 – Showing a Variety of Possible Roles

Show students the variety of roles and career opportunities related to the content and discipline. Students may have limited knowledge about the roles that people play in the course discipline. You can foster students' understanding by explicitly providing a variety of examples, or you could assign students to search online for examples of individuals who use the content area or discipline as part of their jobs. Because new professions are emerging, you could ask students to identify some possible future career opportunities that involve the content area or discipline. The rationale for all of these activities is that by providing a wider variety of possible roles and career opportunities, students will be more likely to see themselves as part of the discipline.

Example C.5.3 – Allowing Students to Share Their Knowledge

Allow students to share their knowledge with others in a way that builds the community in the class. One way to do this is to allow students to research a topic and then share their findings in a poster session in which students create posters, hang them around the class, and walk around to look at other classmates' posters. You may want to divide the class in half so that half can stay by their poster while the others walk around, and then, switch the roles. By walking and talking at the poster session, students are able to discuss a variety of topics with different students; and likely, topics that they're passionate about because they selected the topics themselves. Students may find others in the class with similar interests and identify other similarities between themselves.

The poster session not only creates a caring community, but it is consistent with all of the other components of the MUSIC model. Choosing a research topic of interest is empowering, interesting, and probably considered to be more useful, especially when they select a topic that relates to their goals in life. Sharing their knowledge also makes them more of an "expert" on the topic, which should make them feel successful. All of these factors can contribute to creating a motivating and engaging experience that fosters community.

Example C.5.4 – Providing Assignments to Get to Know Students

Provide assignments that allow you to get to know your students on a more personal level. Strategies such as the "requiring students to describe themselves" strategy presented in a prior section certainly falls into this category. But other types of assignments also provide instructors with a window into students' thinking and lives.

Allison Vaillancourt (2016), a Vice President at the University of Arizona, described how she posed a question at the end of every class period and students responded by writing in a journal. She also urged students to write about any concepts or concerns they had about the course and she read their writing and provided responses each week. Although this assignment might be effective for many reasons, I want to focus on the reason most related to helping students fit into the school culture. Dr. Vaillancourt found that "students began using their journals to ask for advice on school, careers, and even university and community resources. I began to provide academic, career, and life advice on a weekly basis" (para. 5). As a result of these intense interactions, she was able to know her students much better, and I suspect that students have learned a lot from her as well, including how to navigate courses and university life.

Example C.5.5 – Helping Students Interpret Social Situations

Provide students with plausible explanations of social situations that may be threatening or detrimental to their perceptions of belonging. Let me give you an example in the discipline of engineering because women can face a "chilly climate" in engineering programs and professions. Social-belonging and affirmation training interventions have been developed to help first-year women in college feel that they belong in engineering and the results have led to increases in their achievement (Walton, Logel, Peach, Spencer, & Zanna, 2015). Briefly, the social-belonging intervention used in a Walton et al. (2015) study "emphasized that both men and women worry about being treated with respect at first in engineering, but this improves with time; and that even when women do not share some interests with men, they share common interests in engineering" (p. 472). In another study, researchers used similar interventions to help African-American students interpret possible difficulties in their first year college (Walton & Cohen, 2007). Instructors in a variety of disciplines could use similar strategies to help students recognize that difficulties are not unusual and they can be overcome.

It may be helpful to invite upper-level students to your class to explain the struggles they faced as beginning students and how they overcame them over time. Or, create videos of upper-level students providing this type of explanation so that you can use the videos in future semesters or in an online class. In the intervention by Walton et al. (2015), they used a variety of quotations from upper-level students, such as: "When I first got to Waterloo, I worried that I was different from the other students... Now it seems ironic— everybody feels different first year, when really we're all going through the same things" (p. 472-473). These types of interventions can help students realize that their experiences don't necessarily mean that they don't belong; instead, these are common experiences that can be overcome in time.

CHAPTER 9

The MUSIC® Model of Motivation Theory and Research

The purpose of this chapter is to provide a brief explanation about the development of the MUSIC model and research studies directly involving the MUSIC model. This chapter is not needed to help you understand how to effectively *implement* the MUSIC model; therefore, you can skip this chapter if your primary interest is in *using* the MUSIC model.

Why is the MUSIC model needed?

The impetus for developing the MUSIC model arose from my inability to effectively teach university students how to motivate their future or current students (most of my students planned to become teachers or professors and some of them were already teachers who were obtaining a graduate degree in education). In my courses, I thought I'd taught my students all of the relevant motivation theories; but by the end of a course, many of them couldn't readily identify and select appropriate motivation strategies for their instructional design. Instead, they were overwhelmed with the variety of theories, jargon, and overlap among similar motivational concepts.

I also found that effective teachers and professors often learned how to motivate students by trial-and-error, relying on strategies that they experienced as students or that they had used successfully in the past. And who could blame them? What else could they do? An integrated motivation model that incorporated current perspectives of motivation theory simply did not exist (Wentzel & Wigfield, 2009, p. 6). These problems motivated me to find a way to help students and practicing instructors more easily comprehend and implement motivational teaching strategies. The MUSIC model appears to have been successful in achieving my goals, as evidenced by the feedback I've received, including comments such as this statement from a book commissioned by the American Association of State Colleges and Universities:

> *"While academic motivation theories and practices abound, we believe the MUSIC model is especially useful...It is not only inclusive, evidence-based and research-validated, it is also versatile and applied—which makes it relatively straightforward, and therefore, easier to implement, either on campus or online."* (Aldridge & Harvatt, 2014, p. 54)

How was the MUSIC model developed?

I developed the MUSIC model over the span of a decade using an inductive and iterative approach. I found that authors of motivation-related textbooks, handbooks, and journal articles provided implications for instructors based on particular motivation theories. I reviewed as many of these sources and other sources I could find, and I identified patterns in the teaching strategies provided in these sources. These patterns allowed me to group similar motivation strategies together, regardless of the theory from which they were derived. For example, the strategy, "provide students with choices" is one that can be attributed to self-determination theory, flow theory, interest theories, goal orientation theories, expectancy-value theory, and others (Schunk, Meece, & Pintrich, 2014). Although these theories are important, the practical implication for instructors is the same: instructors should provide students with choices to increase students' motivation.

After I developed some initial conceptual groups of motivation strategies, I tried them out in undergraduate and graduate courses at a variety of universities (e.g., Duke University, the University of South Florida St. Petersburg, and Virginia Tech). Over several years, I examined how the groups of strategies facilitated students' conceptual and practical understanding of the motivational strategies. I revised the strategy groups several times over 10 years until I found groups that (a) included the teaching implications of current motivation theories and (b) were easily understandable to students and teachers in ways that would help them design and implement instruction consistent with these theories.

As a result of this approach, I ended-up with five groups of strategies that I labeled using words that were understandable to students and teachers, and that best described the essence of the strategy group: empowerment, usefulness, success, interest, and caring. I presented the MUSIC model formally in an academic journal article in 2009 (Jones, 2009). Since then, I've worked with colleagues and students to use quantitative methods to provide further validity evidence for the five components of the MUSIC model (Jones, Li, & Cruz, 2017; Jones & Skaggs, 2016; Jones & Sigmon, 2016; Jones & Wilkins, 2013; Parkes, Jones, & Wilkins, 2015;

Schram & Jones, 2016). I've also developed the MUSIC Model of Academic Motivation Inventory (Jones, 2017; available at www.theMUSICmodel.com) to assess students' perceptions of the five MUSIC model components.

What theories and research were used to identify the principles of the MUSIC model?

Sometimes people tell me that the MUSIC model is only a combination of this theory and that theory, or three particular theories. That is simply not true. While it may be true that you can identify many MUSIC model strategies by combining only a few theories, that's not the way that I developed the MUSIC model. I developed the model by examining many theories, some of which I list in this section. My intent in creating the model was to be inclusive of as many theories as possible.

Near the beginning of Chapters 4, 5, 6, 7, and 8, I provided a very brief explanation of the primary theories that are most directly relevant to the strategies in the MUSIC model. In this section I list those theories and a few others. This alphabetical list represents *some* of the primary references to *some* of the main theories and research studies that I used to create the MUSIC model; it is not intended to be a comprehensive list:

- arousal theories (Berlyne, 1960; Duffy, 1957),
- attachment theory (Ainsworth, 1979; Bowlby, 1969),
- attribution theory (Weiner, 1986; 2000),
- behaviorist theories (Skinner, 1953; Skinner & Epstein, 1982),
- belonging theories (Baumeister & Leary, 1995; Goodenow, 1993),
- caring theories (Johnson, Johnson, & Anderson, 1983; Noddings, 1984, 1992; Wentzel, 1999),
- competence theories (Elliot & Dweck, 2005; Harter, 1978; White, 1959),
- domain identification theory (Osborne & Jones, 2011)
- emotion theories (Pekrun, 2009),
- expectancy-value theory (Eccles et al., 1983; Wigfield & Eccles, 2000);
- flow theory (Csikszentmihalyi, 1990),
- future time perspective theory (Lens, 1988; Lewin, 1942; Nuttin & Lens, 1985)
- goal orientation theories (Ames, 1992; Elliot, 1999; Maehr & Midgley, 1991; Nicholls, 1984),
- goal setting theories (Locke & Latham, 2002)
- goal theories (Ford, 1992; Locke & Latham, 2002),

- identity and identification theories (Finn, 1989; James, 1890/1981; Voelkl, 1997),
- interest theories (Hidi & Renninger, 2006; Krapp, 2005; Schraw & Lehman, 2001),
- locus of control (deCharms, 1968, 1976)
- rewards and intrinsic/extrinsic motivation theories (Cameron & Pierce, 1994; Deci, 1975; Deci, Koestner, & Ryan, 1999; Deci & Ryan, 1985),
- self-concept theories (Marsh, 1990; Shavelson & Bolus, 1982),
- self-determination theory (Deci & Ryan, 1985, 2000),
- self-efficacy theory (Bandura, 1977, 1986, 1997; Pajares, 1996),
- self-esteem theories (Rosenberg, 1979),
- self-regulation theories (Bandura, 1986; Pintrich & de Groot, 1990; Zimmerman, 2000),
- self-theories of intelligence (Dweck, 1999, 2006; Mueller & Dweck, 1998);
- self-worth theories (Covington, 1992),
- social cognitive theory (Bandura, 1986, 1997), and
- stereotype theories (Aronson & Steele, 2005).

As you can see from this long list of theories, I used motivation strategies that were derived from many different theoretical perspectives when I created the MUSIC model. It's beyond the scope of this book to explain how each of these theories contributed to the model development; however, I have provided some explanations about these relationships in Jones (2016) and in my videos available on my YouTube channel (www.youtube.com/c/brettdjones).

What is the MUSIC Model of Motivation Theory?

The MUSIC® Model of Motivation Theory is explained in Chapter 2. The theory is comprised of a combination of concepts and principles discovered by many researchers over many years. It can be represented graphically as the cycle shown Chapter 2 (please see Chapter 2 for further explanation). A distinguishing feature of the MUSIC model theory is that it specifies five categories of teaching strategies (empowerment, usefulness, success, interest, and caring) as the means through which instructors can most directly affect students' motivation, engagement, and learning. Other researchers have noted the importance of one or more of these categories, but I haven't found another theory that specifies these components as the five distinct categories to consider when designing instruction to motivate students. Theories that do include all five of these components may combine one or more MUSIC constructs or further divide the components into more groups of strategies. In creating the MUSIC model, I wanted to adhere to Occam's razor (the law of parsimony) in order to select the simplest solution that provided a fairly comprehensive explanation. It may be possible to subdivide some of the MUSIC components into further subcategories (Jones & Wilkins, 2013); but doing so unnecessarily complicates the model and, to date, I have not found that subdividing the MUSIC categories provides any significant *practical benefit* to the instructor or students.

Although researchers have provided evidence for many pieces of the model, only since the introduction of the MUSIC model (Jones, 2009) has research begun more earnestly on examining the model with all five MUSIC components included. I encourage researchers studying motivation to not only consider some of the MUSIC model components (e.g., students' perceptions of empowerment/autonomy, usefulness/value, interest), but to include all five MUSIC model components because it is not yet understood how the five MUSIC model components affect each other in different contexts. For example, research by Hulleman and Harackiewicz (2009) documented that a strategy focused on the *usefulness* of science content increased ninth-grade students' *interest* and achievement, but only for students who initially had low *expectations for success*. This study provides vital information about the relationships that can exist between three of the MUSIC model components (i.e., usefulness, interest, success) that would not have been possible if the researchers hadn't included all of these components in their study. Further research is needed to examine whether or not the other two MUSIC model components (empowerment and caring) affect or are affected by changes in usefulness, interest, and success perceptions.

What research has been conducted using the MUSIC model?

The purpose of this section is to summarize some of the research that has been conducted using the MUSIC model. For the most comprehensive and recent information, please visit the "Research" section of my website (www.theMUSICmodel.com).

Since my first explanation of the MUSIC model in a journal article (Jones, 2009), several presentations and articles have been produced to explain the various ways that the MUSIC model can be *used in instruction*, including: in online courses for college students (Jones, 2012b), in "flipping" the classroom for college students (Jones, 2015a), in mental health clinics (Jones, 2015b), in reading instruction with elementary school students (Chittum & Jones, 2015), in educational psychology and motivation courses for college students (Jones, 2016), and in the Reggio Emilia approach to preschool education (Gardner & Jones, 2016).

Empirical research using the MUSIC model can be roughly divided into the three major categories described here and in the following three sub-sections.

1. Examining Students' Motivation
   - These studies use the MUSIC model as a framework to examine students' motivation. Teaching implications often result from these examinations and are often discussed in these studies.
2. Fostering Domain Identification
   - These studies investigate relationships among students' perceptions of the MUSIC model in a course and their identification with (i.e., how much they value) the subject area in the course.
3. Measuring MUSIC Components
   - These studies examine the development and use of different measures (e.g., surveys, interview questions, observation forms) to assess students' MUSIC perceptions.

MUSIC Model Research Related to Examining Students' Motivation

Studies that use the MUSIC model to examine students' motivation vary widely with respect to the school level and subject areas investigated. Table 9.1 includes some examples of the types of studies that have been conducted in higher education settings (the studies are arranged in order from medical school to undergraduate education in alphabetical order by courses/subject areas).

Table 9.1. *Studies in Higher Education That Use the MUSIC Model*

Study Authors and Date	School Level	Courses/Subject Areas
Le, Le, & Pham, 2014	medical school	medical school course
Hall, Jones, Amelink, & Hu, 2013	graduate	nuclear engineering
Martin & Morris, 2017	graduate	teaching composition
Scala, Tomasi, Goncher, & Bursic, 2017	undergraduate	analytics
Kavousi & Miller, 2014a	undergraduate	architecture design studio
Kavousi & Miller, 2014b	undergraduate	architecture design studio

Continued...

Continued...

Chittum, McConnell, & Sible 2017	undergraduate	cancer biology
Dockter, Uvarov, Guzman-Alvarez, & Molinaro, 2017	undergraduate	chemistry
Kafura, Bart, & Chowdhury, 2015	undergraduate	computational thinking
Bart, Whitcomb, Kafura, Shaffer, & Tilevich, 2017	undergraduate	computational thinking
Smith-Orr & Garnett, 2016	undergraduate	computer programming
Jones, Ruff, Snyder, Petrich, & Koonce, 2012	undergraduate	educational psychology
Jones, Tendhar, & Paretti, 2016	undergraduate	engineering
Lee, Brozina, Amelink, & Jones, 2017	undergraduate	engineering
Matusovich, Jones, Paretti, Moore, & Hunter, 2011	undergraduate	engineering
Matusovich, Paretti, Jones, & Brown, 2012	undergraduate	engineering
Mora, Anorbe-Diaz, Gonzalez-Marrero, Martin-Gutierrez, & Jones, 2017	undergraduate	engineering
Jones, Epler, Mokri, Bryant, & Paretti, 2013	undergraduate	engineering capstone courses
Lee, Seimetz, & Amelink, 2014	undergraduate	engineering summer program
Lee, Kajfez, & Matusovich, 2013	undergraduate	engineering support center
Jones, Li, & Lu, 2015	undergraduate	English
Tu & Jones, 2017	undergraduate	neuroscience
Jones, 2010	undergraduate	personal health
Cretu, 2014	undergraduate	pedagogy
Jones, 2012a	undergraduate	personal health
Jones, Watson, Rakes, & Akalin, 2013	undergraduate	personal health
McGinley & Jones, 2014	undergraduate	psychology

Researchers have also used the MUSIC model in preK-12 settings as is evidenced by the studies presented in Table 9.2 (the studies are arranged in order from high school to preschool in alphabetical order by courses/subject areas).

Table 9.2. *Studies in Pre-K to 12 Schools That Use the MUSIC Model*

Study Authors and Date	School Level	Courses/Subject Areas
Evans, Jones, & Akalin, in press	high school	biology
Evans, Jones, & Biedler, 2014	high school	biology
Martin, 2014	high school	English
Remijan, 2017	high school	mathematics
Chittum & Jones, 2017	middle school	science
Chittum, Jones, Akalin, & Schram, 2017	middle school	science/engineering
Schnittka, Brandt, Jones, & Evans, 2012	middle school	science/engineering
Jones, Sahbaz, Schram, & Chittum, 2017	middle school	science/engineering
Jones, Chittum, et al., 2015	middle school	science/engineering
Williams, 2013	elementary	literacy
Chu Yew Yee, 2015	elementary	all
Chittum & Jones, 2015	elementary	reading
Gardner & Jones, 2016	preschool	all

MUSIC Model Research Related to Fostering Domain Identification

Evidence from several studies suggests a positive relationship between students' perceptions of the MUSIC model components in a course and their identification with the subject/field of the course (see Table 9.3). For example, students in a first-year undergraduate engineering course who rated the course higher on the MUSIC components were more likely to be more highly identified with engineering and to plan to pursue engineering as a career (Jones et al., 2014).

Table 9.3. *Studies Examining Relationships Between the MUSIC Variables and Domain identification*

Study Authors and Date	School Level	Courses/Subject Areas
Smith-Orr & Garnett, 2016	undergraduate	computer programming
Jones, Osborne, Paretti, & Matusovich, 2014	undergraduate	engineering
Jones, Tendhar, & Paretti, 2016	undergraduate	engineering
Ruff & Jones, 2016	undergraduate	engineering
Tendhar, Singh, & Jones, 2017	undergraduate	engineering
Jones, Sahbaz, Schram, & Chittum, 2017	middle school	science

When students are more highly identified with a subject or field, that means that they value the subject/field as part of their identity (i.e., as part of their Self), which then, makes them more likely to consider that subject/field as a career (see Figure 9.1).

Increased MUSIC perceptions in a class in a particular subject/field → A higher level of identification in that subject/field → Increased likelihood of a career in that subject/field

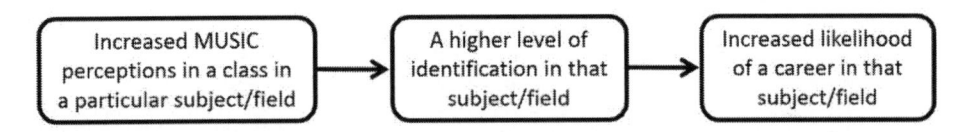

Figure 9.1. *Students' course perceptions can affect the likelihood they choose a career in that discipline.*

The implications of this research are very important because it presents a means through which *teachers* can influence students' beliefs about their careers (of course, other external factors also play an important role, such as parents, peers, and the culture in which students live). It makes sense that students who are motivated and engaged in their courses would consider those course subject/field areas for careers.

Research Related to Measuring MUSIC Components

To assess students' perceptions of the five MUSIC model components, it's useful to have a valid quantitative measure, such as a questionnaire, that can be administered to students quickly and easily. Researchers have been measuring students' perceptions of constructs related to the MUSIC model components for decades;

however, they haven't been measuring all five perceptions in the same study. Rather, they measured only the MUSIC-related constructs that were directly related to the motivation theory they were studying. This approach is appropriate for that purpose. However, to measure students' perceptions of all five of the MUSIC components with items formatted similarly and rated on the same scale, it became necessary to develop a new measure. Therefore, I developed the MUSIC® Model of Academic Motivation Inventory (shortened to the *MUSIC Inventory*; Jones, 2017) to provide the means to measure students' perceptions of all five MUSIC model components with one inventory on the same scale.

The MUSIC Inventory has been validated for use with students of various ages and in different cultural settings, as is evidenced by the list of published peer-reviewed journal articles provided in Table 9.4 (the studies are arranged in order from college to elementary school in alphabetical order by language). The MUSIC inventory has also been translated to other languages and the research is ongoing on five continents (we haven't used it in Australia or Antarctica yet). All of the different versions of the MUSIC Inventory are available in the *User Guide* at www.theMUSICmodel.com.

Table 9.4. *Studies Providing Validity Evidence for the MUSIC Inventory*

Study Authors and Date	MUSIC Inventory Version	Language	Country of Participants
Mohamed, Soliman, & Jones, 2013	college	Arabic	Egypt
Jones, Li, & Cruz, 2017	college	Chinese & Spanish	China & Columbia
Jones & Skaggs, 2016	college	English	U.S.
Pace, Ham, Poole, & Wahaib, 2016	college	English	U.S.
Tendhar, Singh, & Jones, 2017	college	English	U.S.
Chittum & Jones, 2017	middle/high school	English	U.S.
Jones, Sahbaz, Schram, & Chittum, 2017	middle/high school	English	U.S.
Parkes, Jones, & Wilkins, 2015	middle/high school	English	U.S.
Schram & Jones, 2016	middle/high school	Icelandic	Iceland
Jones & Sigmon, 2016	elementary school	English	U.S.

Note: Some of these studies examined the factor structure of the MUSIC Inventory scales (e.g., through confirmatory factor analysis) as part of a study in which validation of the MUSIC Inventory scores wasn't the primary aim.

The fact that the inventory produces valid scores in different cultures provides further evidence of the validity of the five-component MUSIC model. That is, similar to U.S. students, students in other cultures also perceive empowerment, usefulness, success, interest, and caring as separate components in their learning environments.

Several studies have also used qualitative approaches to assess students' MUSIC perceptions. For example, some researchers have interviewed students about their MUSIC perceptions (e.g., Evans et al., 2012; Jones, Epler, et al., 2013) and other researchers have asked open-ended items on questionnaires, typically along with the MUSIC Inventory items (e.g., Jones, Watson, et al., 2012). Examples of interview and open-ended items are provided in the *User Guide* at www.theMUSICmodel.com.

Afterword

As I look back at the strategies and examples in this book, I don't see anything magical or any silver bullets that can be used to solve all student motivation problems. Instead, I see a variety of strategies and examples based on well-grounded research and theories. My final few suggestions for you are provided here.

1. Pay attention to details. Some of these ideas may seem trivial and unimportant, but they may have large effects on students' MUSIC perceptions.

2. Plan, plan some more, and then make sure your plan is ready to implement. I encourage you to try new ideas and make last-minute changes as needed, but effective teaching requires you to think through all aspects of the course design ahead of time.

3. Reflect on your teaching. Use your own observations, feedback from students, and other sources of data to learn about your teaching. The only way to improve is to know what you did well and not so well, and then make changes to address the things that didn't work so well.

Good luck and contact me if you find something that worked great (or not so great) or have any questions. I continue to learn from individuals like you, so I enjoy the feedback I receive and I will try to use it to improve the next edition of this book.

References

Adelson, A. (2015, December 3). *A changed Larry Fedora has North Carolina rolling*. Retrieved from http://www.espn.com/blog/acc/post/_/id/88972/a-changed-larry-fedora-has-north-carolina-rolling

Ainsworth, M. D. S. (1979). Infant-mother attachment. *The American Psychologist, 34*(10), 932-937.

Aldridge, S. C., & Harvatt, K. (2014). *Wired for success: Real-world solutions for transforming higher education*. Washington, DC: American Association of State Colleges and Universities.

Ames, C. (1992). Classrooms: Goals, structures, and student motivation. *Journal of Educational Psychology, 84*, 261-271.

Anderman, E. M., & Patrick, H. (2012). Achievement goal theory, conceptualization of ability/intelligence, and classroom climate. In S. L. Christenson, A. L. Reschly, & C. Wylie (Eds.). *Handbook of research on student engagement* (pp. 173–192). New York, NY: Springer. http://dx.doi.org/10.1007/978-1-4614-2018-7_8

Aronson, J., & Steele, C. M. (2005). Stereotypes and the fragility of academic competence, motivation, and self-concept. In A. J. Elliot, & C. S. Dweck (Eds.), *Handbook of competence and motivation (pp. 436-456)* New York: Guilford.

Assor, A., Kaplan, H., Kanat-Maymon, Y., & Roth, G. (2005). Directly controlling teacher behaviors as predictors of poor motivation and engagement in girls and boys: The role of anger and anxiety. *Learning and Instruction, 15*(5), 397–413.

Atkinson, J. (1964). *An introduction to motivation*. Princeton, NJ: Van Nostrand.

AZ Quotes (2015a). *Brian Tracy*. Retrieved from http://www.azquotes.com/quote/850390

AZ Quotes (2015b). *Joe Paterno*. Retrieved from http://www.azquotes.com/quote/226070

AZ Quotes (2015c). *Saint Augustine*. Retrieved from http://www.azquotes.com/quote/547787

AZ Quotes (2017). *Andy Grove*. Retrieved from http://www.azquotes.com/quote/740591

Baird, T. D., Kniola, D. J., Lewis, A. L., & Fowler, S. B. (2015). Pink time: Evidence of self-regulated learning and academic motivation among undergraduate students, *Journal of Geography, 114*(4), 146-157.

Bandura, A. (1977). Self-efficacy: Toward a unifying theory of behavior change. *Psychological Review, 84*, 191-215.

Bandura, A. (1986). *Social foundations of thought and action: A social cognitive theory.* Englewood Cliffs, NJ: Prentice-Hall.

Bandura, A. (1997). *Self-efficacy: The exercise of control.* New York: Freeman.

Barnes, L. B., Christensen, C. R., & Hansen, A. J. (1994). *Teaching and the case method* (3rd ed.). Boston: Harvard Business School Press.

Barron, B. J. S., Schwartz, D. L., Vye, N. J., Moore, A., Petrosino, A., Zech, L., & Bransford, J. D. (1998). Doing with understanding: Lessons from research on problem- and project-based learning. *The Journal of the Learning Sciences, 7*(3-4), 271–311.

Bart, A. C., Whitcomb, R., Kafura, D., Shaffer, C. A., & Tilevich, E. (2017, March). *Computing with CORGIS: Diverse, real-world datasets for introductory computing.* Paper presented at 2017 ACM SIGCSE Technical Symposium. Seattle, WA. doi:10.1145/3017680.3017708

Bartlett, J. (2002). *Bartlett's familiar quotations* (17th ed.). Boston: Little, Brown and Company.

Bates, S., & Lister, A. (2013, September 23). *Acceptable technology in the classroom: Let the students decide.* Retrieved from http://www.pedagogyunbound.com/tips-index/2013/9/23/acceptable-technology-in-the-classroom-let-students-decide

Baumeister, R., & Leary, M. (1995). The need to belong: Desire for interpersonal attachments as a fundamental human motivation. *Psychological Bulletin, 117,* 497-529.

Berlyne, D. E. (1960). *Conflict, arousal, and curiosity.* New York: McGraw-Hill.

Bernard, L. C. (2012). Evolved individual differences in human motivation. In R. M. Ryan (Ed.), *The Oxford handbook of human motivation* (pp. 381-407). Oxford, England: Oxford University Press.

Bong, M., & Skaalvik, E. M. (2003). Academic self-concept and self-efficacy: How different are they really? *Educational Psychology Review, 15*(1), 1-40.

Boucher, E. (2016, September 2). *It's time to ditch our deadlines.* ChronicleVitae. Retrieved from https://chroniclevitae.com/news/1531-it-s-time-to-ditch-our-deadlines

Bowlby, J. (1969). *Attachment (vol. I).* New York: Basic.

BrainyQuote (2015a). *Joseph Brodsky quotes.* Retrieved from http://www.brainyquote.com/quotes/quotes/j/josephbrod119969.html

BrainyQuote (2015b). *Zhuangzi quotes.* Retrieved from http://www.brainyquote.com/quotes/quotes/z/zhuangzi167907.html

Buzan, T., & Buzan, B. (1993). *The mind map book: How to use radiant thinking to maximize your brain's untapped potential.* New York: Plume.

Cameron, J., & Pierce, W. D. (1994). Reinforcement, reward, and intrinsic motivation: A meta-analysis. *Review of Educational Research, 64,* 363-423.

Cerasoli, C. P., Nicklin, J. M., & Nassrelgrgawi, A. S. (2016). Performance, incentives, and needs for autonomy, competence, and relatedness: A meta-analysis. *Motivation and Emotion, 40,* 781-813.

Cheng, M. (2016, July 27). Attracting more women to study STEM in a world full of geek dude stereotypes. *Forbes.* Retrieved at http://www.forbes.com/sites/michellecheng/2016/07/27/attracting-more-women-to-study-stem-in-a-world-full-of-geek-dude-stereotypes/

Chi, M. T. H., & Wylie, R. (2014). The ICAP Framework: Linking cognitive engagement to active learning outcomes. *Educational Psychologist, 49*(4), 219-243.

Chittum, J. R., & Jones, B. D. (2015). Motivating students to engage during reading instruction: Intentionally designing instruction using a model of academic motivation. *Ohio Reading Teacher, 45*(1), 29-40.

Chittum, J., & Jones, B. D. (2017). Identifying pre-high school students' science class motivation profiles to increase their science identification and persistence. *Journal of Educational Psychology.* Advance online publication. doi:10.1037/edu0000176

Chittum, J. R., Jones, B. D., Akalin, S., & Schram, A. B. (2017). The effects of an afterschool STEM program on students' motivation and engagement. *International Journal of STEM Education, 4*(11), 1-16. doi:10.1186/s40594-017-0065-4

Chittum, J. R., McConnell, K. D., & Sible, J. (2017). SCALE(ing)-UP teaching: A case study of student motivation in an undergraduate course. *Journal of Excellence in College Teaching, 28*(3).

Christenson, S. L., Reschly, A. L., & Wylie, C. (2012). Epilogue. In S. L. Christenson, A. L. Reschly, & C. Wylie (Eds.), *Handbook of research on student engagement* (pp. 813-817). New York: Springer.

ChronicleVitae (2016, July 29). *"Dear Forums...": Jedi mind tricks in the classroom.* Retrieved from https://chroniclevitae.com/news/1493-dear-forums-jedi-mind-tricks-in-the-classroom

Chu Yew Yee, S. L. (2015). Performative authoring: Nurturing Children's creativity and creative self-efficacy through digitally-augmented enactment-based storytelling.

Doctoral Dissertation, Department of Architecture, Texas A&M University. College Station, TX.

Covington, M. V. (1992). *Making the grade: A self-worth perspective on motivation and school reform.* New York: Cambridge University Press.

Covington, M. (2009). Self-worth theory: Retrospection and prospects. In K. R. Wentzel & A. Wigfield (Eds.), *Handbook of motivation at school* (pp. 141-169). New York: Routledge.

Cretu, D. M. (2014). A model for promoting academic motivation. *Procedia – Social and Behavioral Sciences, 180,* 751-758.

Crouch, C. H., & Mazur, E. (2001). Peer instruction: Ten years of experience and results. *American Journal of Physics, 69*(9), 970-977.

Csikszentmihalyi, M. (1990). *Flow: The psychology of optimal experience.* New York: HarperPerennial.

Daves, V. (2015). Pocket Ppoints app rewards students for staying off their phones in class. *USA Today College.* Retrieved from http://college.usatoday.com/2015/09/23/pocket-points-app/

DeCharms, R. (1976). *Enhancing motivation: Change in the classroom.* New York: Irvington.

DeCharms, R. (1968). *Personal causation: The internal affective determinants of behavior.* New York: Academic Press.

Deci, E. L. (1975). *Intrinsic motivation.* New York: Plenum Press.

Deci, E. L., Koestner, R., & Ryan, R. M. (1999). A meta-analytic review of experiments examining the effects of extrinsic rewards on intrinsic motivation. *Psychological Bulletin, 125*(6), 627-668.

Deci, E. L., & Ryan, R. M. (1985). *Intrinsic motivation and self-determination in human behavior.* New York: Plenum.

Deci, E. L., & Ryan, R. M. (1991). A motivational approach to self: Integration in personality. In R. Dientsbier (Ed.), *Nebraska symposium on motivation (Vol. 38).* Lincoln: University of Nebraska Press.

Deci, E. L., & Ryan, R. M. (2000). The "what" and "why" of goal pursuits: Human needs and the self-determination of behavior. *Psychological Inquiry, 11*(4), 227-268.

Delpit, L. (2006). *Other people's children: Cultural conflict in the classroom.* New York: The New Press.

Deresiewicz, W. (2014, August 14). *Spirit Guides.* Retrieved from http://www.slate.com/articles/life/education/2014/08/the_best_teachers_and_p

rofessors_resemble_parental_figures_they_provide.single.html (excerpted from *Excellent Sheep: The Miseducation of the American Elite and The Way to a Meaningful Life* by William Deresiewicz, 2014).

Dick, W., Carey, L., & Carey, J. O. (2015). *The systematic design of instruction* (8th ed.). Boston: Pearson.

Dietrich, J., Viljaranta, J., Moeller, J., & Kracke, B. (2017). Situational expectancies and task values: Associations with students' effort. *Learning and Instruction, 47*, 53-64.

Dockter, D., Uvarov, C., Guzman-Alvarez, A., & Molinaro, M. (2017). Improving preparation and persistence in undergraduate STEM: Why an online summer preparatory chemistry course makes sense. In P. M. Sorensen & D. A. Canelas (Eds.), *Online Approaches to Chemical Education* (pp. 7-33). Washington, DC: American Chemical Society. doi:10.1021/bk-2017-1261

Doolittle, P. E., Hicks, D., Triplett, C. F., Nichols, W. D., & Young, C. A. (2006). Reciprocal Teaching for reading comprehension in higher education: A strategy for fostering the deeper understanding of texts. *International Journal of Teaching and Learning in Higher Education, 17*(2), 106-118.

Donachie, P. (2017, August 17). Data analysis helps SCSU improve student outcomes. *EducationDIVE*. Retrieved from http://www.educationdive.com/news/data-analysis-helps-scsu-improve-student-outcomes/449500/

Duffy, E. (1957). The psychological significance of the concept of "arousal" or "activation." *The Psychological Review, 64*(5), 265-275.

Durik, A. M., Shechter, O. G., Noh, M., Rozek, C. S., & Harackiewicz, J. M. (2015). What if I can't? Success expectancies moderate the effects of utility value information on situational interest and performance. *Motivation and Emotion, 39*, 104-118. doi:10.1007/s11031-014-9419-0

Duvall, S. (n.d.). *Creating a games class: A walkthrough*. Retrieved from http://facstaff.elon.edu/sduvall2/

Dweck, C. S. (1999). *Self-theories: Their role in motivation, personality, and development*. Philadelphia: Psychology Press.

Dweck, C. S. (2006). *Mindset: The new psychology of success*. New York: Random House.

Eccles, J. S., Adler, T. F., Futterman, R., Goff, S. B., Kaczala, C. M., Meece, J. L., & Midgley, C. (1983). Expectancies, values, and academic behaviors. In J. T. Spence (Ed.), *Achievement and achievement motivation* (pp. 75-146). San Francisco, CA: Freeman.

EDUCAUSE (2008). *7 things you should know about Second Life*. Retrieved from http://www.educause.edu/library/resources/7-things-you-should-know-about-second-life

Eggen, P. D., & Kauchak, D. P. (2001). *Strategies for teachers: Teaching content and thinking skills*. Boston: Allyn & Bacon.

Elliot, A. J. (1999). Approach and avoidance motivation and achievement goals. *Educational Psychologist, 34*, 169-189.

Elliot, A. J., & Dweck, C. S. (2005). Competence and motivation: Competence as the core of achievement motivation. In A. J. Elliot, & C. S. Dweck (Eds.), *Handbook of competence and motivation* (pp. 3-12). New York: Guilford.

Evans, M. A., Jones, B. D., & Akalin, S. (in press). Motivating students with game design in out-of-school environments. *Afterschool Matters*.

Evans, M. A., Jones, B. D., & Biedler, J. (2014). Video games, motivation, and learning. In F. C. Blumberg (Ed.), *Learning by playing: Video gaming in education* (pp. 273-289). New York, NY: Oxford University Press.

Finckel, J. (2015, November 3). *The silent professor*. Retrieved from https://www.facultyfocus.com/articles/teaching-and-learning/the-silent-professor/

Finn, J. D. (1989). Withdrawing from school. *Review of Educational Research, 59*(2), 117-142.

Ford, M. (1992). *Motivating humans: goals, emotions, and personal agency beliefs*. Newbury Park, CA: Sage.

Foss, D. J., & Pirozzolo, J. W. (2017). Four semesters investigating frequency of testing, the testing effect, and transfer of training. *Journal of Educational Psychology, 109*(8), 1067-1083.

Fredricks, J. A., Blumenfeld, P. C., & Paris, A. H. (2004). School engagement: Potential of the concept, state of the evidence. *Review of Educational Research, 74*(1), 59-109.

Froiland, J. M., & Davison, M. L. (2016). The longitudinal influences of peers, parents, motivation, and mathematics course-taking on high school math achievement. *Learning and Individual Differences, 50*, 252-259.

Froiland, J. M., & Worrell, F. C. (2016). Intrinsic motivation, learning goals, engagement, and achievement in a diverse high school. *Psychology in the Schools, 53*, 321-336.

Gardner, A. F., & Jones, B. D. (2016). Examining the Reggio Emilia approach: Keys to understanding why it motivates students. *Electronic Journal of Research in Educational Psychology, 14*(3), 602-625.

Garlock, S. (2015, July-August). Is Small Beautiful? Online education beyond the MOOC. *Harvard Magazine*. Retrieved from http://harvardmagazine.com/2015/07/is-small-beautiful

Gazzaley, A., & Rosen, L. D. (2016). *The distracted mind: Ancient brains in a high-tech world.* Cambridge, MA: MIT Press.

Gehlbach, H., Brinkworth, M. E., King, A. M., Hsu, L. M., McIntyre, J., & Rogers, T. (2016). Creating birds of similar feathers: Leveraging similarity to improve teacher-student relationships and academic achievement. *Journal of Educational Psychology, 108,* 342–352.

Gilley, B. H., & Clarkston, B. (2014). Collaborative testing: Evidence of learning in a controlled in-class study of undergraduate students. *Journal of College Science Teaching, 43*(3), 83-91.

Goldman, R., & Papson, S. (1998). *Nike culture: The sign of the swoosh.* Thousand Oaks, CA: Sage.

Gooblar, D. (2015, October 21). Make your office hours a requirement. *ChronicleVitae*. Retrieved from https://chroniclevitae.com/news/1167-make-your-office-hours-a-requirement

Goodenow, C. (1993). Classroom belonging among early adolescent students: Relationship to motivation and achievement. *Journal of Early Adolescence, 13*(1), 21-43.

Gose, B. (2017, October 22). Bringing history alive. *The Chronicle of Higher Education*. Retrieved from http://www.chronicle.com

Green, G. & Watson, E. (2015, July). *Strategies for effectively engaging students in large classes.* Teaching Large Classes Conference. Blacksburg, VA.

Guerrero, M., & Rod, A. B. (2013). Engaging in office hours: A study of student-faculty interaction and academic performance. *Journal of Political Science Education, 9*(4). 403-416.

Hall, S., Jones, B. D., Amelink, C., & Hu, D. (2013). Educational innovation in the design of an online nuclear engineering curriculum. *The Journal of Effective Teaching, 13*(2), 58-72.

Harrison, D. (2009, February 18). *Real-life teaching in a virtual world.* Retrieved from http://campustechnology.com/Articles/2009/02/18/Real-Life-Teaching-in-a-Virtual-World.aspx?Page=2

Hart, T. (2004). Opening the contemplative mind in the classroom. *Journal of Transformative Education, 2*(1), 28-46.

Hartanto, A., & Yang, H. (2016). Is the smartphone a smart choice? The effect of smartphone separation on executive functions. *Computers in Human Behavior, 64,* 329-336.

Harter, S. (1978). Effectance motivation reconsidered: Toward a developmental model. *Human Development, 21,* 34-64.

Harvard Kennedy School of Government. (2017). *Case studies.* Retrieved from https://www.hks.harvard.edu/centers/research-initiatives/crisisleadership/publications/case-studies

Harvard Law School. (2017). *The case study teaching method.* Retrieved from http://casestudies.law.harvard.edu/the-case-study-teaching-method/

Hebb, D. O., Drives and the C.N.S. (Conceptual Nervous System). *The Psychological Review, 62*(4), 243-254.

Hidi, S. (2016). Revisiting the role of rewards in motivation and learning: Implications of neuroscientific research. *Educational Psychology Review, 28,* 61-93. doi:10.1007/s10648-015-9307-5

Hidi, S., & Renninger, K. A. (2006). The four-phase model of interest development. *Educational Psychologist, 41*(2), 111-127.

Hsee, C. K., & Ruan, B. (2016). The Pandora effect: The power and peril of curiosity. *Psychological Science, 27*(5). Advance online publication. doi:10.1177/0956797616631733

Hulleman, C. S., & Harackiewicz, J. M. (2009). Promoting interest and performance in high school science classes. *Science, 326,* 1410–1412.

Hulleman, C. S., Kosovich, J. J., Barron, K. E., & Daniel, D. B. (2017). Making connections: Replicating and extending the utility value intervention in the classroom. *Journal of Educational Psychology, 109*(3), 387-404.

Husman, J., Derryberry, W. P., Crowson, H. M., & Lomax, R. (2004). Instrumentality, task value, and intrinsic motivation: Making sense of their independent interdependence. *Contemporary Educational Psychology, 29,* 63–76.

Husman, J., & Lens, W. (1999). The role of the future in student motivation. *Educational Psychologist, 34,* 113-125.

Institute for the Study of Diplomacy at Georgetown University. (2017). *Case Studies Summaries.* Retrieved from https://casestudies.isd.georgetown.edu/

Ishida, A. (2014-2015). Media and contexts in teaching building materials. *Pedagogy in Practice.* Virginia Tech: University Printing Services.

iz Quotes (2015a). *Albert Einstein quote.* Retrieved from http://izquotes.com/quote/282667

iz Quotes (2015b). *Gail Godwin quote.* Retrieved from http://izquotes.com/quote/72240

iz Quotes (2015c). *Isaac Asimov quote.* Retrieved from http://izquotes.com/quote/207682

iz Quotes (2015d). *Victor Kiam quote.* Retrieved from http://izquotes.com/quote/101731

James, W. (1890/1981). *The Principles of Psychology.* Cambridge, MA: Harvard University Press.

Jang, H. (2008). Supporting students' motivation, engagement, and learning during an uninteresting activity. *Journal of Educational Psychology, 100*(4), 798-811.

Jenkins, R. (2015). Cross-training for the brain. *ChronicleVitae.* Retrieved from https://chroniclevitae.com/news/907-cross-training-for-the-brain

Jenkins, R. (2017, June 19). The "realistic" research paper. *ChronicleVitae.* Retrieved from https://chroniclevitae.com/news/1832-the-realistic-research-paper

Jepma, M., Verdonschot, R. G., van Steenbergen, H., Rombouts, S. A. R. B., & Nieuwenhuis, S. (2012). Neural mechanisms underlying the induction and relief of perceptual curiosity. *Frontiers in Behavioral Neuroscience, 6*, 1-9.

Johnson, D. W., Johnson, R., & Anderson, A. (1983). Social interdependence and classroom climate. *Journal of Psychology, 114*(1), 135-142.

Jones, B. D. (2009). Motivating students to engage in learning: The MUSIC Model of Academic Motivation. *International Journal of Teaching and Learning in Higher Education, 21*(2), 272-285.

Jones, B. D. (2010). An examination of motivation model components in face-to-face and online instruction. *Electronic Journal of Research in Educational Psychology, 8*(3), 915-944.

Jones, B. D. (2012a, August). *Factors that impact students' motivation, instructor ratings, and course ratings in an online course.* Research presented at the International Conference on Motivation 2012. Frankfurt, Germany.

Jones, B. D. (2012b, February). How to motivate students in online courses: Using the MUSIC Model of Academic Motivation to connect research to practice. *Proceedings of the 2012 Conference on Higher Education Pedagogy*, Blacksburg, VA.

Jones, B. D. (2017). *User guide for assessing the components of the MUSIC® Model of Motivation.* Retrieved from http://www.theMUSICmodel.com

Jones, B. D. (2015a, February). Designing a flipped classroom to motivate students. *Proceedings of the 2015 Conference on Higher Education Pedagogy*, Blacksburg, VA.

Jones, B. D. (2015b, June). *Instructional approaches to enhance motivation for learning.* Cognitive Remediation in Psychiatry Conference, Columbia University, New York, New York.

Jones, B. D. (2016). Teaching motivation strategies using the MUSIC® Model of Motivation as a conceptual framework. In M. C. Smith, & N. DeFrates-Densch (Eds.), *Challenges and innovations in educational psychology teaching and learning* (pp. 123-136). Charlotte, NC: Information Age Publishing.

Jones, B. D., Chittum, J. R., Akalin, S., Schram, A. B., Fink, J., Schnittka, C.,...Brandt, C. (2015). Elements of design-based science activities that affect students' motivation. *School Science and Mathematics, 115*(8), 404-415. doi:10.1111/ssm.12143

Jones, B. D., Epler, C. M., Mokri, P., Bryant, L. H., & Paretti, M. C. (2013). The effects of a collaborative problem-based learning experience on students' motivation in engineering capstone courses. *Interdisciplinary Journal of Problem-based Learning, 7*(2). doi:10.7771/1541-5015.1344

Jones, B. D., Li, M., & Cruz, J. M. (2017). A cross-cultural validation of the MUSIC® Model of Academic Motivation Inventory: Evidence from Chinese- and Spanish-speaking university students. *International Journal of Educational Psychology, 6*(1), 366-385. doi:10.17583/ijep.2017.2357.

Jones, B. D., Li, M., & Lu, P. (2015, July). *Using the MUSIC® Model of Motivation to redesign instruction in a large course.* Paper presented at the Conference on Teaching Large Classes, Blacksburg, VA.

Jones, B. D., Llacer-Arrastia, S., & Newbill, P. B. (2009). Motivating foreign language students using self-determination theory. *Innovation in Language Learning and Teaching, 3*(2), 171-189. doi:10.1080/17501220802358210

Jones, B. D., Osborne, J. W., Paretti, M. C., & Matusovich, H. M., (2014). Relationships among students' perceptions of a first-year engineering design course and their engineering identification, motivational beliefs, course effort, and academic outcomes. *International Journal of Engineering Education, 30*(6A), 1340-1356.

Jones, B. D., Ruff, C., & Osborne, J. W. (2015). Fostering students' identification with mathematics and science. In K. A. Renninger, M. Nieswandt, & S. Hidi (Eds.), *Interest in mathematics and science learning* (pp. 331-352). Washington, DC: American Educational Research Association.

Jones, B. D., Ruff, C., Snyder, J. D., Petrich, B., & Koonce, C. (2012). The effects of mind mapping activities on students' motivation. *International Journal for the Scholarship of Teaching and Learning, 6*(1), 1-21.

Jones, B. D., Sahbaz, S., Schram, A. B., & Chittum, J. R. (2017). Using psychological constructs from the MUSIC Model of Motivation to predict students' science identification and career goals: Results from the U.S. and Iceland. *International Journal of Science Education.* Advance online publication. doi:10.1080/09500693.2017.1319093

Jones, B. D., & Sigmon, M. L. (2016). Validation evidence for the elementary school version of the MUSIC® Model of Academic Motivation Inventory. *Electronic Journal of Research in Educational Psychology, 14*(1), 155-174. Retrieved from http://dx.doi.org/10.14204/ejrep.38.15081

Jones, B. D., & Skaggs, G. E. (2016). Measuring students' motivation: Validity evidence for the MUSIC Model of Academic Motivation Inventory. *International Journal for the Scholarship of Teaching and Learning, 10*(1). Retrieved from http://digitalcommons.georgiasouthern.edu/ij-sotl/vol10/iss1/7

Jones, B. D., Tendhar, C., & Paretti, M. C. (2016). The effects of students' course perceptions on their domain identification, motivational beliefs, and goals. *Journal of Career Development, 43*(5), 383-397. doi:10.1177/0894845315603821

Jones, B. D., Watson, J. M., Rakes, L., & Akalin, S. (2012). Factors that impact students' motivation in an online course: Using the MUSIC Model of Academic Motivation. *Journal of Teaching and Learning with Technology, 1*(1), 42-58.

Jones, B. D., & Wilkins, J. L. M. (2013). Testing the MUSIC Model of Academic Motivation through confirmatory factor analysis. *Educational Psychology: An International Journal of Experimental Educational Psychology, 33*(4), 482-503. doi:10.1080/01443410.2013.785044

Joyce, B., Weil, M., & Calhoun, E. (2004). *Models of teaching.* New York: Pearson.

Kafura, D., Bart, A. C., & Chowdhury, B. (2015). Design and preliminary results from a computational thinking course. *Proceedings of the 2015 ACM Conference on Innovation and Technology in Computer Science Education, Lithuania,* 63-68. doi:10.1145/2729094.2742593

Kauffman, D. F., & Husman, J. (2004). Effects of time perspective on student motivation: Introduction to a special issue. *Educational Psychology Review, 16*(1), 1–7. doi:10.1023/B:EDPR.0000012342.37854.58

Kavousi, S., & Miller, P. (2014a, February). *Student motivation and learning in the design studio: Rethinking the MUSIC model.* Proceedings of the 8th International Conference on Design Principles and Practices, Vancouver, Canada.

Kavousi, S., & Miller, P. (2014b, March). *Increasing the academic motivation towards landscape architecture studio course, finding center landscape+values.* CELA 2014 Conference Proceedings University of Maryland, Baltimore, Maryland.

Knight, D. D. (2008). A useful strategy for assessing class participation. *Faculty Focus.* Retrieved from https://www.facultyfocus.com/articles/educational-assessment/educational-assessment-a-useful-strategy-for-assessing-class-participation/

Knowles, E. (Ed.) (2004). *The Oxford dictionary of quotations* (6th ed.). Oxford: Oxford University Press.

Koestner, R., Ryan, R., Bernieri, F., & Holt, K. (1984). Setting limits on children's behavior: The differential effects of controlling vs. informational styles on intrinsic motivation and creativity. *Journal of Personality, 52*(3), 233–248.

Kovas, Y., Malykh, S., & Petrill, S. A. (2014). Genetics for education. In D. Mareschal, B. Butterworth, & A. Tolmie (Eds.), *Educational Neuroscience* (pp. 77-109). West Sussex, UK: John Wiley & Sons.

Krajcik, J. S., & Shin, N. (2014). Project-based learning. In R. K. Sawyer (Ed.), *The Cambridge Handbook of the Learning Sciences* (pp. 275-297). New York, NY: Cambridge University press.

Krapp, A. (2005). Basic needs and the development of interest and intrinsic motivational orientations. *Learning and Instruction, 15*, 381-395.

Lakeoff, G. (2004). *Don't think of an elephant! Know your values and frame the debate.* White River Junction, VT: Chelsea Green Publishing.

Larsen, A. S. (2015). Who cares? Developing a pedagogy of caring in higher education (Doctoral dissertation). Retrieved from http://digitalcommons.usu.edu/etd/4287

Le, H. H., Le, H. D. T., & Pham, B. N. (2014). Applying MUSIC model to explore students' academic motivation in an ESP course. *Sino-US English Teaching, 11*(10), 719-725.

Lee, W. C., Brozina, C., Amelink, C. T., & Jones B. D. (2017). Motivating incoming engineering students with diverse backgrounds: Assessing a summer bridge program's impact on academic motivation. *Journal of Women and Minorities in Science and Engineering, 23*(2), 121-145. doi:10.1615/JWomenMinorScienEng.2017017960

Lee, W. C., Kajfez, R. L., & Matusovich, H. M. (2013). Motivating engineering students: Evaluating an engineering student support center with the MUSIC model of academic motivation, *Journal of Women and Minorities in Science and Engineering, 19*(3), 245-271.

Lee, W. C., Seimetz, C. N., & Amelink, C. T. (2014, June). *Examining the transition to engineering: A multi-case study of six diverse summer bridge program participants.* Paper presented at the ASEE Annual Conference & Exposition, Indianapolis, IN.

Lens, W. (1988). The motivational significance of future time perspective. The homecoming of a concept. *Psychologica, 1,* 27-46.

Leonard, E. (n.d.). *Great expectations: Students and video in higher education: A SAGE white paper.* Retrieved from www.sagepub.com/repository/binaries/pdfs/StudentsandVideo.pdf

Lewin, K. (1942). Time perspective and morale. In G. Watson (Ed.), *Civilian morale* (pp. 48-70). New York: Reynal & Hitchcock.

Light, R. J. (2015, July 31). How to live wisely. *The New York Times.* Retrieved from http://www.nytimes.com/2015/08/02/education/edlife/how-to-live-wisely.html

Lin-Siegler, X., Ahn, J. N., Chen, J., Fang, F.-F. A., & Luna-Lucero, M. (2016). Even Einstein struggled: Effects of learning about great scientists' struggles on high school students' motivation to learn science. *Journal of Educational Psychology, 108*(3), 314-328.

Linnenbrink-Garcia, L., Patall, E. A., & Messersmith, E. E. (2013). Antecedents and consequences of situational interest. *British Journal of Educational Psychology, 83,* 591-614. doi:10.1111/j.2044-8279.2012.02080.x

Locke, E. A., & Latham, G. P. (2002). Building a practically useful theory of goal setting and task motivation: A 35-year odyssey. *American Psychologist, 57,* 705-717.

Locke, E. A., & Latham, G. P. (2006). New directions in goal-setting theory. *Current Directions in Psychological Science, 15*(5), 265-268.

Loftus, M. (2011). Whet their appetite. *PRISM, 20*(7&8). Retrieved from http://www.asee-prism.org/march-april-2011/

Lohani, V. K. (2014-2015). Technology enhanced pedagogy in engineering instruction. *Pedagogy in Practice.* Virginia Tech: University Printing Services.

Maehr, M. L., & Midgley, C. (1991). Enhancing student motivation: A schoolwide approach. *Educational Psychologist, 26,* 399-427.

Marsh, H. W. (1990). A multidimensional, hierarchical self-concept: Theoretical and empirical justification. *Educational Psychology Review, 2,* 77-172.

Marshall, K. (2015, June, 1). *Rethinking Twitter in the classroom.* Retrieved from https://chroniclevitae.com/news/1021-rethinking-twitter-in-the-classroom

Martin, J. (2014). *Motivational factors related to a secondary English teacher's use of new literacies with voice and writing instruction* (Unpublished doctoral dissertation). Virginia Tech, Blacksburg, VA.

Martin, J. M., & Morris, S. L. (2017). Teaching composition together: Democracy, perceptions, and new literacies. *International Journal for the Scholarship of Technology Enhanced Learning, 1*(2), 18-24.

Matos, N. (2017, August, 15). "Don't take our failures personally." ChronicleVitae. Retrieved from https://chroniclevitae.com/news/1880-don-t-take-our-failures-personally

Matusovich, H., Jones, B. D., Paretti, M., Moore, J., & Hunter, D. (2011, June). Problem-based learning: A student perspective on the role of the facilitator. *Proceedings of the 118th American Society for Engineering Education Annual Conference*, Vancouver, Canada.

Matusovich, H. M., Paretti, M., Jones, B. D., & Brown, P. (2012, June). How problem-based learning and traditional engineering design pedagogies influence the motivation of first-year engineering students. *Proceedings of the 119th American Society for Engineering Education Annual Conference*, San Antonio, TX.

Mazur, E. (2012). Eric Mazur shows interactive teaching. Retrieved from https://www.youtube.com/watch?v=wont2v_LZ1E

McGinley, J., & Jones, B. D. (2014). A brief instructional intervention to increase students' motivation on the first day of class. *Teaching of Psychology, 41*(2), 158-162. doi: 10.1177/0098628314530350

Mohamed, H. E., Soliman, M. H., & Jones, B. D. (2013). A cross-cultural validation of the MUSIC Model of Academic Motivation and its associated inventory among Egyptian university students. *Journal of Counseling Quarterly Journal, 36*, 2-14.

Mora, C. E., Anorbe-Diaz, B., Gonzalez-Marrero, A. M., Martin-Gutierrez, J., & Jones, B. D. (2017). Motivational factors to consider when introducing problem-based learning in engineering education courses. *International Journal of Engineering Education, 33*(3), 1000-1017.

Mueller, C. M., & Dweck, C. S. (1998). Praise for intelligence can undermine children's motivation and performance. *Journal of Personality and Social Psychology, 75*(1), 33-52.

Murray, H. A. (1938). *Explorations in Personality.* New York: Oxford University Press.

Myers, G. C. (1914). Recall in relation to retention. *Journal of Educational Psychology, 5,* 119–130. http://dx.doi.org/10.1037/h0075769

Newbury, P. (2013, August 23). *You don't have to wait for the clock to strike to start teaching.* Retrieved from http://www.peternewbury.org/2013/08/you-dont-have-to-wait-for-the-clock-to-strike-to-start-teaching/

Nicholls, J. G. (1984). Achievement motivation: Conceptions of ability, subjective experience, task choice, and performance. *Psychological Review, 91,* 328-346.

Noddings, N. (1984). *Caring: A feminine approach to ethics and moral education.* Berkeley: University of California Press.

Noddings, N. (1992). *The challenge to care in schools: An alternative approach to education.* New York: Teachers College Press.

Noels, K., Clément, R., & Pelletier, L. (1999). Perceptions of teachers' communicative style and students' intrinsic and extrinsic motivation. *The Modern Language Journal, 83*(1), 23–34.

Novak, J. D., & Gowin, D. B. (1984). *Learning how to learn.* New York: Cambridge University Press.

Nuttin, J., & Lens, W. (1985). *Future time perspective and motivation: Theory and research method.* Leuven, Belgium: Leuven University Press.

Ormrod, J. E. (2011). *Our minds, our memories: Enhancing thinking and learning at all ages.* Boston: Pearson.

Ormrod, J. E. (2012). *Human learning* (6th ed.). Upper Saddle River, NJ: Pearson.

Ormrod, J. E., & Jones, B. D. (2018). *Essentials of educational psychology: Big ideas to guide effective teaching* (5th ed.). Boston: Pearson.

Osborne, J. W., & Jones, B. D. (2011). Identification with academics and motivation to achieve in school: How the structure of the self influences academic outcomes. *Educational Psychology Review, 23*(1), 131–158.

Pace, A. C., Ham, A.-J.L., Poole, T. M., & Wahaib, K. L. (2016). Validation of the MUSIC® Model of Academic Motivation Inventory for use with student pharmacists. *Currents in Pharmacy Teaching & Learning, 8,* 589-597. doi:10.1016/j.cptl.2016.06.001

Painter, A. (2017, November 20). *White meat or dark meat? Serving up big data to decipher Thanksgiving dinner.* Retrieved from https://vtnews.vt.edu/articles/2017/11/cals-whitemeatordark.html

Pajares, F. (1996). Self-efficacy beliefs in academic settings. *Review of Educational Research, 66*(4), 543-578.

Parkes, K., Jones, B. D., & Wilkins, J. (2015). Assessing music students' motivation using the MUSIC Model of Academic Motivation Inventory. *UPDATE: Applications of Research in Music Education*. Advance online publication. doi:10.1177/8755123315620835

Parkes, K. A., & Kajder, S. (2010). Eliciting and assessing reflective practice: A case study in Web 2.0 technologies. *International Journal of Teaching and Learning in Higher Education, 22*(2), 218-228.

Patterson, R. W. (2015). *Can behavioral tools improve online student outcomes? Experimental evidence from a massive open online course*. Retrieved from http://www.ilr.cornell.edu/sites/ilr.cornell.edu/files/cheri_wp165_0.pdf

Pekrun, R. (2009). Emotions at school. In K. R. Wentzel & A. Wigfield (Eds.), *Handbook of motivation at school* (pp. 575-604). New York: Routledge.

Piaget, J. (1932). *The moral judgment of the child*. New York, NY: Free Press.

Pintrich, P. R., & de Groot, E. V. (1990). Motivational and self-regulated learning components of classroom academic performance. *Journal of Educational Psychology, 82*, 32-40.

Prince, M., & Felder, R. (2007). The many faces of inductive teaching and learning. *Journal of College Science Teaching, 36*(5), 14-20.

Reeve, J. (2009). Why teachers adopt a controlling motivating style toward students and how they can become more autonomy supportive. *Educational Psychologist, 44*(3), 159–175.

Reeve, J., Jang, H., Carrell, D., Jeon, S., & Barch, J. (2004). Enhancing students' engagement by increasing teachers' autonomy support. *Motivation and Emotion, 28*, 147-169.

Remijan, K. W. (2017). Project-based learning and design-focused projects to motivate secondary mathematics students. *Interdisciplinary Journal of Problem-Based Learning, 11*(1). doi:10.7771/1541-5015.1520

Reynolds, G. (2015, June 23). *Presentation Zen*. Retrieved from http://www.presentationzen.com

Rieger, G. W., & Heiner, C. E. (2014). Examinations that support collaborative learning: The students' perspective. *Journal of College Science Teaching, 43*(4), 41-47.

Roberts, J. L. (2013, November-December). The power of patience: Teaching students the value of deceleration and immersive attention. *Harvard magazine*. Retrieved from http://harvardmagazine.com/2013/11/the-power-of-patience

Rosenberg, M. (1979). *Conceiving the self*. New York: Basic Books.

Rosenblum, D. (2017, January 2). Leave your laptops at the door to my classroom. *The New York Times.* Retrieved from https://www.nytimes.com/2017/01/02/opinion/leave-your-laptops-at-the-door-to-my-classroom.html

Ruff, C. (2013). *Examining and supporting domain identification and student interest in first year college students* (Unpublished doctoral dissertation). Virginia Tech, Blacksburg, VA.

Ruff, C., & Jones, B. D. (2016). Becoming a scientist: Using first-year undergraduate science courses to promote identification with science disciplines. *International Journal for the Scholarship of Teaching and Learning, 10*(2). Retrieved from http://digitalcommons.georgiasouthern.edu/ij-sotl/vol10/iss2/12/

Ryan, R. (1982). Control and information in the intrapersonal sphere: An extension of cognitive evaluation theory. *Journal of Personality and Social Psychology, 43*(3), 450–461.

Ryan, R. M. (Ed.). (2012). *The Oxford handbook of human motivation.* Oxford, England: Oxford University Press.

Saltzman, A. (n.d.). *Mindfulness: a guide for teachers.* Retrieved from http://www.contemplativemind.org/resources/k-12

Sana, F., Weston, T., & Cepeda, N. J. (2013). Laptop multitasking hinders classroom learning for both users and nearby peers. *Computers & Education, 62,* 24-31.

Savery, J. R. (2006). Overview of problem-based learning: Definitions and distinctions. *Interdisciplinary Journal of Problem-Based Learning, 1*(1), 9-20.

Scala, N. M., Tomasi, S., Goncher, A., & Bursic, K. M. (2017). Motivation and analytics: Comparing business and engineering students. INFORMS Transactions on Education. Advance online publication. doi:10.1287/ited.2017.0187

Schippers, M. C., Scheepers, A. W. A., & Peterson, J. B. (2015). A scalable goal-setting intervention closes both the gender and ethnic minority achievement gap. *Palgrave Communications, 1,* 1-12. doi: 10.1057/palcomms.2015.14

Schnittka, C. G., Brandt, C. B., Jones, B. D., & Evans, M. A. (2012). Informal engineering education after school: Employing the studio model for motivation and identification in STEM domains. *Advances in Engineering Education, 3*(2), 1-31.

Schram, A. B., & Jones, B. D. (2016). A cross-cultural adaptation and validation of the Icelandic version of the MUSIC Model of Academic Motivation Inventory. *Icelandic Journal of Education, 25*(2), 159-181.

Schraw, G., Flowerday, T., & Lehman, S. (2001). Increasing situational interest in the classroom. *Educational Psychology Review, 13*(3), 211-224.

Schraw, G., & Lehman, S. (2001). Situational interest: A review of the literature and directions for future research. *Educational Psychology Review, 13*(1), 23-52.

Schiefele, U. (2009). Situational and individual interest. K. R. Wentzel & A. Wigfield (Eds.), *Handbook of motivation at school* (pp. 197-222). New York, NY: Routledge.

Schunk, D. H., & Ertmer, P. A. (1999). Self-regulatory processes during computer skill acquisition: Goal and self-evaluative influences. *Journal of Educational Psychology, 91*(2), 251-260.

Schunk, D. H., Meece, J. L., & Pintrich, P. R. (2014). *Motivation in education: Theory, research, and applications.* Columbus, OH: Pearson.

Schunk, D. H., & Mullen, C. A. (2012). Self-efficacy as an engaged learner. In S. Christenson, A. Reschly, & C. Wylie (Eds.). *Handbook of research on student engagement.* New York: Springer. doi:10.1007/978-1-4614-2018-7_10

Schwartz, B. (2005). *The paradox of choice: Why more is less.* New York, NY: Harper Collins.

Shaftel, F., & Shaftel, G., (1967). *Role playing of social values.* Englewood Cliffs, NJ: Prentice-Hall.

Shah, J. Y., & Gardner, W. L. (Eds.). (2008). *Handbook of motivation science.* New York, NY: The Guilford Press.

Shambaugh, N., & Magliaro, S. G. (2006). *Instructional design.* Boston, MA: Pearson.

Shavelson, R. & Bolus, R. (1982). Self concept: The interplay of theory and methods. *Journal of Educational Psychology, 74,* 3-17.

Skinner, B. F. (1953). *Science and human behavior.* New York: Macmillan.

Skinner, B. F., & Epstein, R. (1982). *Skinner for the classroom.* Champaign, IL: Research Press.

Skinner, E. A. (1996). A guide to constructs of control. *Journal of Personality and Social Psychology, 71*(2), 549-570.

Smith-Orr, C. S., & Garnett, A. (2016, October). *Motivation and identity in C++ the effects of music in an engineering classroom.* Paper presented at 2016 IEEE Frontiers in Education Conference, Erie, PA.

Sojourners, P. (2014). *Desks to destinations: 25 students, 49 countries, 175 pages of reflection.* CreateSpace.

Sperber, M. (2005, September). Notes from a career in teaching. The Chronicle of Higher Education. Retrieved from http://www.chronicle.com/article/Notes-From-a-Career-in/4851

Tendhar, C., Singh, K., & Jones, B. D. (2017). Using the domain identification model to study major and career decision-making processes. *European Journal of Engineering Education.* Advance online publication. doi:10.1080/03043797.2017.1329280

The Eberly Center for Teaching Excellence & Educational Innovation at Carnegie Mellon University. (2015). *Case studies.* Retrieved from https://www.cmu.edu/teaching/designteach/teach/instructionalstrategies/casestudies.html

The President and Fellows of Harvard College. (2015). *Reflecting on your life.* Retrieved from http://fdo.fas.harvard.edu/pages/reflecting-your-life

Tu, H.-W., Jones, B. D. (2017). Redesigning a neuroscience laboratory course for multiple sections: An action research project to engage students. *The Journal of Undergraduate Neuroscience Education, 15*(2), A137-A143.

Tulving, E., & Kroll, N. (1995). Novelty assessment in the brain and long-term memory encoding. *Psychonomic Bulletin and Review, 2*(3), 387–390.

Turner, J. C., & Nolen, S. B. (2015). Introduction: The relevance of the situative perspective in educational psychology. *Educational Psychologist, 50*(3), 167-172.

Usher, E. L., & Pajares, F. (2008). Sources of self-efficacy in school: Critical review of the literature and future directions. *Review of Educational Research, 78*(4), 751-796.

Vaillancourt, A. M. (2016, February 29). Blue books energized my teaching. *ChronicleVitae.* Retrieved from https://chroniclevitae.com/news/1308-blue-books-energized-my-teaching

Van de Veen, E. (2015, November 27). *Even at Harvard, students don't read the book. Unless...* Retrieved from https://www.linkedin.com/pulse/even-harvard-students-dont-read-book-have-so-how-does-van-de-veen

Voelkl, K. E. (1997). Identification with school. *American Journal of Education, 105,* 294-318.

Walsh, C. (n.d.). *The blank syllabus.* Retrieved from a link for the PDF provided at http://www.pedagogyunbound.com/tips-index/2013/8/14/the-blank-syllabus

Walton, G. M., & Cohen, G. L. (2007). A question of belonging: Race, social fit, and achievement. *Journal of Personality and Social Psychology, 92,* 82–96. doi:10.1037/0022-3514.92.1.82

Walton, G. M., Logel, C., Peach, J. M., Spencer, S. J., & Zanna, M. P. (2015). Two brief interventions to mitigate a "chilly climate" transform women's experience, relationships, and achievement in engineering. *Journal of Educational Psychology, 107*(2), 468-485.

Weiner, B. (1986). *An attributional theory of motivation and emotion.* New York: Springer-Verlag.

Weiner, B. (2000). Intrapersonal and interpersonal theories of motivation from an attributional perspective. *Educational Psychology Review, 12*(1), 1-14.

Wentzel, K. (1999). Social-motivational processes and interpersonal relationships: Implications for understanding students' academic success. *Journal of Educational Psychology, 91,* 76-97.

Wentzel, K. R., & Wigfield, A. (2009). Introduction. K. R. Wentzel & A. Wigfield (Eds.), *Handbook of motivation at school* (pp. 1-8). New York, NY: Routledge.

White, R. W. (1959). Motivation reconsidered: The concept of competence. *Psychological Review, 66*(5), 297-333.

Wieman, C. E., Rieger, G. W., & Heiner, C. E. (2014). Physics exams that promote collaborative learning. *The Physics Teacher, 52,* 51-53.

Wigfield, A., & Eccles, J. S. (2000). Expectancy-value theory of achievement motivation. *Contemporary Educational Psychology, 25,* 68-81.

Wikiquote (2015a). *Aristotle.* Retrieved from https://en.wikiquote.org/wiki/Aristotle

Wikiquote (2015b). *Edward Young.* Retrieved from https://en.wikiquote.org/wiki/Edward_Young

Wikiquote (2015c). Yogi Berra. Retrieved from https://en.wikiquote.org/wiki/Yogi_Berra

Williams, A. W. (2013). *An action research study using the MUSIC Model of Academic Motivation to increase reading motivation in a fourth-grade classroom* (Unpublished doctoral dissertation). Virginia Tech, Blacksburg, VA.

Willingham, D. T. (2004). The privileged status of story. *American Educator.* Retrieved from http://www.aft.org/periodical/american-educator/summer-2004/ask-cognitive-scientist

Young, J. R. (2013, May 20). What professors can learn from "hard-core" MOOC students. *The Chronicle of Higher Education.* Retrieved from http://chronicle.com/article/What-Professors-Can-Learn-From/139367/

Zaromb, F. M., & Roediger, H. L., III (2010). The testing effect in free recall is associated with enhanced organizational processes. *Memory & Cognition, 38*(8), 995-1008.

Zimmerman, B. J. (2000). Attaining self-regulation: A social cognitive perspective. In M. Boekaerts, P. R. Pintrich, & M. Zeidner (Eds.), *Handbook of self-regulation* (pp. 13-39). San Diego: Academic Press.

APPENDICES

APPENDIX A

Tips for Succeeding (see Example S.2.2)

This is an example of a "Tips for Succeeding" document. This isn't a complete document, but it's intended to give you some ideas for what you can include.

Learning and Studying from the Course Readings

Students often say: "I read the assigned readings and I didn't get an A, it must be a bad test." Certainly, it could be that the test is bad, but more often, when I probe into students' true understanding I find that they don't really understand the concepts. Reading an educational psychology textbook is not like reading a novel. You must pause, think about what you are learning, and take steps to learn the information. What steps can you take? Please read on to find out…

An excellent strategy that can help you to understand and remember what you read is the PQ4R strategy (Thomas & Robinson, 1972). PQ4R is an acronym for Preview, Question, Read, Reflect, Recite, and Review.

Preview: Skim through the reading and pay attention to the general topics and the structure of the chapter by reading the various headers and titles. The purpose of previewing is to identify the main topics of the reading and to "activate" any prior knowledge you might have regarding these topics.

Question: Think of questions related to the major sections of the reading. It's possible to turn the major section headers into questions.

Read: After previewing and questioning, it's time to read. Try to answer your questions while reading. Note main ideas, terminology, concepts, evidence, and applications of main ideas.

Reflect: While reading, it is important to take the time to think about what you're reading. Stop occasionally and determine whether or not you understand what you're reading. Connect the reading to your own experiences. Reflect to connect! You can also take notes, underline, write outlines, create concept maps, and do anything that helps you to actively process the information. Simply underlining or highlighting the text without actively processing the concepts is an ineffective way to learn.

Recite: After reading a topic or section, stop and try to answer your questions aloud. Try to recall what you read and summarize it. If you are in a public space, such as a coffee shop, do these things in your head. Reread any sections that you forgot or that are confusing.

Review: When you are all finished, try to recall the main points. For better recall and understanding, try to recall the main points again a couple days later or at the beginning of your next study session. Spending just a few minutes every few days trying to recall the main ideas can enhance your memory of the content significantly.

Tips for Taking Online Quizzes

Students often benefit from thinking about strategies to use when taking online quizzes. The purpose of this section is to list a few tips that have worked for students in the past. Some of these may seem obvious, but at least some students in the past have not known these strategies and have found them helpful.

1. Read the textbook before you take the online quizzes. There is not enough time to look-up the answers and take the quizzes at the same time if you are not already familiar with the material in the chapter. There should be time, however, to look up a few specific things if you have already read over the material. The main reason students don't do well on the quizzes is because they don't understand the material well enough to apply it to the questions.
2. Read the questions carefully. Often when students tell me that the answer to a particular question is incorrect, they have misread the question and actually know the correct answer if they had simply read the question correctly. Take the time to read the questions carefully.
3. Read all of the answer choices before selecting an answer. There may be an answer that is partially correct, but another answer that is always correct; and thus, it's the best answer. Think about whether your answer is always true or if there are cases where this answer is not always true and there may be a better answer.
4. If you don't know the answer to a question, move on to the next question. Don't spend too much time on one question. Write down the number of every skipped question so that you can go back to it when you have answered all of the questions that you know. In your first pass through the quiz, you should spend no more than 45 to 60 seconds on each question.
5. Once you've read every question and responded to the ones that you are sure of, look at your time and figure out how much time you can now devote to the remaining questions you have to answer.
6. If you cannot figure out the best answer, start by excluding the answers that you know to be incorrect. Then narrow down your selections and choose the best answer.

7. The questions require you to understand the concepts in the textbook, so focus on the concepts as you study and answer the questions. If you understand the concept behind the question, it is generally easy to narrow the choices and select the correct answer. Some questions may seem tricky, but if you understand the concepts, they're fairly straightforward.
8. Don't go beyond the information in the question. Read the question as if you were a judge and you had to make a decision based on the facts. Students often read something into the question that is not there. For instance, one answer says that "Roy works hard to keep his grades up so he can get into a good college and make his parents proud." A student interpreted this to mean that "he must have observed his parents successes in going to college and used their input on the importance of getting into a good college." Yet, the answer says nothing about his parents going college. Do not infer things that are not there. Simply read the questions and answers as they are.
9. The best test taking strategy is to study well and master the material. You will encounter some difficult ideas, theories, and concepts. Be sure you understand not only each idea but also how ideas relate to each other. Summarize sections of the text in your mind and on paper, organize your thoughts and understanding, elaborate on ideas, connect the ideas you study to your own experiences, test yourself frequently, try discussing ideas with others, reflect frequently on ideas and their meanings, review regularly, and monitor your understanding as you study.
10. If you do not understand, seek help. You can ask the instructor, ask fellow students, look for explanations in other books, search the Internet for explanations, or participate in a study group.

APPENDIX B

My Study Strategies in This Course assignment (see Example S.2.9)

This is an example of an assignment that requires students to reflect on their study strategies and to consider other possible strategies they could use to be more effective learners.

Purpose

The purpose of this assignment is for you to reflect on your study strategies in this course and to consider other possible strategies that you could use to improve the efficiency of your learning. Effective study strategies can help you learn the concepts better, make your study time more efficient, and help you to achieve a higher grade in this course.

Instructions

- Write a single-spaced paper that answers the following three questions:

    1. What was your process as you studied Chapters 1 and 2 (please complete this after you have finished the tests related to Chapters 1 and 2)?
    2. How effective was the process you described in #1 above?
    3. What could you do differently to study more effectively for the remainder of this course?

- For questions #1 and #2: Please be honest in your answers. You will not be graded lower if you didn't use effective study strategies. The goal is simply to be accurate in documenting your study processes. Your response should be between 150 and 750 words total for questions #1 and 2 combined. Write enough to explain what you did, but longer isn't necessarily better. Use bullet points if it's helpful.
- For question #3: As you prepare your answer for the third question, consider the ideas in the "Tips for Succeeding in EDEP 5154" document, but don't be limited by these strategies because there are many strategies that are not listed in that document. Whether or not you actually *use* the strategies is less important (although it would be great if you used effective strategies); rather, you need to understand how to use effective strategies if you want to do so. Your response should be between 400 and 800 words.

- Create three sections in your paper with three sections headers labeled: "Question 1," Question 2," and "Question 3," respectively. Answer the corresponding question in each section.
- <u>How to submit it</u>: Submit it as a Word document by uploading it to the Assignments section of the course website.

This assignment will be <u>graded</u> on the following criteria:

- The assignment is typed and single spaced.
- There are between 150 and 750 words for questions #1 and 2 combined. This will be checked using the word count feature in Word.
- There are between 400 and 800 words for question #3.
- The response for question #3 includes strategies that are consistent with the strategies in the "Tips for Succeeding in EDEP 5154" document or any other resources you used.
- There are 3 separate sections with appropriately labeled headers (i.e., Question 1, 2, and 3).
- Please include your last name as part (or all) of the title of the Word document that you submit.

APPENDIX C

Retaking Tests (see Example S.2.12)

This is an example of an explanation as to why you're allowing students to retake tests.

There are no extra-credit assignments in this course because I don't want you to learn extra things, I want you to learn the objectives in this course. However, I would like to offer you the following opportunity to improve your learning and grades.

I am most interested in you learning the concepts in this course. Therefore, I am going to allow you to retake up to three of the 14 chapter tests. I believe it is fair to allow you to go back and learn things that you didn't quite understand the first time and re-taking tests is one way to accomplish that. I also realize that some of you might have had a bad day or week and didn't score as well as you might have otherwise on the tests. If your grades have been good on the tests or if you are happy with your grades, you do not need to retake any tests. You don't have to retake three tests, you can retake only one or two tests, it's up to you.

After you retake a test, you don't get the higher of the two test grades; rather, you get the grade you earned on it the second time, whether it was higher or lower than the first time you took it because the computer will delete your first attempt after you start re-taking it. My experience is that most students do the same or better, but there is a chance that your grade will go down. Therefore, use this opportunity to retake your very worst tests.

The procedure for re-taking tests is to…

APPENDIX D

Example Email to Students Doing Well (see Example S.2.15)

This is an example of an email that can be sent to students who are doing well in your course. This type of message can be sent to solicit their strategies, which can then be shared with the other students in the class.

Hi,

I see that you are doing well in the course, keep up the good work! I was writing today because a few students are really struggling in the course and I've been giving them advice on how to improve their grades. I've found that it can also be helpful if other students give them advice.

Because you're doing so well in the course, I was wondering if you would be willing to take a few minutes to write-up a summary of what you do each week to prepare for the quizzes. Even the smallest things that you do can be included. I don't want you to feel obligated to do so. Whether you agree or not will not affect your grade in any way. But if you are willing, it might be helpful to some others to hear what you do. I'm sending this message to a few other students as well, so you won't be the only one submitting strategies.

I would like to send out your summary to the entire class because everyone can benefit from hearing the different types of strategies that others use in this course. I won't provide your name along with your summary (unless you specifically ask me to). I'm happy to have your name on it, but some students would rather not have the other students know who it is, it's up to you.

Let me know what you think – either way is fine. And again, it won't affect your grade in any way, but it might help others. And maybe you will see some strategies that others are using that could be useful to you.

Thanks!

APPENDIX E

Example Tables to Include in a Syllabus (see Example S.5.1)

These two tables are examples of tables that can be included on your syllabus to help make course expectations explicit to students.

Graded Attendance, Assignments, and Exams	Point Value	% of Total Grade
1. Attendance/Participation (15 @ 2 points each)	1. 30 points	23%
2. Assignment A (12 @ 2 points each)	2. 24 points	18%
3. Assignment B (2 @ 8 points each)	3. 16 points	12%
4. Assignment C (2 @ 8 points each)	4. 16 points	12%
5. Tests (3 @ 5 points each)	5. 15 points	11%
6. Final Exam	6. 30 points	23%
Total	131 points	100%

Class Number, Date, and Topic	Attendance	Assignment A	Assignment B	Assignment C	Tests/ Final Exam
1. 1/20 Topic 1	1				
2. 1/27 Topic 2	2				
3. 2/3 Topic 3	3	A 1			
4. 2/10 Topic 4	4	A 2	B 1		
5. 2/17 Topic 5	5	A 3		C 1	
6. 2/24 Topic 6	6	A 4			Test 1
7. 3/3 Topic 7	7	A 5			
3/10 Spring Break					
8. 3/17 Topic 8	8	A 6, A 7			Test 2
9. 3/24 Topic 9	9		B 2		
10. 3/31 Topic 10	10	A 8			
11. 4/7 Topic 11	11			C 2	
12. 4/14 Topic 12	12	A 9			
13. 4/21 Topic 13	13	A 10			Test 3
14. 4/28 Topic 14	14	A 11			
15. 5/5 Topic 15	15	A 12			
16. 5/12 Final					Final Exam
Total points = 131	30	24	16	16	45

Note: The letters A, B, and C are used to signify different types of assignments. For example, Assignment A might be a one-page paper due almost every week.

APPENDIX F

Strategies to Learn Students' Names (see Example C.1.1)

This appendix includes strategies that you can use to more effectively learn students' names.

It's possible to learn 20 to 30 students' names after the first or second class. But to do so, you need to use memory strategies intentionally and frequently. Here, I provide you with a few specific strategies for learning names.

First, review the list of names before your first class. My university provides me access to students' identification photos along with their names, which allows me to begin connecting names to faces prior to the first class. Use some type of visual image to connect their name to an image. You might picture:

- Diana Campbell sitting on top of a large can of Campbell's tomato soup,
- Amanda Black dressed entirely in black like a ninja (maybe even as a "man" to remember A<u>man</u>da),
- Jose Ramirez ramming his head into a wall (using the first part of his last name "Ram"),
- Dong Nguyen or Edwin Smith at the finish line winning a 100-meter dash race (Nguyen is roughly pronounced "win" and Edwin contains the word "win").

You're more likely to remember unusual images. Create a specific image with as many details as possible and think about the image in your mind for several seconds. The more you practice this strategy the better you'll get at it. If you can't think of an image, try to connect the name to something else, perhaps to another person with the same first or last name, someone famous, or something you learned from a conversation with him or her. Use one of his physical or personality features if needed, such as tall Tim, short Shakira, or gabby Gabriella. If you're unable to do this prior to the first class, try to do it as students arrive to the first class or soon after the end of the first class.

During the first class, arrive early and walk around the class with the roster and ask students for their names. After they say their name, listen to it, and repeat it back to them, possibly several times if needed to get the pronunciation correct. Take a good look at them so that you know what they look like. Check them off your roster and try to form a visual image with their name. During the first class, have students fold piece of paper in the shape of a basic tent with their name on it to display on their desk and ask them to bring this to class for at least one or two more classes. Use their name during class as much as possible. After the first class, look at every students' name and try to recall the image or create an image if you can picture the student. You might also attach information you learned about them from a short conversation with them. As students arrive for the second class, see if you can remember their names without asking them and check them off your roster if you remember them. For the students you don't remember, walk around the room and ask students to remind you of their names. Continue with this process until you have learned everyone's name. Taking attendance and trying to remember students' names at the beginning of every class is a very effective way to remember names, especially if you attach visual images to their names. You can also spend a few minutes to take attendance during some class activities if you're unable to complete your attendance check prior to class.

About the Author

Brett D. Jones, Ph.D., is a Professor and the Educational Psychology program leader in the School of Education at Virginia Tech. He received his B.A.E. in Architectural Engineering from The Pennsylvania State University (1992) and his M.A. and Ph.D. in Educational Psychology from the University of North Carolina at Chapel Hill (1999). He has held faculty positions as an educational psychologist at Duke University, the University of South Florida St. Petersburg (USFSP), and Virginia Tech, and has taught courses as an adjunct professor at the University of the Virgin Islands and North Carolina Central University. He has taught 24 different types of courses related to motivation, cognition, and teaching strategies, and has conducted workshops and invited presentations at several universities. His teaching awards include the *Teaching Excellence Award* for the College of Education at USFSP (2003), the university-wide *Undergraduate Teaching Award* at USFSP (2003-2004), and the *Favorite Faculty* award (2007) and the *Teacher of the Week* award (2013) at Virginia Tech.

As an educational psychologist and motivation scientist, Dr. Jones' research includes investigating how students' beliefs impact their motivation and examining methods professors can use to design instructional environments that support students' motivation and learning. He has received more than $2 million from the National Science Foundation (NSF) to conduct his research and has published more than 90 articles, books, and book chapters. He has also contributed to the discipline by conducting more than 130 presentations at regional, national, and international conferences. For his research, Dr. Jones received the North Carolina Association for Research in Education's *Distinguished Paper Award* (2000); the *Scholar of the Week* recognition at Virginia Tech (2009); the *Best Paper Award* from the American Society for Engineering Education, K-12 Engineering Division (2010); and the Virginia Tech College of Liberal Arts and Human Sciences *Excellence in Research and Creative Scholarship Award* (2010-2011). He was inducted into the East Stroudsburg Area School District *Meritorious Hall of Fame* in 2010.

Email: brettdjones@gmail.com

Website: www.theMUSICmodel.com

YouTube: www.youtube.com/c/brettdjones

Twitter: @brettdjones, www.twitter.com/brettdjones

Made in the USA
Columbia, SC
29 August 2019